The Syriac Writers of Qatar in the Seventh Century

Gorgias Eastern Christian Studies

38

Gorgias Eastern Christian Studies brings to the scholarly world the underrepresented field of Christianity as it developed in the Eastern hemisphere. This series consists of monographs, edited collections, texts and translations of the documents of Eastern Christianity, as well as studies of topics relevant to the world of historic Orthodoxy and early Christianity.

The Syriac Writers of Qatar in the Seventh Century

Edited by

Mario Kozah

Abdulrahim Abu-Husayn

Saif Shaheen Al-Murikhi

Haya Al Thani

gorgias press

2014

Gorgias Press LLC, 954 River Road, Piscataway, NJ, 08854, USA

www.gorgiaspress.com

2014 ܐ,

ISBN 978-1-4632-0355-9 **ISSN 1539-1507**

Library of Congress Cataloging-in-Publication Data

A Cataloging-in-Publication record is available from the Library of Congress

Printed in the United States of America

❖ ܕܒܝܬ ܩܛܪ̈ܝܐ ❖

"To the People of Qatar"

(Ishoʿyahb III, Patriarch of the Church of the East d. 659. Letter 18)

TABLE OF CONTENTS

Table of Contents vii
Acknowledgments ix
Introduction 1
MARIO KOZAH
An Archaeological Survey of Beth Qatraye 23
HAYA AL THANI
Christianity in Arabia: An Overview (4th–9th Centuries CE) 37
SULEIMAN A. MOURAD
The Quranic Word *ḥanīf* and its Explanation in the Light of the Syriac Root 61
ABDUL RAHMAN CHAMSEDDINE
The Manuscript Heritage of Isaac of Nineveh: A Survey of Syriac Manuscripts 71
GRIGORY KESSEL
Remembrance of God and its Relation to Scripture in Isaac III Including insights from Islamic and Jewish Traditions 93
MARY HANSBURY
Two Discourses of the "Fifth Part" of Isaac the Syrian's Writings: Prolegomena for Apokatastasis? 123
SABINO CHIALÀ
Syriac Biblical Interpretation from Qatar: Ahob of Qatar 133
BAS TER HAAR ROMENY
Gabriel of Beth Qatraye as a Witness to Syriac Intellectual Life c. 600 CE 155
SEBASTIAN BROCK
The Future of the Past: The Reception of Syriac Qaṭraye Authors in Late Medieval Iraq 169
THOMAS A. CARLSON

Dadishoʿ Qaṭraya's Compendious Commentary on the Paradise of the Egyptian Fathers in Garshuni — A Case of Manuscript Mistaken Identity....195
MARIO KOZAH

Lost and found: Dadishoʿ Qatraya's Commentary on the Paradise of the Fathers as a witness to the works of Theodore of Mopsuestia....207
DAVID PHILLIPS

The Book of Monks: Ethiopian Monasticism via Beth Qatraye ..231
ROBERT A. KITCHEN

The Influence of Christianity Among the Arab Tribes in the Gulf Area During the Sixth and Seventh Centuries A.D......249
SAIF SHAHEEN AL-MURIKHI

Bibliography....269
Index....281

ACKNOWLEDGMENTS

This book was made possible by NPRP grant # [NPRP 4–981–6–025] from the Qatar National Research Fund (a member of Qatar Foundation). The statements made herein are solely the responsibility of the authors.

INTRODUCTION

MARIO KOZAH
AMERICAN UNIVERSITY OF BEIRUT

THE BACKGROUND

Scholars in the field of Syriac studies have identified and written on the subject of at least seven Syriac writers from around the seventh century who were born and educated in Beth Qaṭraye (the region or territory of the Qataris). Included amongst them is the famous Isaac of Nineveh or Isaac the Syriac,[1] who is referred to in a number of biographical notices and manuscripts as Isaac Qaṭraya,[2] bishop of the town of Nineveh, and who is considered to be the most influential of all Syriac monastic writers whose writings, translated into many languages, continue to exert a strong influence in monastic circles today. Many of the others like Dadishoᶜ Qaṭraya, Gabriel bar Lipah Qaṭraya, Abraham bar Lipah, Gabriel Arya, and Aḥūb Qaṭraya—all, it seems, from around the seventh century—were important Syriac writers on spirituality and monasticism, or liturgical commentators and biblical exegetes within the Church of the East. This group of writers who all originated in Beth Qaṭraye and, it seems, were educated there reveals the presence of an im-

[1] As opposed to the more commonly used but rather misleading "Isaac the Syrian" since all his writings are in Syriac but he was never associated with "Syria" at any stage in his life.

[2] As attested, for instance, in the rubric of MS 181 at St Mark's Monastery in Jerusalem dated 1561/2: ܩܕܝܫܐ ܡܪܝ ܐܝܣܚܩ ܩܛܪܝܐ "Holy Mar Isaac Qaṭraya".

portant centre of education that rivalled the other more well-known centres such as the School of Nisibis or the School of Edessa. This standard of learning is proven by the Syriac writers of Beth Qaṭraye themselves who produced some of the most sophisticated writing to be found in Syriac literature from the seventh century.

The demonym "Qaṭraya" (Syriac for Qatari/of Qatar) is found added to the names of all of the writers above in the ancient Syriac manuscripts now to be found in the British Library, Paris Bibliotheque Nationale, Vatican Library, and the Mingana collection in Birmingham. In addition, the name Beth Qaṭraye (Syriac for the region or territory of the Qataris) was used by the Syriac speaking communities who lived there and throughout the Middle East to refer to the whole region of what is now Qatar, Bahrain and the adjacent Eastern coast of Arabia. Identifying Beth Qaṭraye as a vibrant site of cultural production in the seventh century is important because it offers new centres of learning that shift the emphasis from the traditional centres of the time, namely Syria, Mesopotamia and Fars. The Syriac writers of Beth Qaṭraye and their works are a vivid example of the product of this vibrant cultural environment. Highlighting Beth Qaṭraye as a centre and disseminator of cultural and literary production complicates the structure of "centre and periphery" of learning, drawing the Arabian peninsula during that time as a key player in the cultural production within and beyond its borders. Thus, studying the role and writings of Syriac authors from Beth Qaṭraye, and in so doing, identifying scholarly communities in the Arabian Peninsula that have actively shaped the production of knowledge from the seventh century across the region and beyond, serves to enrich the cultural map of the Middle East during that time as well as in following centuries, given the long and rich translation history of at least two of these authors, and encourages scholars to rethink the ways in which the field of Middle Eastern Studies is constructed and defined. More concentrated study of the contributions of the Syriac writers from Beth Qaṭraye will, it is hoped, help align the rich heritage of pre-Islamic Arabia (especially the Arabic poetic tradition) with other voices, speaking different languages and producing different knowledge, yet sharing the same or adjacent territory. This will create crossings in the cultural and historical studies of Syriac and Arabic, pre-Islamic Arabia, Fars and Byzantium. It will also highlight the Peninsula's role in producing and contributing to intellectual, cultural and religious debates at the time, showing a diversity of writings and ideas with wide ranging effects, emerging from and going back and forth between the Arabian Peninsula and the surrounding empires.

ĪSHŌʿYAHB III (D. 659)

The name Beth Qaṭraye along with the place names of specific locations within this region are to be found in five letters written by Īshōʿyahb III, the Patriarch of the Church of the East from 649–659, to the church authorities, priests, monks and lay people of Beth Qaṭraye. It would seem that the Syriac community in Beth Qaṭraye were behaving independently of the authorities in Fars and Seleuca-Ctesiphon to the dismay of the Patriarch. In letter XXI addressed "To the Monks of Beth Qaṭraye" (ܠܘܬ ܕܝܪܝܐ ܡܫܒܚܐ ܕܒܝܬ ܩܛܪܝܐ) he writes:

> I have written many letters to Beth Qaṭraye (ܠܒܝܬ ܩܛܪܝܐ): some to the bishops by name only; some to particular individuals; and some to Nimparūk bar Dūstar (ܢܡܦܪܘܟ ܒܪ ܕܘܣܬܪ), from Ḥaṭṭa (ܚܛܐ). I sent those to Nimparūk from time to time, since I thought that he would give them all for everyone (ܕܠܟܠܗܘܢ ܠܟܠܢܫ) to read. But, as he himself has now written to me, he showed none of them to anyone, not only from those which had been written to him, but not even from those which had been written to others. If he acted so, then he acted very badly. You, however, ask from him all the letters which I wrote for him (ܕܟ̈ܬܒܐ ܠ̈ܗ) and the others, and read them in front of everyone, because there perhaps will be found one who has the fear of God and is afraid of the evil which stains the Qataris (ܠܟܢ̈ܦܐ ܕܩܛܪܝܐ) with impiety towards God; and there perhaps will be found there [those] who, reading and understanding [the letters], perhaps shall groan and be tormented over the folly of the bishops-by-name of Beth Qaṭraye (ܒܝܬ

> ܩܛܪܝܐ) and over the slothfulness and wretchedness of the christians-by-name who are subject to error.[3]

In letter XVIII addressed to the Qatari people (ܠܥܡܐ ܩܛܪܝܐ), Īshōʿyahb III mentions a number of locations in Beth Qaṭraye:

> You, however, priests and deacons (ܩܫܝܫܐ ܘܡܫܡܫܢܐ), carry out your noble Church [ministry] in all that is within the rule of the law separate from the communion of those who used to be called your bishops (ܐܦܝܣܩܘܦܝܟܘܢ). Until a priestly chair is established for you by the Church of God according to the rule and ordinance of the spiritual canons. And you faithful individuals who possess auxiliary rule (ܡܫܠܛܢܘܬܐ ܡܥܕܪܢܝܬܐ) over the islands (ܓܙܪܬܐ) and the dwellers of the desert (ܥܡܡܐ ܡܕܒܪܐ), that is to say, Dayrīn (ܕܝܪܝܢ) and Mashmahīg (ܡܫܡܗܝܓ) and Tilūn (ܛܠܘܢ) and Ḥaṭṭa (ܚܛܐ) and Hagar (ܗܓܪ), take pains at this time more than at any time in guarding your faith and in the legal establishment of the priesthood by which you have been consecrated, more so than in worldly affairs.[4]

---

[3] From my complete English translation and edition of the five letters by Īshōʿyahb III relating to Beth Qaṭraye (see *The Syriac Writers of Beth Qatraye – an Anthology*). For an older Syriac edition see R. Duval, *Išōʿyahb Patriarchae III, Liber Epistularum*, *CSCO* 11–12: Scr. Syr. 11–12. Paris, 1904–5, p. 282.

[4] Ibid., p. 267.

Map showing the location of Beth Qaṭraye.

Map taken from: J.M. Fiey, *Communautés syriaques en Iran et Irak des origines á 1552*. London: Variorum Reprints, 1979.

Most of these place names, first investigated by Mingana in his article "The Early Spread of Christianity in India",[5] have now been identified in a number of cartographical studies of the region.[6] Mashmahīg (ܡܫܡܗܝܓ) has been identified as the island of Muḥarraq in the Bahrain archipelago[7] and is referred to in the Acts of the Synod of Seleucia-Ctesiphon in 410 as an episcopal see[8] bearing witness to the fact that Christianity was already well established in

---

[5] A. Mingana, "The Early Spread of Christianity in India", *BJRL* 10, 1926, pp. 435–514.

[6] Most recently by H. Bin Seray, "The Arabian Gulf in Syriac Sources", *New Arabian Studies* 4, 1997, pp. 205–232.

[7] J. Beaucamp and C. Robin, "L'Évêché nestorien de Mâšmâhīg dans l'archipel d'al-Baḥrayn (Ve–IXe Siècle)", in D.T. Potts (ed.), *Dilmun: New Studies in the Archaeology and Early History of Bahrain*. Berlin, 1983, pp. 171–96.

[8] J.B. Chabot, *Synodicon Orientale*. Paris, 1902, pp. 35–36 (text)/273–275 (French tr.).

Beth Qaṭraye by this time and representing the oldest episcopal see in Beth Qaṭraye to be mentioned in the acts of the thirteen synods held by the Church of the East from 410 to 775 preserved in the eighth century collection known as the *Synodicon Orientale*. Tilūn (ܬܝܠܘܢ) has been identified with the island of Bahrain also comprising Failaka and Tārūt islands and does not seem to have been an episcopal see. Ḥaṭṭa (ܚܛܐ) which was an episcopal see has been located on the Arabian coast of the Gulf and is usually identified with al-Qaṭīf.[9] Hagar (ܗܓܪ) was also an episcopal see and most likely referred to a town with its surrounding region identified by some scholars with the present-day oasis of al-Hufūf[10] or Thāj.[11] Dayrīn (ܕܝܪܝܢ) was another old episcopal see in Beth Qaṭraye mentioned in the synod of 410 and most probably identifiable today as the island of Tārūt east of al-Qaṭīf.

SYNOD OF DAYRĪN 676 IN BETH QAṬRAYE

It is in Dayrīn that in 676, approximately twenty years after Īshōʿyahb III's letters to Beth Qaṭraye, that the issue of the acknowledgement of the supreme authority of the catholicos is finally resolved, not by Īshōʿyahb III himself, however, but by his successor Gīwargīs I (c. 659–680) at a local synod which took place there and whose acts are recorded in the *Synodicon Orientale*:

> And in this month of May, in the 57th year of the rule of the Arabs (ܛܝܝ̈ܐ), after visiting the islands (ܓܙܪ̈ܬܐ)[12] and other locations, we reached the holy church on the island of Dayrīn (ܕܝܪܝܢ). Those of us present there were:

---

[9] J. Beaucamp and C. Robin, "L'Évêché nestorien de Mâšmâhīg dans l'archipel d'al-Baḥrayn (Ve–IXe Siècle)", p. 171.

[10] Ibid.

[11] D.T. Potts, "Thāj and the Location of Gerrha", *PSAS* 14, 1984, pp. 87–91.

[12] The word "islands" (ܓܙܪ̈ܬܐ) designates in the acts of the thirteen synods held by the Church of the East all the islands situated in the Gulf which included seven episcopal sees.

I, Gīwargīs (ܓܝܘܪܓܝܣ), by the grace of God, patriarch of the East (ܦܛܪܝܪܟܝܣ ܕܡܕܢܚܐ);
I, Tūmā (ܬܐܘܡܐ), by the grace, metropolitan (ܐܦܝܣܩܘܦܐ ܡܝܛܪܦܘܠܝܛܝܣ) of Beth Qaṭraye (ܕܒܝܬ ܩܛܪܝܐ);
I, Īshōʿyahb (ܝܫܘܥܝܗܒ), by the grace, bishop (ܐܦܝܣܩܘܦܐ) of the island of Dayrīn (ܕܝܪܝܢ ܓܙܪܬܐ);
I, Sargīs (ܣܪܓܝܣ), by the grace, bishop of Ṭrīhan (ܛܪܝܗܢ);
I, Estaphanūs (ܐܣܛܦܢܘܣ), by the grace, bishop of the Mazunaye (ܡܙܘܢܝܐ);
I, Pūsai (ܦܘܣܝ), by the grace, bishop of Hagar (ܗܓܪ);
I, Shahīn (ܫܗܝܢ), by the grace, bishop of Ḥaṭṭa (ܚܛܐ).[13]

What is noticeable here is that we now have a metropolitan for Beth Qaṭraye thus making it independent of Rev Ardashir (modern Zaydūn) which was the main ecclesiastical see in Fars that included under its authority the bishops of Beth Qaṭraye, and which was the source of the revolt against the Catholicosate begun by the rebel metropolitan Shemʿūn (ܫܡܥܘܢ) during the patriarchate of Īshōʿyahb III. It would seem that this was a concession made by Gīwargīs in order to win back the loyalty of the bishops of Beth Qaṭraye and that this synod in Dayrīn was the occasion for the reconciliation of Beth Qaṭraye with the Catholicosate.

ISAAC OF NINEVEH / ISAAC QAṬRAYA (FL. END SEVENTH CENTURY)

Also most probably present at this synod was a certain monk by the name of Isaac who would later be known as Isaac of Niniveh, and Isaac Qaṭraya. The origins of Isaac Qaṭraya are mentioned in a notice to be found in the *Book of Chastity* (ܟܬܒܐ ܕܢܟܦܘܬܐ) or *History of the founders of monasteries in the realms of the Persians and the Arabs*[14] by the ninth-century East Syriac author Īshōʿdnaḥ (ܝܫܘܥܕܢܚ)

[13] J.B. Chabot, *Synodicon Orientale.* Paris, 1902, p. 216 (text)/ p. 482 (tr.).

[14] ܫܪܒܐ ܕܡܫܩܠܐ ܕܟܠܗܘܢ ܐܒܗܬܐ ܐܝܠܝܢ ܕܒܢܘ ܕܝܪܐ ܒܡܠܟܘܬܐ ܕܦܪܣܝܐ ܘܕܛܝܝܐ : J.B. Chabot, "Le livre de la chasteté composé par Jésusdenah, évéque de Baçrah", in *Mélanges d'archéologie et d'histoire.* Ecole française de Rome, T. XVIe, Rome, 1896.

(fl. c. 860) who states in a short notice about Isaac that: "His origin, then, was from Beth Qaṭraye".[15] Furthermore, two thirteenth-century manuscripts of Isaac's works describe him as "the holy Mar Isaac Qaṭraya, bishop of the town of Niniveh".[16] One of these manuscripts, Mardin 46, was used by P. Bedjan for his edition of Isaac's works.[17] A more detailed fifteenth century notice however from a Syriac Orthodox biographical notice and to be found published in the *Studia Syriaca* of I.E. Rahmani provides us with interesting biographical details such as the fact that Isaac was born in the region of Beth Qaṭraye and having been educated there in the writings of the Church Fathers became a monk and teacher himself in Beth Qaṭraye. These details reveal that this region was an important centre of education and learning proven by the fact that writers such as Isaac and Dadishoʿ Qaṭraya, who wrote some of the most sophisticated works to be found in Syriac literature of the seventh century, are salient examples of the literary figures that it helped produce. This same notice also tells us that when the patriarch Gīwargīs came to Beth Qaṭraye, almost certainly to the synod referred to above held in Dayrīn, he took Isaac back with him to Beth Aramaye (Seleuca-Ctesiphon) due to the fact that a relative of his was Gabriel Qaṭraya, known as the "Interpreter of the Church". The notice further informs us that Gīwargīs later appoints him as bishop of Niniveh, and that he subsequently resigns and retreats to live the life of a hermit in Beth Hūzaye (ܒܝܬ ܗܘܙܝܐ)/Khusistan:

> This Mar Isaac of Niniveh originated from the region of the Qataris (ܐܬܪܐ ܕܩܛܪܝܐ) beneath India (ܠܬܚܬ ܡܢ ܗܢܕܘ). When he had become instructed in the writings of the Church and in the commentaries he became a monk and a teacher in his country (ܠܐܬܪܗ). And when Mar Gūrgīs (ܓܘܪܓܝܣ) the catholicos went to his country, he took Isaac with him to Beth

[15] ܓܢܣܗ ܕܝܢ ܡܢ ܒܝܬ ܩܛܪܝܐ ܐܝܬܘܗܝ (Ibid., p. 64).

[16] The two manuscripts are Mardin 46 and Seert 76.

[17] P. Bedjan (ed.), *Mar Isaacus Ninivita. De Perfectione Religiosa.* Paris/Leipzig, 1909.

> Aramaye (ܒܝܬ ܐܪ̈ܡܝܐ), because he was a relative of Mar Gabrā'īl Qaṭraya (ܡܪܝ ܓܒܪܐܝܠ ܩܛܪܝܐ), the Interpretor of the Church (ܡܦܫܩܢܐ ܕܥܕܬܐ). Mar Isaac was ordained a bishop of Niniveh in the monastery of Beth ʿAbe (ܒܝܬ ܥ̈ܒܐ).[18]

In his *Book of Chastity* Īshōʿdnaḥ describes Isaac's appointment and resignation in the following concise statements:

> He was appointed bishop of Niniveh by the Catholicos Mar Gīwargīs (ܡܪܝ ܓܝܘܪܓܝܣ ܩܬܘܠܝܩܐ) in the monastery of Beth ʿAbe (ܒܝܬ ܥ̈ܒܐ). After having governed the diocese of Niniveh for five months, as the successor of the bishop Moses (ܡܘܫܐ ܐܦܣܩܘܦܐ), he resigned from his position of bishop for a reason that God knows and went away to live in the mountains (ܠܛܘܪ̈ܐ)... Isaac after having left the see of Niniveh (ܟܘܪܣܝܐ ܕܢܝܢܘܐ), went up to the mountain of Matout (ܡܬܘܛ) which surrounds the region of Beth Hūzaye (ܒܝܬ ܗܘܙܝ̈ܐ) and lived in solitude with the anchorites (ܢܘܟܪ̈ܝܐ) who were there.[19]

The works of Isaac in Syriac survive today in three confirmed "parts" (ܦ̈ܠܓܘܬܐ). "The First Part" edited by P. Bedjan[20] was translated into English by A.J. Wensinck in 1923.[21] "The Second Part" was almost entirely edited and translated by S. Brock.[22] Only the third chapter, which consists of four "Centuries" of Kephalaia (or "Headings") on spiritual knowledge, remains unedited and currently with no English translation. "The Third Part" which was recently discovered has been edited by S. Chiala and was published[23] while

[18] I.E. Rahmani, *Studia Syriaca*, I. Charfet, 1904, p. ܟܒ.

[19] J.B. Chabot, "Le livre de la chasteté compose par Jésusdenah, évéque de Baçrah", p. 63.

[20] P. Bedjan, *Mar Isaacus Ninivita, de Perfectione Religiosa*. Paris/Leipzig, 1909; repr. Piscataway NJ, 2007.

[21] A.J. Wensinck, *Mystic Treatises by Isaac of Nineveh*. Amsterdam, 1923; repr. Wiesbaden, 1969.

[22] S.P. Brock, *Isaac of Nineveh (Isaac the Syrian): 'The Second Part', Chapters IV–XLI*, *CSCO*: Scr. Syr. 224 (text) and 225 (tr.). Louvain, 1995.

[23] S. Chialà, *Isacco di Ninive. Terza Collezione*, *CSCO* 637/8, Syr. 246/7. Louvain, 2011.

translations in French and Italian have now also been published by A. Louf and S. Chiala.[24] However, the question as to how many "parts" Isaac wrote remains unresolved and even the earliest sources that refer to him provide contradictory information. In the *Book of Chastity* Īshōʿdnaḥ states:

> He wrote books (ܟܬܒ̈ܐ) on the divine way of life (ܕܘܒܪ̈ܐ ܐܠܗܝܐ) of the solitaries (ܝܚܝܕ̈ܝܐ). He wrote three works (ܬܠܬܐ ܡܘܫܒ̈ܪܐ) which were disapproved of (ܠܐ ܐܬܩܒܠܘ) by many people.[25]

If the three works (ܬܠܬܐ ܡܘܫܒ̈ܪܐ) referred to by Īshōʿdnaḥ, or "propositions" as Chabot gives in his translation, can be considered an allusion to three "parts" (ܦ̈ܠܓܘܬܐ) in the form that Isaac's works survive today then we must look no further. However, the Syriac Orthodox biographical notice published by Rahmani states the following:

> He wrote five volumes (ܚܡܫ ܦܢܩܝ̈ܬܐ) which are known to this day [consisting of] sweet teaching (ܡܠܦܢܘܬܐ). This is attested by Mar Dāzedeq (ܡܪܝ ܕܐܙܕܩ) in the letter which he wrote to his pupil Būshīr (ܒܘܫܝܪ), to the monastery of Mar Shabūr (ܡܪܝ ܫܒܘܪ), saying thus: I thank our Lord for of your diligence which has sent me the teaching of Mar Isaac of Nineveh.[26]

Could it be that these "volumes" are the equivalent to the "parts" as they survive today? In which case two further "parts" remain potentially undiscovered or unidentified. There are, in fact, reports of a number of manuscripts of a "Fifth Part". All of these manuscripts are reported to exist in various libraries in the Middle East apart from one incomplete manuscript in the Vatican. This "Fifth

[24] A. Louf , *Isaac le Syrien, Oeuvres spirituelles – III, d'après un manuscrit récemment découvert*. Spiritualité orientale 88, 2009. S. Chialà, *Isacco di Ninive. Discorsi ascetici, terza collezione*. Communità di Bose, 2004.

[25] J.B. Chabot, "Le livre de la chasteté compose par Jésusdenah, évéque de Baçrah", p. 64.

[26] I.E. Rahmani, *Studia Syriaca*, I. Charfet, 1904, p. ܠܒ.

Part", now edited and published by S. Chialà,[27] is, according to him, fairly short and having now analysed the text does seem to resemble Isaac's writings.[28] The possible existence of a "Fifth Part" would suggest that there was once a "Fourth Part" as well. However, no traces of it have so far been discovered in Syriac manuscripts.

To complicate matters further, there exist a number of Garshuni manuscripts which are translations of the writings of Isaac divided into four "parts" (ܓܙܘ). The oldest of these manuscripts are a couple which date back to the thirteenth and fourteenth centuries and are to be found in the Charfet collection.[29] Another very old Garshuni manuscript is to be found in the St Mary Al Sourian Monastery in Egypt.[30] Later manuscripts which contain or refer to four parts include a sixteenth century manuscript in the Vatican Library,[31] one in the Bodleian Library,[32] and a seventeenth century manuscript in the Cambridge University Library.[33] Finally, an eighteenth century manuscript with a fourth part is to be found in the Kaslik collection.[34] Although some variation is encountered in the content of the Garshuni "fourth part" (ܐܠܓܙܘ ܐܠܪܐܒܥ) as it has been preserved in the above mentioned manuscripts, the majority of them include much of the same material

---

[27] S. Chialà, *Dall'ascesi eremitica alla misericordia infinita. Ricerche su Isacco di Ninive e la sua fortuna.* Biblioteca della Rivista di Storia e Letteratura Religiosa, Studi 14. Florence, 2002, p. 71–72.

[28] For a discussion of the "Fifth Part" see S. Chiala's article in this volume: "Two discourses of the 'Fifth Part' of Isaac the Syrian's Writings: Prolegomena for Apokatastasis?".

[29] Charfet ar. 7/2 and Charfet ar. 7/3. I would like to thank Grigory Kessel for alerting me to the existence of these manuscripts.

[30] MS 153.

[31] Vat. sir. 198. A partial copy of this MS is found in Borg. ar. 133 although it does not include the fourth part despite the fact that it is found listed in the contents page.

[32] Bodleian Syr. 150.

[33] Cambridge D.d.15.2. Another MS which may contain fragments of a fourth part is Cambridge 3279.

[34] Kaslik, OLM 1580.

under congruent headings. So far, scholars who have studied the Garshuni corpus have only managed to find an approximate correlation with the extant Syriac texts. It is hoped that a full edition and translation of the Syriac "third part" and Garshuni "fourth part" will help with the identification of any of this material in the extant Syriac texts and by doing so identify any new material that is extant only in the Garshuni corpus.[35] As a result significant progress would have been achieved in making the writings of Isaac Qaṭraya more accessible for advanced study and the deeper appreciation that they deserve.

The final resting place of Isaac Qaṭraya was the Monastery of Rabban Shabūr[36] where he spent his last days in prayer, study and composition.[37] It is with this same Monastery that the late seventh century monastic writer Dadishoʿ Qaṭraya was associated and

---

[35] A full edition of the "fourth part" is currently underway using the above-listed MSS. Edition: Mario Kozah.

[36] The location of this monastery is identified by A. Scher as being in the environs of the town of "Šouštar" (or Tustar). See A. Scher, "Notice sur la vie et les oeuvres de Dadishoʿ Qaṭraya", *Journal Asiatique*, 10:7, 1906, p. 109, n. 1. J-M. Fiey, suggests that if the monastery was founded to the south of the town of "Tuster" in the direction of the village of Dūlāb, the birthplace of Rabban Shabūr himself, then it might be identified with "Dayr Ḥamīm" mentioned in the Muslim sources. See J-M. Fiey, "L'Elam, première des metropoles ecclésiastiques syriennes orientales", *Melto* 5, 1969, p. 247, n. 126. For a more recent article on the Monastery of Rabban Shabūr but which does not make any advance on Fiey's conclusions concerning its location see F. Jullien, "Le couvent de Rabban Shapour et le renouveau monastique en Perse", in M. Vannier, *Connaissance des Pères de l'Eglise, N° 119, septembre 20 : Isaac de Ninive*. Nouvelle Cité, 2010.

[37] "Afterwards he grew old and advanced in years (ܥܠ ܒܫ̈ܢܝܐ) and departed to our Lord. He was buried in the Monastery of Mar Shabūr (ܐܬܩܒܪ ܒܥܘܡܪܐ ܕܡܪܝ ܫܒܘܪ)". See I.E. Rahmani, *Studia Syriaca*, I. Charfet, 1904, p. ܩܠ. "When he became very advanced in age, he departed from temporal life (ܚ̈ܝܐ ܙܒܢܝܐ) and his body was buried in the Monastery of Shabūr (ܐܬܬܩܒܪ ܦܓܪܗ ܒܥܘܡܪܐ ܕܫܒܘܪ)". See J.B. Chabot, "Le livre de la chasteté composé par Jésusdenah, évéque de Baçrah", p. 64.

which he himself mentions on a number of occasions in his writings.[38]

DADISHOʿ QAṬRAYA (FL. END OF THE SEVENTH CENTURY)

See my article in this volume.

GABRIEL QAṬRAYA BAR LIPAH (FL. MID SEVENTH CENTURY)

The seventh century East Syriac liturgical commentator Gabriel Qaṭraya bar Lipah is known through a single thirteenth century manuscript at the British Library (BL. Or. 3336) where the following colophon is to be found:

> The writing of this book is complete, filled with ardent life, consisting of the explanation of the liturgy (ܕܦܘܫܩ ܠܬܫܡܫܬܐ), written and arranged by a man in whom the spirit dwells completely, Rabban Gabriel Qaṭraya (ܪܒܢ ܓܒܪܐܝܠ ܩܛܪܝܐ) known as [Bar] Lipah (ܒܪ ܠܝܦܗ).[39]

In 1966 S.H. Jammo wrote an article[40] on the contents of this manuscript and its author in which he argues on the basis of the content that Gabriel bar Lipah was writing before the liturgical reforms of the Patriarch Īshōʿyahb III (649–659).[41] In addition, the

---

[38] ܗܘܐ ܕܝܢ ܠܗ ܒܗܘ ܙܒܢܐ ܕܗܘܐ ܒܥܘܡܪܐ ܕܪܒܢ ܫܒܘܪ See A. Scher, "Notice sur la vie et les oeuvres de Dadishoʿ Qaṭraya", *Journal Asiatique*, 10:7, 1906, p. 111.

[39] BL. Or. 3336, f. 229ᵛ. The word ܒܪ is missing as a result of damage to the folio.

[40] S.H. Jammo, "Gabriel Qaṭraya et son commentaire sur la liturgie chaldéenne" in *Orientalia Christiana Periodica* 32, 1966, pp. 39–52.

[41] This argument was first made by R.H. Connolly regarding the liturgical commentary written by Abraham bar Lipah in the preface, written in Latin, of his edition and Latin translation of this work: R. H. Connolly, *Anonymi auctoris Expositio Officiorum Ecclesiae Georgio Arbelensi vulgo ascripta. II. Accedit Abrahae Bar Lipeh Interpretation Officiorum. CSCO* 72, 76, Scr. Syri 29, 32, 1913–15, p. 148.

fact that he at one point mentions that Shubḥalmaran, metropolitan of Karka d-Beth Slokh and a contemporary of Īshōʿyahb III as still alive[42] leads Jammo to conclude that Gabriel belongs to the first half of the seventh century. The commentary consists of five *memre* each of which is divided up into chapters. The topics of these five *memre* are given in this same article by Jammo who later produced a Latin translation[43] of chapter two in the fifth *memra* on the Eucharistic liturgy. This same chapter has consequently been translated into English twice the most recent by S. Brock[44] who also provided a full listing in English of all the chapter headings in the five *memre*. Nevertheless, this leaves much of this very important commentary still largely unedited, untranslated and unexplored.

ABRAHAM QAṬRAYA BAR LIPAH (FL. MID SEVENTH CENTURY)

A second liturgical commentator of the seventh century from Beth Qaṭraye is Abraham bar Lipah who is the author of a short *Commentary on the Liturgy* in a question and answer format edited and translated into Latin by R.H. Connolly.[45] His name appears in the opening rubric of the Syriac text to be found in the Vatican manuscript which Connolly relied on for his edition:

> The explanation [commentary] of the liturgy (ܦܘܫܩ ܠܡܫܡܫܢܘܬܐ) written by Mar Abraham Qaṭraya bar Lipah (ܡܪܝ ܐܒܪܗܡ ܩܛܪܝܐ ܒܪ ܠܝܦܗ)[46]

In the preface to his translation, both of which are in Latin, Connolly makes the argument that the work belongs to the first half of the seventh century since there is no mention in the commentary

---

[42] BL. Or. 3336, f. 109ʳ.

[43] S.H. Jammo, *La structure de la messe chaldéenne. Orientalia Christiana Analecta* 207, 1979.

[44] S. Brock, "Gabriel of Qatar's Commentary on the Liturgy", in *Hugoye* vol. 2, no. 2, July 2003.

[45] R.H. Connolly, op. cit.

[46] Vat. sir. 504, f. 119ʳ. The same rubric is to be found in another copy of the same commentary in Mingana 566, f. 154ʳ.

of the liturgical reforms undertaken by the Patriarch Īshōʿyahb III (649–659). This same argument as we have seen was later taken up by S.H. Jammo and used to date the commentary written by Gabriel bar Lipah.[47] However, Connolly leaves the possibility open that Abraham's commentary is from the early eighth century once again using the content to argue that the author is silent about the recitation of the Lord's Prayer both at the beginning and at the end of the evening office, and indeed about any second recitation of it towards the end of the liturgy. He states that there was no law that the Lord's Prayer should be used at those places in the office until Timothy I required it at the end of the eighth century. This is, however, not a definite indication of date; since there continued to be a variety of practices in this matter amongst the churches even after the law had been promulgated by Timothy. Nevertheless, Connolly continues, if Abraham bar Lipah had lived after Timothy, one might still have expected him to say something about that law.[48]

However, it should be borne in mind that the argument that takes the reforms undertaken by the Patriarch Īshōʿyahb III (649–659) as a fixed point for the purpose of dating the content of both Gabriel and Abraham's commentaries needs to take into consideration the fact that during the period of Īshōʿyahb III's patriarchate he himself was writing letters to Beth Qaṭraye complaining to the church authorities, priests, monks and lay people there that they had lost all ecclesiastical legitimacy, as discussed above. It would, therefore, seem rather unlikely that the Syriac community in Beth Qaṭraye who were behaving independently of the authorities in Fars and Seleuca-Ctesiphon and in a state of open ecclesiastical rebellion, to the dismay of the Patriarch, would at the same time be implementing his liturgical reforms. It is only at a local synod in Dayrīn in 676, approximately twenty years after Īshōʿyahb III's letters to Beth Qaṭraye, that the issue of the acknowledgement of the supreme authority of the catholicos is finally resolved by Īshōʿyahb III's successor Gīwargīs I (c. 659–680). This later date of

[47] S.H. Jammo, "Gabriel Qaṭraya et son commentaire sur la liturgie chaldéenne" in *Orientalia Christiana Periodica* 32, 1966, p. 42.

[48] R.H. Connolly, op. cit.

676 does not affect the early seventh century dating of Gabriel's commentary given the reference in his commentary to Shubḥalmaran, metropolitan of Karka d-Beth Slokh, but allows us to bring forward Abraham's commentary to the second half of the seventh century since what is certain is that his commentary was written after that of Gabriel which is clearly demonstrated by the fact that *memra* 5 chapter 2 of Gabriel's commentary is abbreviated in its entirety in Abraham's work. This observation first made by Jammo[49] was later confirmed by Brock[50] in his English translation of this *memra* where he italicizes passages taken up by Abraham:

Gabriel bar Lipah:	Abraham bar Lipah:[51]
Memra 5, Chapter 2 (On the Eucharistic Liturgy)[52]	
(Italics indicate passages taken up by Abraham bar Lipah)	The equivalent passage from my complete English translation of Abraham bar Lipah's commentary (see *Anthology*).[53]
58. *The first Peace which the priest gives [200b] to the people is a prayer of the priesthood where* he *prays for the people that there may remain* with him, and beside him, *that peace which Christ left behind before he died*, saying "*My peace I leave to*	The first "peace" which the priest gives the people, is the prayer of the priesthood, which is prayed for the people (ܕܡܨܠܝܐ ܥܠ ܥܡܐ), that it might remain in that peace (ܕܢܗܘܐ ܠܗܘ ܫܠܡܐ ܗܘ) which Christ left for it

[49] S.H. Jammo, ibid., p. 41: "En effet, R.H. Connolly a publié un commentaire sur la liturgie ayant le meme titre que l'ouvrage que nous étudions et ayant un contenu et souvent un texte semblable".

[50] S. Brock, ibid.: "In his article of 1966 Jammo…rightly observes that the published Commentary by Abraham bar Lipeh is nothing but an abbreviation of Gabriel's work".

[51] Taken from my critical edition and translation of Abraham bar Lipah's *Commentary on the Liturgy*. See *Anthology*.

[52] The translation is that of S. Brock, "Gabriel of Qatar's Commentary on the Liturgy", in *Hugoye* vol. 2, no. 2, July 2003.

[53] The Syriac text is to be found in R.H. Connolly, op. cit., pp. 176–177.

you". (John 14:27)	(ܕܫܒܩ ܠܗ) before he died: "My peace I leave to you" [1 Jn 14, 27].
59. *After the people respond to the priest "May you have peace with the spirit of priesthood which you have received", then the herald bids the people "Give the peace to one another in the love of Christ"; that is to say, "Show in action your peace with one another, and root out from your hearts resentment* and enmity, *so that you may become worthy to receive the life-giving Mysteries*, and be forgiven your sins". (cp Matt. 6:14*) For with this peace we fulfil the words of our Lord, "Forgive*, so that *you may be forgiven*", and again, "When you offer up your offering on the altar [201a] and there remember that your brother holds some resentment against you, leave your offering there on the altar", and the rest. (Matt. 5:23–4).	And after the people answer the priest: "To you also let there be peace with the spirit of priesthood which you have received", then the herald orders the people: "Give one another the peace in the love of Christ"; that is to say, "Show your peace towards one another in deed; and root out of your hearts anger (ܐܟܬܐ), that you may become worthy to receive the life-giving mysteries". For with this peace we accomplish the word of our Lord (ܠܡܠܬܗ ܕܡܪܢ): "Forgive and it shall be forgiven unto you". [3 Lk 6, 37]
60. The fact that at this point they *read the Book of the Living and the Dead…*	The reading of the book of the living and the dead (ܣܦܪ ܚܝ̈ܐ ܘܡܝ̈ܬܐ)…

Only a full edition and translation of both commentaries will truly reveal the textual relationship at least between these two bar Lipah's from Beth Qaṭraye.

AḤŪB QAṬRAYA (C. SEVENTH CENTURY) AND RABBAN GABRIEL QAṬRAYA

Aḥūb Qaṭraya (ܐܚܘܒ ܩܛܪܝܐ)[54] is mentioned in the Catalogue of ʿAbdishoʿ bar Brikā as having composed a scholion (ܢܘܗܪܐ) on the whole of the New Testament (ܘܕܟܠܗ ܚܕܬܐ), the Law (ܐܘܪܝܬܐ) and all the Prophets (ܘܕܟܠܗܘܢ ܢܒܝܐ) excluding the scholion of Beth Mawtbe (ܢܘܗܪ ܒܝܬ ܡܘܬܒܐ). Although none of these works survive Aḥūb is in fact cited in a number of East Syriac biblical commentaries and in particular the so-called *Anonymous Commentary* which in its most extended form covers both the Old and New Testaments. Most manuscripts, however, contain only the Old Testament Part, or even only the Pentateuch section. So far only a facsimile edition with English translation of the *Anonymous Commentary* on Genesis 1:1–28:6 has been published by A. Levene.[55] This facsimile is from MS Mingana Syr. 553 which is in fact a very late copy. A more complete and older source of the *Anonymous Commentary* which contains both the Old and New Testaments is MS (olim) Diyarbakır 22 which contains 530 folios and was written before 1605, possibly in the fourteenth century. A full survey of the complex manuscript tradition associated with the *Anonymous Commentary* was first given by T. Jansma[56] and additions were later made by L. Van Rompay.[57]

---

[54] J.S. Assemanus, *Bibliotheca Orientalis Clementino-Vaticana*, III/1, p. 175, incorrectly transcribes his name as Ayyub (ܐܝܘܒ) as first argued by J.B. Chabot, "AḤÔB DU QAṬAR", in *Journal Asiatique*, 10:8, 1906, pp. 273–4. This error is confirmed by consulting the manuscripts in which his name features such as BL. Or. 9354, f. 1ᵛ: ܥܒܕܗ ܐܚܘܒ ܩܛܪܝܐ.

[55] Abraham Levene, *The Early Syrian Fathers on Genesis from a Syriac Ms. on the Pentateuch in the Mingana Collection*. London, 1951.

[56] T. Jansma, "Investigations into the Early Syrian Fathers on Genesis", in P.A.H. de Boer (ed.), *Studies on the Book of Genesis*. Leiden: Brill, 1958, pp. 69–181.

[57] L. Van Rompay, "A Hitherto Unknown Nestorian Commentary on Genesis and Exodus 1–9, 32 in the Syriac Manuscript (olim) Dijarbekr 22", *Orientalia Lovaniensia Periodica* 5, 1974, pp. 53–78.

Interestingly, in addition to citations from Aḥūb Qaṭraya, the *Anonymous Commentary* also includes glosses containing words in the language of Qatar or Qatari (ܩܛܪܐܝܬ)[58] spoken by Qataris (ܩܛܪ̈ܝܐ) who appear to be distinguished from Arabs (ܛܝܝ̈ܐ) who have their own language.[59] There is also the possibility that a full edition of this commentary may not only yield many more references to words in Qaṭari but also more citations from Aḥūb as well as reveal more anonymous or not yet recognized references to authors from Beth Qaṭraye.

Aḥūb Qaṭraya is also the author of the "Cause of the Psalms" (ܥܠ̈ܬܐ ܕܡܠܘܗܝ ܕܡܙܡܘܪ̈ܐ) which is a short introduction to the Psalter that survives in a number of manuscripts. There is an edition and Latin translation of this introduction by B. Vandenhoff,[60] however, this is based on a single, now lost manuscript. Surveys[61] of this manuscript tradition have revealed seven other surviving manuscripts. Finally, important material from Aḥūb Qaṭraya also features in an unpublished commentary[62] or scholion on the Psalms (ܢܘܗܪܐ ܕܡܠܬܐ ܕܡܙܡܘܪ̈ܐ)[63] attributed according to some manuscripts to Rabban Denḥa the teacher (ܡܠܦܢܐ ܪܒܢ ܕܢܚܐ),[64] possibly a student of

---

[58] A. Levene, op. cit., pp. 37–38.

[59] Ibid., p. 41: ܪܩܒܐ ܐܝܟ ܗܢܝܢ ܕܫܩܠܝܢ ܛܠܝ̈ܐ ܛܝܝ̈ܐ ܕܩܪܝܢ ܠܗܘܢ ܡܫܟ. ܘܩܛܪ̈ܝܐ ܕܝܢ ܫܘܢ : "A water skin (*raqba*) like those which Arab boys carry and which they call *mshak*, and the Qaṭaris call *shūn*".

[60] B. Vandenhoff, *Exegesis Psalmorum imprimis messianicorum apud Syros Nestorianos e codice adhuc inedito illustrata.* Rheine: Altmeppen, 1899, pp. 3–9, Latin translation on pp. 17–20.

[61] W. Bloemendaal, *The Headings of the Psalms in the East Syrian Church.* Leiden: Brill, 1960, p. 16; L. Van Rompay, *Théodore de Mopsueste: Fragments syriaques du Commentaire des Psaumes* [trad.]. *CSCO* 436 / Syr. 190. Leuven: Peeters, 1982, pp. ix–xiv.

[62] The MSS which contain this commentary are the same as those which include Aḥūb's "Cause of the Psalms". Cf. W. Bloemendaal, op. cit., and L. Van Rompay, *Théodore de Mopsueste*, op. cit. In addition, the earliest versions of this commentary are to be found in MS Paris, BnF syr. 367 (olim Seert 29), dated to 1252; MS Paris, BnF syr. 351.

[63] Mingana 58, f. 17ᵛ; BL. Or. 9354, f. 17ᵛ.

[64] Ibid.

Ishoʿ bar Nun, and by others to a monk called Gregory (ܘܐܚܪ̈ܢܐ ܘܐܡܪܝܢ ܠܒܪܡ ܠܓܪܝܓܘܪ ܝܚܝܕܝܐ).[65]

The commentary incorporates a number of earlier works including material from Theodore of Mopsuestia. It seems that the material from Aḥūb is not included in the earliest copies of this commentary[66] but was added at a later stage in the manuscript tradition in the margins as well as possibly in the text itself.[67] What is evident even from a very cursory consideration of this commentary is that the citations taken from Aḥūb are very closely interwoven with a number of other sources of East Syriac exegesis such that only a context-based analysis of this material would allow for a true appreciation of its worth and that of its author.

The so-called *Anonymous Commentary* contains quotations from another biblical commentator, relied upon as an authority for both the Old and the New Testaments, from Beth Qaṭraye who is at times referred to as Rabban Gabriel Qaṭraya (ܪܒܢ ܓܒܪܐܝܠ ܩܛܪܝܐ)[68] and at others as Mar Abba Gabriel Qaṭraya (ܡܪܝ ܐܒܐ ܘܓܒܪܐܝܠ ܩܛܪܝܐ)[69] or simply as Gabriel or Rabban.

A Rabban Gabriel is also mentioned in the colophon of Vat. sir. 24 f. 153 as having written this commentary on Bible readings to be found in the East Syriac Office. It has been convincingly argued by S. Brock that this Rabban Gabriel is the same person as Gabriel Qaṭraya, the relative of Isaac of Niniveh, and Gabriel Arya.[70] Brock concludes his ground-breaking article on the Syriac writers of Beth Qaṭraye by stating that both "Ahob and Gabriel the Commentator, serve as fine examples of the high level of biblical scholarship in the Church of the East at this time, whose influence

---

65 Ibid.

66 MS Paris, BnF syr. 367 (olim Seert 29), dated to 1252; MS Paris, BnF syr. 351.

67 This is a matter which still needs to be ascertained.

68 A. Levene, op. cit., p. 57.

69 Ibid., p. 56.

70 S.P. Brock, "Syriac Writers from Beth Qaṭraye", in *Aram*, 11–12, 1999–2000, p. 90.

continued to be felt in the later commentary tradition, long after their deaths".[71]

ANONYMOUS MONK FROM BETH QAṬRAYE (SEVENTH CENTURY)

Finally, mention should be made of a surviving work, edited and translated into German by E. Sachau, written by an anonymous monk who refers to himself in his preface as one of the brother strangers/monks from the territory of Beth Qaṭraye (ܚܕ ܡܢ ܐܚ̈ܐ ܐܟܣܢ̈ܝܐ ܡܢ ܐܬܪܐ ܕܒܝܬ ܩܛܪ̈ܝܐ).[72] The work itself is a translation from Persian into Syriac (ܕܬܘܪܓܡܗ̇ ܠܟܬܒܐ ܗܢܐ ܡܢ ܦܪܣܝܐ ܠܣܘܪܝܝܐ) of the Law Book of Mar Shemʿūn the metropolitan bishop of Rev Ardashir (ܡܪܝ ܫܡܥܘܢ ܐܦܣܩܘܦܐ ܡܝܛܪܦܘܠܝܛܐ ܕܪܝܘܐܪܕܫܝܪ). He states that he carried out the difficult task of translating this work at the request of a certain priest and teacher also by the name of Shemʿūn (ܡܪܝ ܫܡܥܘܢ ܩܫܝܫܐ ܘܡܠܦܢܐ).[73]

CONCLUSION

In conclusion, the Syriac writers of Beth Qaṭraye highlight the existence of a variety of voices that have emerged from the Arabian peninsula and who have played a role in shaping cultural production throughout the whole Middle Eastern region. It is hoped that a grant by the Qatar National Research Fund (QNRF), a member of the Qatar Foundation, to fund a three year project[74] whose purpose is to introduce, edit and translate many of the remaining extant

---

[71] Ibid., p. 95.

[72] E. Sachau, *Syrische Rechtsbücher*, 3. Berlin, 1914, p. 209.

[73] See *Anthology* for my edition and English translation of this anonymous monk from Beth Qaṭraye's preface.

[74] The project is funded by the National Priorities Research Program (NPRP), the flagship program and largest funding activity of the Qatar National Research Fund (www.qnrf.org) a member of the Qatar Foundation. Project title: "The Syriac Writers of Qatar in the 7th Century CE". Principal Investigators: Abdulrahim Abu-Husayn (AUB), Saif al-Murikhi (University of Qatar), Haya al-Thani (Qatar Museums Authority), Mario Kozah (AUB). Project number: NPRP 4-981-6-025.

texts of this group of Syriac authors will also help to contextualize them within a wider cultural and regional setting, from the seventh century past to the present. This is an important aim which the present edited volume sets out to achieve being the product of an international conference, "The Syriac Writers of Qatar in the Seventh Century CE", which took place in Qatar University on 26–27 February, 2014 as part of the QNRF funded project.

In a globalized world, where multiculturalism and multilingualism are increasingly important to the way people identify and relate to one another, a volume such as this is an opportunity to move from a narrow subject within Syriac Studies to a study of multiculturalism in seventh century Arabia. The place of Beth Qaṭraye in the seventh century, its cultural interactions with Byzantium and Persia, and the relationship of Syriac to Arabic through Garshuni, are all issues which will be rigorously addressed in this volume. By reflecting the multicultural landscape in seventh century Arabia and Beth Qaṭraye, an important result is a necessary rethinking of disciplinary boundaries and their corresponding models of expertise. Thus the implications of the research in this volume will not only advance our knowledge of important Syriac writers from Beth Qaṭraye, of which modern day Qatar is a geographical part, but may also offer new scholarly paradigms that move us beyond narrowly defined fields.

AN ARCHAEOLOGICAL SURVEY OF BETH QATRAYE

HAYA AL THANI
QATAR MUSEUMS AUTHORITY

ABSTRACT

The Syriac sources of the Church of the East (the Nestorian Church) state that North-Eastern Arabia was part of a region known as Bet Qatraye, which contained monasteries from at least the mid-fourth to early ninth or tenth centuries. Over the years a significant amount of Christian archaeological evidence has accumulated in the Arabian Gulf, and recently from the Qatar peninsula too. This will cast a new light on the history of the Church of the East in the region, and provide us with greater understanding of the existence of Syriac writers who originated in Bet Qatraye.

In the 7th – 8th centuries a notable literary culture emerged among the Nestorian ascetics of the Arabian Gulf, the expansion of coenobitic institutions was clearly established, with archaeological evidence which has been discovered recently around the Gulf region connected to the same period.

The Syriac sources of the Church of the East (the Nestorian Church) state that North-Eastern Arabia was part of a region known as Bēt Qatraye, which contained monasteries at least from the mid-fourth to early ninth-tenth century.

There is no doubt that the Gulf region was considered during the beginning of this period as the main transit area for Church of the East to be embraced among the Arab tribes of Abd al-Qais and Baker b. Wail. The presence of the Nestorians in the region followed a series of persecutions by the Romans, in 399 they were granted permission by Yazdigird I the Persian ruler to hold their first synod. In 410 the organization of the Oriental church in Seleucia-Ctesiphon was established. By 424 Rev-Ardašir, located near Bushire in southern Fars was added as a sixth province in ecclesiastical provinces. Bēt Qatraya was known in Syriac Nestorian sources as northeastern Arabia and was considered part of the Rev-Ardašir catholicosate in Fars. The Nestorian church in Bēt Qatraya which developed in the westernmost region, encompassed al-Baḥrayn, Darīn, alKhaṭṭ (AlQaīf) and Al-Ḥasā (al-Aḥsā'oasis), the Qatar peninsula and UAE presumably should be part of it (see map on p. 5 in this volume). Bēt Mazūniye the eastern administrative unit of the Nestorian church on the Arabian shore with its Centre at Ṣuḥhār in Oman (Potts 1990: 241–247, Carter 2008: 71).

Over the years a significant amount of Christian archaeological evidence has accumulated in the Arabian Gulf, and recently from the Qatar peninsula too, this will cast a new light on the history of the Church of the East in the region, and provide us with greater understanding of the existence of Syriac writers who originated here in Bēt Qatraya.

This study will focus on this archaeological evidence from the Arabian Gulf, and in more detail concerning what has been recently discovered and speculated in Qatar itself, associated with the Nestorian sphere.

NESTORIAN CHRISTIANITY

A church in the UAE (Abu-Dhabi)

The Nestorian complex, which was discovered on the Sir Bani Yas island of Abu Dhabi in the UAE in the Gulf is considered to be the most important Christian Nestorian monastery revealed till now.

Excavations took place between 1993 and 1996 and the complex consist of a monastery, church and courtyard houses, measuring c.1.5km east-west and 2km north-south, reevaluated by Carter as dating back to the late 7th to middle of 8th century AD (King 1997: 221; Carter 2008: 72–3)

Sir Bani Yas monastery

The Sir Bani Yas church shares many characteristics of Eastern churches like al-Qusur and Kharg (King 1997 a: 226–227; Elders 2003). The ceramics of Sir Bani Yas indicate that all were imported, parallelling that which has been recovered from many Nestorian sites around the Gulf: turquoise glaze from southern Mesopotamia, buff ware from Bahrain, pottery from India and possibly the hard gritty ware from the lower Gulf, though still undefined there is also the presence of the Persian ceramics on the site (Carter 2008: 93–5).

Carter in his study of the Sir Bani Yas ceramics concluded that the variety of pottery revealed from the Sir Bani Yas Nestorian complex shows that it "was well integrated into the region's networks of the trade and communication" (Carter 2008: 97).

Nestorian churches in Kuwait

In Kuwait two archaeological sites have so far been identified: one in Al-Qusur on Failaka Island and the other in Akkaz, a small island facing mainland Kuwait.

The Al-Qusur church on Failaka Island, excavated by a French team (1991), has architecture and stuccowork similar to that of Sir Bani Yas, Kharg (Iran) and Jubayl. The Akkaz church—although poorly preserved—appears to resemble al-Qusur, Sir Bani Yas and Kharg on the Iranian coast (Gachet 1998: 69–79; Bernard, J-F Salles 1991:7–21).

Nestorian churches in Saudi (KSA)

Jubayl

In 1987, the Saudi Department of Antiquities excavated a church in Jubayl yet no sufficient report has been published yet. Langfeldt in 1994 described this church in an article as consisting of a walled courtyard and on its east side three rooms. He emphasized that its architecture resembled that of other churches in the 'East Syrian church' and had the same elaborate stucco and Nestorian cross also known in Gulf churches (Langfeldt 1994:32–42). Carter, in his review of the Jubayl church, stated that although it is difficult to precisely date it, the stucco shows that it is comparable with other Nestorian structures (monasteries and churches) in the Gulf such as Al-Quser, Sir Bani yas and Kharg (on the Iranian coast) (ibid).

Jubayl Church

On a website[1] a brief description of the Jubayl Nestorian church and pictures are presented captured by Robert and Patricia McWhorter in 1986 after it was recovered by the Department of Antiquities. The layout appears to share some similarities with the

[1] http://forums.catholic.com/showthread.php?t=625600

7th century building in Qasr Al Malehat site which was uncovered recently in the south of Qatar (see further discussion on Qatar and Nestorian communities).

Thaj

A church was identified here based on the presence of stone slabs incised with crosses flanking the entrance. There is a deficiency in providing real data concerning the Thaj church structure or its date, nevertheless it undoubtedly indicates the presence of a Christian community at Thaj (Langfeldt 1994:44–7).

Jabal Berri

A bronze and mother-of-pearl cross uncovered from Jabal Berri, south of Jubayl; the bronze cross resembling those in the Eastern Church (Potts 1994). The settlement ruins appear nearby, which makes Carter speculate on the existence of a Christian community close to Jubayl (2008: 98)

Hinnah

Carter (ibid) emphasized Langfeldt's interpretation of many stones engraved with crosses from Hinnah, near Thaj, as Langfeldt understood them to be gravestones in a Christian cemetery (1994: 49).

Darin

Deirin (Dayrin, Diren) and Ardai all are identified as the extended village of Darin on Tarut Island, opposite Qatif. It was also sometimes written as Darai (Bin Seray 1996: 320).

Darin is the main town in Tarut, Todoru Island, opposite the Qatif. Three gravestones were discovered there. Potts (1984) mentions that in 1914 a letter from an American missionary to a German orientalist revealed that these stelae were in Bahrain and they are on display in the Bahrain Museum (Potts 1984: 29).

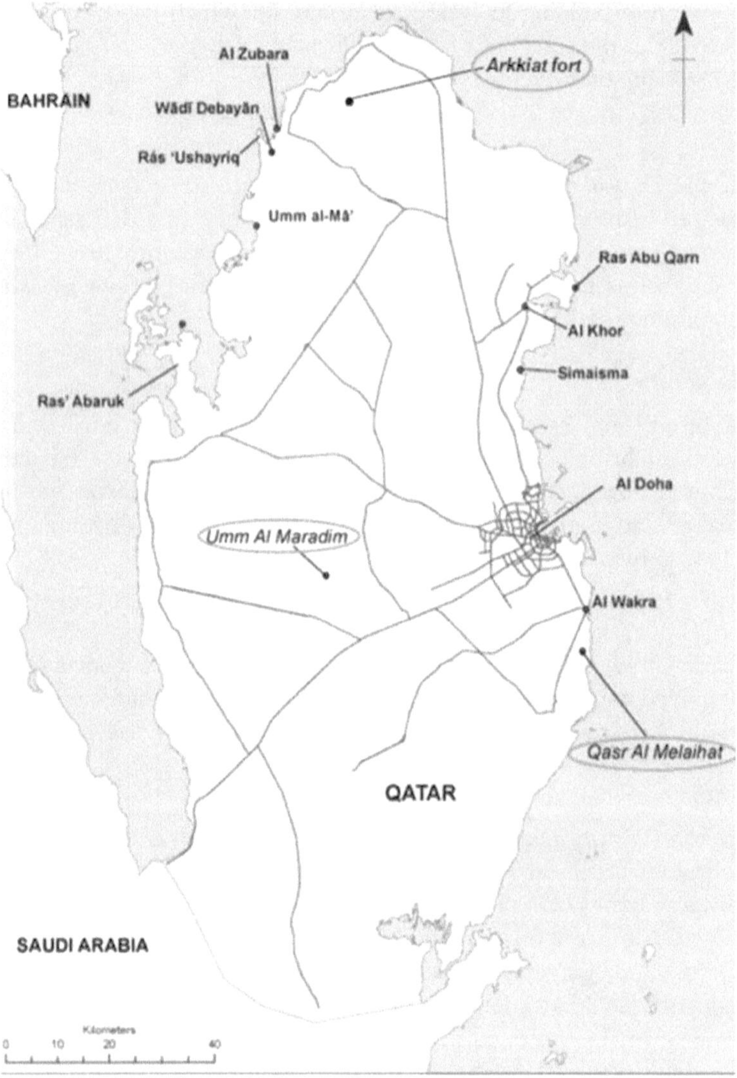

Qatar map and key sites mentioned in this paper

Nestorian Christianity in Bahrain

Mešmahik, Samahiğ village on Muharraq Island in Bahrain still preserves the name of the Nestorian Bishopric Mešmahig. Potts mentions that in 1914 on the Coast of Bahrain on Muharraq Island an "old foundation" of a Nestorian monastery was uncovered (1990: 124).

Al Dayer (الدير), in Aramaic "cloister" or "monastery", is a village to the west of Muharraq. Potts suggests that it is only a matter of time before more archaeological evidence is uncovered in Bahrain, dovetailing with the literary evidence, to reveal an extensive Nestorian population on Bahrain from the fifth–seventh centuries (1990: 125).

Evidence available on Bahrain during the Sassanian period is contained in Syriac religious scripts, which record events in the history of the Church of the East (Potts 1990: 150).

A NESTORIAN CHRISTIAN COMMUNITY IN QATAR

During the last two years many clues associated with the Nestorian Christian community have come to light from different sites around Qatar. Discussion about some of the suggestions and hypotheses related to the existence of this monastic community will be conducted in this paper.

Umm AlMaradim

Description and discussion of the Nestorian Cross discovered in central Qatar

At the end of Dec 2013, a Nestorian cross was discovered in Central Qatar. Our modest observation of this cross in terms of its appearance, is that it is made of hard stone and measures between 4-3 cm, broken in the middle and a crack divides the engraved cross in to 2 parts, the upper part of the stone and the head of the cross is lost.

Engraved and very shallow small holes are found around the cross, at the bottom of it an incised little wide line, which may give a clue regarding the function of the cross. On the back of this hard stone, 2 incised lines. The cross appears to have been a mold in 2 parts, the second part is lost. It would have been filled with copper or bronze or silver or any kind of metal, to produce a cross shape model for different uses. The back of the stone appears as though a string or cord was tied around it which suggests two stones attached together.

The Nestorian cross: front (left) and back (right). Photos courtesy of the Qatar Museum Authority.

No feature of structures could be observed on the site. There are 2 hearths and many pottery shreds scattered throughout the place, (QNHER) -Birmingham University team conducted a surface survey at end of Dec. 2013 and should be continuing their work in excavation at the beginning of 2014.

Umm AlMaradim: Pottery shreds scattered at the site. Photos taken by the author.

Qasr Al Malehat

Qasr Al Malehat is located on the south east coast of Qatar, near Al Wakra. In 2011 QNHER (the Birmingham University team) conducted a survey on the New Port area prior to development taking place, and discovered a building structure measuring 11.5m x 6.15m comprising three stone-built rooms aligned approximately east-west and built directly on the limestone bedrock. Inside the structure were the remains of a hearth and a small 'tabun' or oven.

The radiocarbon dates suggest that occupation at the site began early in the 7th century AD (600–630 AD), and the substantial pottery assemblage suggests occupation continued until the mid to late 8th century.

This isolated dwelling bears various characteristics which could be perceived as those of a solitary Nestorian cell, although no sign of a cross has been found. The ceramics from the site reveal a general resemblance with the ceramics of Nestorian monasteries in the Gulf, from Iran to AlQaser in Kuwiat, from AlMuharraq in Bahrain, from Sir Bani Yas in Abu Dhabi and Kush in Iran. These pottery collections are evidence of large trade networks that connected southern Iraq, Iran and India in the period in question.

The domestic structure found to the south of Al Wakra comprised three stone-built rooms aligned approximately east-west. Parallels in its structure and features can be seen with the Jubayl church in the Eastern Province of Saudi Arabia.

Qasr Al Malehat site

Arkkiat Fort and the possibility of it being a Nestorian monastery

The fortress of Arkkiyat is located about 94 km northwest of Doha city, about 8km northeast of Zubarah town, and about 2 km from Althaqb (Alkhulaifi, Archeogological sites 2003: 80). The fortress has a distinctive residential/defensive architectural shape. Al Shibani mentions that Arkkiyat was an inhabited ruin possessing potable water (Al Shibani 1962: 224).

Arkkiyat is considered to be amongst the bigger fortresses in the Qatari peninsula. In the proximity of the fort there is still an active potable water well with a depth of 5m, the other indicator to the availability of water in the Arkkhiyat area is the presence of small farms around the fort, and during in the winter and the spring vegetation growth is visible which attests to the fertility of the area.

Architectural Description of the Fort

The fort has a general rectangular shape with the dimensions of 28m X 22m. Like all Qatari forts, Arkkiyat has 4 watchtowers located in the four corners, three of which are rectangular in shape located in the NE, NW and SE corners. The fourth watchtower located on the SW corner is a semi-circular shaped tower which was discovered by the surface excavations undertaken by the Department of Museums and Antiquities.

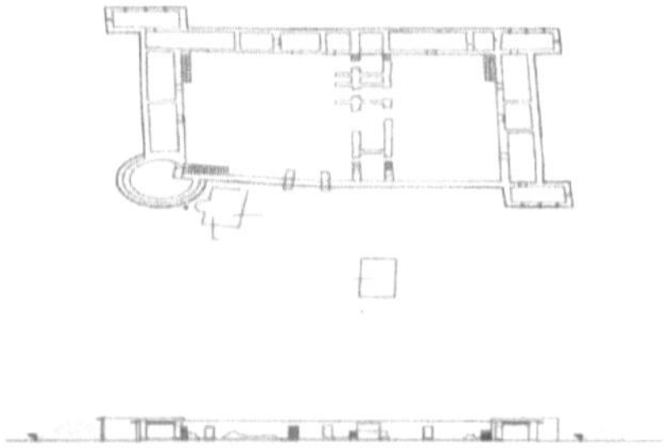

AlThani (2013), pp. 57–9.

It is notable that the fort has only one main entrance located on the southern wall attesting to the use of the fort as a defensive center as well as being the residence of one of the pillars of society. Connected living corners are adjoined to the northern, eastern and western walls, plus there is archeological evidence of foundations for a rectangular room in the middle of the courtyard of the fort.

The fort has three stairs; the first is located in the SW corner of the courtyard and leads up to the semi-circular watchtower. The second is located in the NE corner and the third is located in the NW and they both lead to the roof of the fort.

Two types of material were used in the construction of the fort; the lower part is constructed of limestone and mud and rises to a height of 1.5m from the foundation, and the top part is constructed from Lubnah (a locally produced mud/clay brick). (Al Khulaifi, Traditional Architecture 2003: 80).

The Department of Museums and Archaeology started restoration works on the fort in the beginning of 1988 with the assistance of some Qatari builders under the supervision of archaeologists. The walls were dilapidated and piles of rubble were strewn about the fort, the general situation of the ruins did not allow the visibility of the true dimensions and layout of the fort, only after the renovation work did the fort look complete and the visitor to the fort can now view the natural dimensions of the fort.

The most important finds resulting from the restoration work undertaken on the fort was the flooring to previous residential quarters plus some rooms in the central courtyard, and a pressing room for date molasses (Madbassa). A bronze coin was also found with the inscription '*there is no God but ALLAH alone with no partner on one side and Muhammad is the Messenger of ALLAH*' in Arabic. This coin appears to belong to the period of the beginning of the Abbasid State, specifically to the time period between 132–232 H (= 749–846 AD). The discovery of this coin is a new indicator of the history of the fort, as coined currency can be used as substantial evidence in the determination of the age of historical sites / buildings. Al Khulaifi notes that the discovery of this coin cannot necessarily be substantiated as evidence that the fort belonged to the first Abbasid Era. (Traditional Architecture 2003:76)

The history of the fort according to modern data dates back to between the 17th and 19th centuries, and it is not to be ruled out that the fort was inhabited until the beginning of the 20th century. Historical data presents an alternative dimension for determining the inhabitation time period of the fort through the fort being located in an area that is rich in archeological findings belonging to the early Islamic era, and the possibility of a site being inhabited at different varying time periods cannot be ruled out (H. AlThani 2013:52, in Arabic).

What follows is a brief description of one of the monasteries in northeast Iraq. It will be presented to undertake a comparison between it and Arkkiyat fortress. Qatari researchers are debating and discussing now widely the issue of the similarity and dissimilarity between the architectural characteristics of these two structures in north Qatar and in north Iraq, in reality both orbit within the Christian sphere of the Church of the East.

Dair Mar Elia (known in English as Saint Elijah's Monastery دير مار إيليا) is a Christian monastery in North Iraq, dating from the 6th century. It is located south of Mosul. The monastery was founded around 595 AD by Mar Elia, a monk who studied at al-Hirah, in southern Iraq and it was the center of the Christian community in the region for centuries.

It was renovated in the 17th century and in beginning of the 20th century, some restoration was undertaken on a few halls and rooms. The structure, along with its neighboring reservoir and natural mineral water springs, were cared for by the Chaldean Church, and Christian pilgrims continue to visit the ruins.

Dair Mar Elia Monastery in north Iraq

The structure and the layout of Dair Mar Elia monastery bears the same features and characteristics of Arkkiyat fort. The rooms are adjusted to the fortress wall and the middle wall is divided into two parts while the stairs leads up to the top of both forts. All these features and others indicate and show that there are common denominators.

It is a matter of fact that more exploration, surveying and examination must be conducted in the northern area of Qatar where many early Islamic sites and many forts have been identified. Unfortunately, some of these fortress and Qela'aa have already been restored, with no systematic survey done.

CONCLUSION

This has paper briefly discussed many archaeological discoveries associated with the Church of the East in the last twenty years in the Gulf region and focused in particular on what has been identified in Qatar.

Tangible evidence has been presented from the Qatari peninsula establishing its central geographical position in the Bēt Qatraya region. It also sheds light on the Church of the East Syriac writers who originated here and produced intellectually sophisticated Syriac literature during the 7th century.

It is to be hoped that more investigation will be seriously undertaken, when the excavation or restoration of early Islamic sites in Qatar begins.

CHRISTIANITY IN ARABIA: AN OVERVIEW (4TH–9TH CENTURIES CE)

SULEIMAN A. MOURAD
SMITH COLLEGE, USA

Christianity in Arabia remains a topic in need of further research and study. The lack of sources and more importantly the lack of knowledge of some existing sources have allowed broad generalizations to shape the scholarly outlook regarding the spread of Christianity in the Arabian Peninsula and the status of Christians there. Some recent scholarship, with help from archaeology and Syriac manuscripts, has furnished very valuable information about Christianity in the Gulf region in the period between the fourth and ninth centuries CE,[1] although this is still largely unfamiliar except for the few specialists in these small fields.[2] Christian communities

[1] See the excellent surveys in D. T. Potts, *The Arabian Gulf in Antiquity, Volume 2: From Alexander to the Coming of Islam* (Oxford: the Clarendon Press, 1990); Hamad M. Bin Seray, "Christianity in East Arabia", *Aram* 8 (1996): 315–332; and R. A. Carter, "Christianity in the Gulf during the first centuries of Islam", *Arabian Archaeology and Epigraphy* 19 (2008): 71–108. See also John Healey, "The Christians of Qatar in the 7th Century A.D.", in *Studies in Honour of Clifford Edmund Bosworth, Vol. 1*, ed. Ian R. Netton (Leiden: Brill, 2000), 222–237.

[2] For instance, the absence of anything on Christianity in eastern Arabia in Gerald Hawting, "Pre-Islamic Arabia / The Jahiliyya", in *Oxford Bibliography Online* (www.oxfordbibliographiesonline.com) (2011). Even in Robert Hoyland's survey, he makes a very broad and brief mention of Christianity in Arabia: see Robert G. Hoyland, *Arabia and the Arabs: From*

did indeed flourish in the eastern Arabian Peninsula (modern Qatar, Bahrain, northeastern Saudi Arabia, Kuwait, United Arab Emirates and Oman), in the southwestern Arabian Peninsula (modern Yemen and southwestern Saudi Arabia), and in the northwestern parts (Jordan, southern Palestine and the areas adjacent to them from the south). Their history can shed important lights on history, religion and culture in Arabia, as well as the world in which Islam was born. This paper will provide a broad survey of the history of Christianity in Arabia between the fourth and ninth centuries CE, by looking at a variety of Christian and Islamic sources. A special focus will be made on the seventh century CE, the period of the emergence of Islam. Given that the classical definition of Arabia extends to such regions as modern Jordan and northeastern Egypt, I will restrict my examination to the regions of Hijaz, Najran and eastern Arabia.

There are three types of sources about Christianity in Arabia: 1) Christian sources, 2) Islamic sources, and 3) archaeological sources. The Christian sources are predominantly in Syriac, with the overwhelming majority coming from Iraq. The Islamic sources include the Qur'an and *Sira* literature (accounts of the life and career of the Prophet Muhammad) as well as chronicles, *tabaqat* (prosopographies) and *ansab* (genealogies) works. The archaeological sources comprise remains of churches and monasteries, as well as a variety of objects of material culture that can be clearly identified as Christian (e.g. crosses) from sites discovered in eastern Arabia.

THE CHRISTIAN SOURCES

The Christian sources on Christianity in Arabia are mainly chronicles or correspondences between Christian centers, especially the

---

the Bronze Age to the Coming of Islam (London: Routledge, 2001), 30–31. In this respect, there is a need for a new survey study of Christianity in Arabia to replace J. Spencer Trimingham's very influential though now outdated *Christianity among the Arabs in Pre-Islamic Times* (London: Longman, 1979) and incorporate the findings of recent research and archaeological breakthroughs.

Nestorian patriarchate in Seleucia-Ctesiphon, and Christian bishops and communities in Beth Qatraye (which in Syriac literature refers to the coastal region of the northeastern Arabian Peninsula along with the adjacent islands, which corresponds today to the stretch from Kuwait to the northern UAE). These correspondences are overwhelmingly in Syriac. We also have a list of well-known Christian scholars from Beth Qatraye who flourished in the sixth and seventh centuries CE and whose works have survived (such as Isaac of Nineveh, Dadishoᶜ, Gabriel bar Lipeh, Abraham bar Lipeh, Gabriel Arya, and Ahob).[3] Although their works do not provide the historians with direct information about Christianity in Arabia, yet, the fact that these authors were initially educated into the monastic order in the region testifies to the presence of active and well developed religious centers in the region of Beth Qatraye, and their works can thus reflect some of the Christian customs and practices in the region.

The Christian textual sources have certain limitations in that in some cases they do not provide the historian with accurate information about the exact location of Christian sites and communities in Arabia. For instance, *the Life of Jonah* speaks of a monastery built on the borders of the Black Island between 343 and 346 CE,[4] and *the Chronicle of Seert* tells of a monk named ᶜAbdisho who built between 363 and 371 CE a monastery on the island of Ramath.[5]

---

[3] On these authors, see Sebastian P. Brock, "Syriac Writers from Beth Qatraye", *Aram* 11–12 (1999–2000): 85–96; and Mario Kozah, "Syriac Writers of Qatar in the 7th Century CE: An Overview of the Current State of Studies", in *Syriac in its Multi-Cultural Context*, eds. H. Teule, E. Keser-Kayaalp, K. Akalın, N. Doru, and M. S. Toprak (Louvain: Peeters, forthcoming).

[4] See Arthur Vööbus, *History of Asceticism in the Syrian Orient, Vol. 1: The Origin of Asceticism. Early Monasticism in Persia—CSCO Vol. 184, part 14* (Louvain: Secrétariat du Corpus Scriptorum Christianorum Orientalium, 1958), 308–309; and Potts, *The Arabia Gulf*, 245 and 333.

[5] See *Histoire nestorienne inédite: Chronique de Séert*, ed. and trans. Addai Scher (Paris: Firmin-Didot, 1908–1950), 1.2:311–312; and Potts, *The Arabia Gulf*, 245.

But we do not know for sure where either island was.[6] I will return to the Christian sources with more details later in this paper.

THE ISLAMIC SOURCES

The Qur'an and *Sira* literature feature a number of references to Christianity and Christians who came into contact, be it directly or indirectly, with the Prophet Muhammad. Such references include descriptions of encounters and disputations Muhammad had with Christians, sermons he delivered about Christianity, or letters he sent to Christian rulers. Undoubtedly, there are problems with the historicity of some of these encounters and stories in that they were employed in discourses on the legitimization of Islam and its prophet as well as in anti-Christian polemics and disputations. Hence, some of these stories could have been edited to suit the objectives of medieval Muslim scholars and polemicists. Another issue regarding the reliability of some narratives on Christians and Christianity in Arabia is that they do not necessarily reflect historical knowledge. They were rather exegetical attempts to explain particular verses in the Qur'an.[7]

Some of these earliest Islamic sources include *Sirat Rasul Allah (The Life of the Messenger of God)* by Ibn Ishaq (d. 150 H/767 CE), which is preserved almost in its entirety in the work with the same title by Ibn Hisham (d. 218 H/833 CE). Other works from the first two centuries of Islam are not extent except as quotations in later works. The principle sources for these quotations are *Ansab al-Ashraf (The Pedigrees of Aristocrats)* by al-Baladhuri (d. 270 H/883 CE), which discusses the genealogies of some notable Arab clans and tribes from Mecca and Medina, and *Ta'rikh al-Umam wa-l-Muluk (The History of Peoples and Kings)* by al-Tabari (d. 310 H/922 CE).

---

[6] The problem with identifying the locations of sites mentioned in Syriac texts is discussed in Carter, "Christianity in the Gulf", 100–103; and Healey, "The Christians of Qatar", 233–235.

[7] This issue has been raised in several modern studies, such as in Wim Raven, "Some early Islamic texts on the Negus of Abyssinia", *Journal of Semitic Studies* 33.2 (1988): 197–218.

The accounts that report on encounters between Muhammad and Christians exhibit some interesting features. First, they reflect an effort on the part of early Muslim scholars to show that the authenticity and veracity of Muhammad's claim to prophethood was evident to those learned in the Christian scripture.[8] In other words, the early Muslims believed that Muhammad exhibited to Christians in and around Arabia all the signs of true prophet and that Christian scripture foretold his coming. One finds this emphasized in almost every legend of Christians' encounter with Muhammad and his followers: when they saw him or he was described to them, they knew in their hearts that he is a true prophet, the one they have been expecting. But, according to our Islamic sources, the Christians were not always able to publicly profess this for various reasons, such as eagerness to adhere to their belief, fear of loss of status in their communities, or due to their wickedness and malice. Second, we notice as well in many of the Islamic stories that some narratives of encounters with Christians were also meant to prophecy the victory of Islam, be it the success of Muhammad and his followers in defeating their enemies in Arabia or the Islamic conquests of Syria and defeat of the Byzantines.[9]

---

[8] For a discussion of early Muslim belief that Muhammad's prophethood is attested and foretold in Christian and Jewish scriptures, see Uri Rubin, *The Eye of the Beholder: The Life of Muḥammad as Viewed by the Early Muslims, A Textual Analysis* (Princeton: The Darwin Press, 1995), 21–43.

[9] Indeed, the theme of a Christian ruler acknowledging the truthfulness of Islam and its beliefs, despite the objection of his clergy and generals, is repeated in almost every story of an encounter between Muslims and a Christian ruler (as in the cases of the Negus of Abyssinian, Emperor Heraclius of Byzantium, leader of the Christians of Najran, etc.). Similarly is the case of the prophecies about the victory of Islam. They must be treated as literary topoi inserted into these legends to demonstrate that the veracity of Muhammad's prophethood, soundness of the teachings of Islam, and its imminent victory were evident to the leaders of the Christians: see Suleiman A. Mourad, "Christians and Christianity in the *Sira* of Muḥammad", in *Christian-Muslim Relations: A Bibliographical History, Volume*

To put the issue of reliability aside, what do the Islamic sources (including the Qur'an) tell us about the form (or forms) of Christianity present in Arabia at the time of Muhammad and the emergence of Islam? This question has attracted many scholars over the centuries, some of whom were interested in polemics. Some Christian scholars were eager to prove that the Qur'an is misinformed about Christianity, whereas some Muslim scholars were interested in proving that the revealed text exposes the fallacy of Christian beliefs. It is of utmost importance therefore to understand that some of the modern studies on Christianity in the Qur'an reflect polemics,[10] counter polemics,[11] and, recently, dialogue and rapprochement, and not necessarily history.[12] Even some scholarly studies were preconditioned by the domination and infiltration of polemics into mainstream academic circles. In other words, despite the fact that many scholars were not polemicists, they were "framed" to read the stories as polemics or from the perspectives of the polemicists. And all of this highlights the many

1 (600–900), eds. David Thomas and Barbara Roggema (Leiden: Brill, 2009), 57–71.

[10] See, for instance, Richard Bell, *The Origin of Islam in its Christian Environment* (London: Macmillan & Co, 1926). Nilo Geagea, *Mary of the Koran: A Meeting Point Between Christianity and Islam*, trans. and ed. Lawrence T. Fares (New York: Philosophical Library, 1984) [originally published as: *Maria nel messagio coranico* (Rome: Edizioni del Teresianum, 1973)]; Giuseppe Rizzardi, *Il problema della cristologia coranica*, (Milano: Istituto Propaganda Libraria, 1982); Christoph Luxenberg, *The Syro-Aramaic Reading of the Koran: A Contribution to the Decoding of the Language of the Koran* (Amherst: Prometheus Books, 2009) [originally published as: *Die Syro-Aramäische Lesart des Koran: Ein Beitrag zur Entschlüsselung der Koransprache* (Berlin: Das Arabische Buch, 2000)].

[11] See, for instance, Rashid al-Mulayki, "*al-Masihiyya fi al-islam: tafsir jami' al-ayat al-qur'aniyya al-lati yastashid biha al-masihiyyun*", *Muntadayat Hurras al-'Aqida* http://www.hurras.org/vb/showthread.php?t=9384 (accessed on 3 February 2014).

[12] See, for instance, W. Montgomery Watt, "The Christianity Criticized in the Qur'an", *Muslim World* 57:3 (1967): 197–201.

difficulties that face the historian when researching the topic of Christianity in Arabia.

Recent efforts to better understand the Qur'an and its environment have yielded very interesting and promising observations. Summed briefly, the Qur'an shows close affinity with mainstream Christianity and Rabbinic Judaism in sixth and early seventh century CE Near East, and this is achieved by comparing the Qur'an to Christian Syriac and Rabbinic literatures.[13] This is certainly not surprising given the fact that the Qur'an and its worldview only make sense in the context of Judeo-Christian monotheism. In this respect, and leaving the issue of the Qur'an's polemical tone against Jews and Christians, the Qur'anic stories of such figures as Mary, Jesus and John the Baptist, parallel what one finds in mainstream Christian texts, be they canonical or extra-canonical.[14] My point here is to say that it is absurd to postulate on the basis of the Qur'an, as many scholars have done, that the forms of Christianity

---

[13] See, for instance, Sidney H. Griffith, "When Did the Bible Become an Arabic Scripture?" *Intellectual History of the Islamicate World* 1 (2013): 7–23; idem, "Christian Lore and The Arabic Qur'an" The "Companions of the Cave" in *Surat al-Kahf* and in Syriac Christian Tradition", in *The Qur'an in Its Historical Context*, ed. Gabriel S. Reynolds (New York: Routledge, 2008), 109–137; Michael E. Pregill, "The Hebrew Bible and the Quran: The Problem of the Jewish 'Influence' on Islam", *Religion Compass* 1.6 (2007): 643–659; and Joseph Witztum, "Joseph among the Ishmaelites: Q 12 in Light of Syriac Sources", in *New Perspectives on the Qur'an: The Qur'an in Its Historical Context 2*, ed. Gabriel S. Reynolds (New York: Routledge, 2011), 425–448.

[14] Such as the annunciation story in *Surat Al 'Imran* (Chapter 3: the Family of Amram) 45–49 which parallels what we find in the *Protevangelium of James* 11.1–3, whereas the annunciation story in *Surat Maryam* (Chapter 19: Mary) 16–22 parallels the one in the *Gospel of Luke* 1.26–38: see Suleiman A. Mourad, "From Hellenism to Christianity and Islam: The Origin of the Palm tree Story concerning Mary and Jesus in the Gospel of Pseudo-Matthew and the Qur'ān", *Oriens Christianus* 86 (2002): 206–216.

that flourished in Arabia were strange heresies completely different from the forms of Christianity that dominated in the Near East.[15]

ARCHAEOLOGICAL EVIDENCE

Archaeological evidence for Christianity in Arabia comes mostly from the Gulf region. It shows that Christian communities flourished there starting in the fourth century CE, and that sizeable Christian presence, including monastic settlements, existed up till the ninth century CE or so. I will return to this with more details later on.

A. CHRISTIANITY & CHRISTIANS IN THE HIJAZ

Our knowledge of Christianity in the Hijaz comes dominantly from the Islamic sources. On the basis of these sources, one can say that there were no Christian groups of any significance in and around Mecca and Medina during the period under examination. For instance, there were probably no more than five Christians in Mecca at the time of the emergence of Islam. According to Ibn Habib (d. 245 H/859 CE), there were two Christians in Mecca during the lifetime of Muhammad: ʿUthman ibn al-Huwayrith and Waraqa ibn Nawfal.[16] Ibn Habib related an interesting story about the conversion of Waraqa. Allegedly, Waraqa got into trouble with ʿAmr ibn Abi Shamr (brother of the Ghassanid king al-Harith ibn Abi Shamr) because of a satiric poem, and ʿAmr pledged to boil him in a pot if he were to catch him. When Waraqa heard of this, he fled to Bahrain. There, a Christian advised him on how to get ʿAmr to pardon him: "Hold on to the king's mantle and say: 'I seek shelter

---

[15] See, for instance, Joshua Finkel, "Jewish, Christian and Samaritan Influences on Arabia", in *The Macdonald Presentation Volume* (Princeton: Princeton University Press, 1933), 145–166; and François de Blois, "Nasrani and Hanif: Studies on the Religious Vocabulary of Christianity and Islam", *Bulletin of the School of Oriental and African Studies* 65 (2002): 1–30.

[16] Ibn Habib, *Kitab al-Muhabbar* (Beirut: Dar al-Afaq al-Jadida, n.d.), 171; and idem, *Kitab al-Munammaq fi Akhbar Quraysh*, ed. Khurshid A. Fariq (Haydarabad: Daʾirat al-Maʿarif al-ʿUthmaniyya, 1964), 152–153.

in Christ from this king.'" So Waraqa left straight to the court of ʿAmr, asked to have an audience with him and recited a eulogy in which he paraphrased what the Christian from eastern Arabia told him. ʿAmr knew right away that the poet was none other than Waraqa and pardoned him. As a result of this, Waraqa's heart warmed up to Christianity and he converted.[17]

There was a third Meccan who converted to Christianity: ʿUbayd Allah ibn Jahsh who was the husband of Umm Habiba (this is the same Umm Habiba who later married the prophet Muhammad after the death of ʿUbayd Allah). But it is likely that he converted to Christianity upon his migration to Abyssinia.[18] All three individuals (ʿUthman, Waraqa and ʿUbayd Allah) were cousins and belonged to the Asad ibn ʿAbd al-ʿUzza clan of Quraysh.

Al-Yaʿqubi (d. 284 H/897 CE) had noticed that the few Meccans who converted to Christianity around the time of the Prophet Muhammad belonged to the Asad ibn ʿAbd al-ʿUzza clan. But he only listed the same ʿUthman ibn al-Huwayrith and Waraqa ibn Nawfal, as in Ibn Habib.[19] On the basis of this, we cannot speculate that the direct families of these individuals were also Christians. Actually, some evidence points to the opposite. For instance, according to al-Baladhuri, ʿUthman ibn al-Huwayrith was indeed a Christian (*mata ʿala al-nasraniyya*), but his son al-Huwayrith was a polytheist and fought on the side of Mecca against the Muslims at the Battle of Badr in 2 H/624 CE.[20]

---

[17] Ibn Habib, *Kitab al-Munammaq*, 158–159.

[18] Both Ibn Ishaq and Ibn Habib stated that ʿUbayd Allah became Christian in Abyssinia: Ibn Hisham, *al-Sira*, 1:180; Ibn Ishaq, *The Life of Muhammad*, 99; Ibn Habib, *Kitab al-Muhabbar*, 172; and idem, *Kitab al-Munammaq*, 154. Al-Masʿudi, however, alleged that when still in Mecca ʿUbayd Allah was already familiar with Christianity (*kana qad qara'a al-kutuba fa-mala ila al-nasraniyyati*): al-Masʿudi, *Muruj al-Dahab wa-Maʿadin al-Jawhar*, ed. Charles Pellat (Beirut: The Lebanese University, 1966), 1:82.

[19] Al-Yaʿqubi, *Ta'rikh al-Yaʿqubi* (Beirut: Dar Sadir, 1992), 1:257. Al-Yaʿqubi also named other Arab clans and tribes outside the Hijaz that adopted Christianity, such as Taghlib, Tanukh, Ghassan and Lakhm.

[20] See al-Baladhuri, *Ansab al-Ashraf, Vol. 5*, ed. Ihsan ʿAbbas (Wiesbaden: Franz Steiner, 1996), 74.

We also know of one additional Christian in Mecca, named Abu Tijrat ibn Yasar, originally from Yemen, who made and sold wooden idols in Mecca during the time of Muhammad.[21] His two sisters, Baraka and Fukayha, converted to Islam and migrated with their husbands to Abyssinia, and his two daughters, Barra and Habiba, also converted to Islam in Mecca.[22] But we do not have any information if these women were Christians before they converted to Islam.

Besides, al-Azraqi (d. ca. 245 H/859 CE) alleged that there was inside the Kaʿba an ornamented statue of Mary holding in her lap the child Jesus and it stayed there until the Kaʿba was destroyed during the revolt of Ibn al-Zubayr in 72 H/692 CE.[23] There was also inside the Kaʿba an icon for Mary and Jesus.[24] The presence of the statue and icon do not necessarily suggest that Christianity was widespread in Mecca and the Hijaz. For all practical purposes, their placement there could have been done either by or to please Christian tribes outside the Hijaz who used to come to Mecca for the pilgrimage in pre-Islamic times. Indeed, we know from al-Azraqi that the Monophysite Christian tribe of Ghassan (in southern Syria) had a house (*dar*) in Mecca in which they lodged when they came to Mecca for the pilgrimage.[25] In this respect, the legend reported by Ibn Ishaq about a Syriac parchment found under the Kaʿba fits well in this hypothesis. Ibn Ishaq stated that when Quraysh decided to rebuild the Kaʿba around the year 605 CE, they excavated the foundations where they found a parchment paper on which a short text in Syriac was written. It reads:

---

[21] See al-Waqidi, *Kitab al-Maghazi*, ed. Marsden Jones (Beirut: ʿAlam al-Kutub, 1984), 2:870. See also al-Baladhuri, *Ansab al-Ashraf, Vol. 4.1*, ed. Ihsan ʿAbbas (Wiesbaden: Franz Steiner, 1979), 479.

[22] See Ibn Saʿd, *al-Tabaqat al-Kubra*, 8:246–247, and 4:104 and 202; and Ibn Habib, *Kitab al-Muhabbar*, 408–409.

[23] See al-Azraqi, *Akhbar Makka*, ed. Rushdi S. Malhas (Beirut: Dar al-Andalus, 1969), 1:167–168.

[24] See al-Azraqi, *Akhbar Makka*, 1:168–169.

[25] See al-Azraqi, *Akhbar Makka*, 1:125 and 2:255.

> I am God, the Lord of Bakka. I created it the day I created the heavens and the earth and shaped the sun and the moon. I established around it seven *hanif* angels; they will not perish until its two mountains perish. Blessed for its people are its water and milk.[26]

Clearly, there is nothing in this alleged text that points directly to Christianity in Mecca, although one can speculate that a Christian from Syria could have left the parchment there (obviously if there was ever such a parchment).

Aside from Mecca, there were possibly three Christians in Medina as well. According to al-Masʿudi (d. 345 H/956 CE), two monastics lived in Medina: one named Sirma ibn Abi Anas of al-Najar tribe and the other named Abu ʿAmir ibn Sayfi of al-Aws tribe (al-Baladhuri used the expression *tarahhaba wa-labisa al-musuh* to describe their religious status and observance). Sirma in particular had a monastic cell to which he would not allow any one. When the Prophet came to Medina in 622 CE, Sirma converted to Islam, but Abu ʿAmir did not and left to Syria where he became Christian and died there.[27] We cannot ascertain if the expression *tarahhaba wa-labisa al-musuh* meant precisely that they were Christians, although this might have been the case (if we read the expression to mean: they became monastics and wore monastic attires). But we know for sure that there was a Christian named ʿAddas, originally from Nineveh (likely brought to Arabia as a slave), who first met the Prophet Muhammad in Ta'if. He was killed, while still a Christian, during the Battle of Badr in 2 H/624 CE fighting alongside the Muslim army.[28]

---

[26] See Ibn Hisham, *al-Sira*, 1:159; Ibn Ishaq, *The Life of Muhammad*, 85–85. Translation is mine. Bakka is one of the names of Mecca and is also attested in Qur'an 3.96. I want to thank Mario Kozah for bringing the story of the Syriac parchment in Ibn Ishaq to my attention. On the meaning of *hanif*: see Uri Rubin, "Hanafiyya and Kaʿba: An Inquiry into the Arabian Pre-Islamic Background of Din Ibrahim", *Jerusalem Studies in Arabic and Islam* 13 (1990): 85–112.

[27] See al-Masʿudi, *Muruj al-Dahab*, 1:81–82.

[28] See al-Masʿudi, *Muruj al-Dahab*, 1:81.

From this sketch, one can say that Christianity in the Hijaz was not yet widespread, and that it was restricted to a few individuals. With the particular case of Mecca, the few Christians there were from the Asad ibn ʿAbd al-ʿUzza clan, and they likely were Monophysites. It is also interesting that the two local Christians in Medina, if one were to accept that they were Christians, were monastics.

B. CHRISTIANITY IN NAJRAN

B1. The Introduction of Christianity to Najran

According to Ibn Ishaq, Christianity was introduced in Najran by a Christian monk named Euphemius (Arabic, Fimyun), who was brought there as a slave.[29] At the time, the people of Najran worshiped a palm-tree. Euphemius was asked one day to produce a miracle so that the people of Najran would leave their religious customs and follow Christianity. The monk prayed to God that the palm-tree they worshiped be cursed. As a result, a strong wind came and uprooted it. Hence, the people of Najran became Christians.[30]

A different version of this story states that Euphemius came to Najran and built for himself a tent in a village there. A young

---

[29] Nöldeke suggested that Fimyun is from the Greek name Euphemion: see Theodor Nöldeke, *Geschichte der Perser und Araber zur Zeit der Sasaniden* (Leiden: Brill, 1879), 177, note 3. Jacques Ryckmans, however, following A. Moberg, pointed to the similarity between the Fimyun story and that of the Persian Christian martyr Pethion: see Jacques Ryckmans, "Le Christianisme en Arabie du Sud préislamique", in *Accademia Nazionale dei Lincei. Atti del Convegno internazionale sul thema l'Oriente christiano nella storia della civilità* (Rome: Accademia Nazionale dei Lincei, 1964), 441–442.

[30] See Ibn Hisham, *al-Sira al-Nabawiyya*, ed. Ibrahim al-Saqqa et al. (Beirut: Dar al-Khayr, 1990), 1:28–30; and Ibn Ishaq, *The Life of Muhammad: A Translation of Ishaq's* Sirat Rasul Allah, trans. Alfred Guillaume (Lahore: Oxford University Press, 1967), 14–16; al-Tabari, *Ta'rikh al-Umam wa-l-Muluk*, (Beirut: Dar al-Kutub al-ʿIlmiyya, 1991), 1:434–435; and idem, *The History of al-Tabari, Vol. 5*, trans. C. E. Bosworth (Albany: SUNY Press, 1999), 193–202.

boy named ʿAbd Allah ibn al-Thamir, who was the son of one of the leaders, became his pupil and learned from him about monotheism. It was ʿAbd Allah ibn al-Thamir who introduced and spread Christianity in Najran. Then the Jewish king of Yemen Dhu Nu'as invaded Najran in the hope to convert its people to Judaism, but they refused. Accordingly, they were massacred, thrown in a trench (*ukhdud*) and burnt; hence the Qur'anic reference in *Surat al-Buruj* (Chapter 85: the Constellations), verses 4–9: *Perish the people of the Trench, with its fire and its faggots, as they sat above it witnessing what they did to the faithful! All they held against them was their belief in God, Almighty, All-Praiseworthy, He to Whom belongs sovereignty over the heavens and the earth; And God is witness over all things.*[31] Among those killed that day was ʿAbd Allah ibn al-Thamir.[32] In this respect, the legend suggests the mid to late fifth century CE as a date for the introduction of Christianity into Najran.

Nestorian sources, however, allege that Christianity was introduced into Najran by a certain merchant named Hannan or Hayyan, who had learned about Nestorian Christianity while in Hira. When he later returned to Najran, he converted his family and subsequently the people of Najran to Christianity.[33] Here too, the date for the introduction of Christianity into Najran is roughly, like in the Islamic sources, the mid to late fifth century CE.

As it is well known among historians, it was the massacre of the Christians of Najran in the early sixth century CE that led to the Abyssinian invasion of Yemen, and the failed attempt of its leader Abraha to conquer Mecca. The Islamic sources date the year of the Elephant (*ʿam al-Fil*) to 570 CE, that is the year Muhammad was supposedly born.[34] This legend as well is tied to the Qur'an,

---

[31] All quotations from the Qur'an are based on *The Qur'an*, trans. Tarif Khalidi (New York: Penguin Books, 2009).

[32] See Ibn Hisham, *al-Sira*, 1:30–31; Ibn Ishaq, *The Life of Muhammad*,16–18; al-Tabari, *Ta'rikh*, 1:435; and idem, *History of al-Tabari*, 5:202.

[33] See *Histoire nestorienne inédite*, 1.1:330–331.

[34] Although we now know that the year of the Elephant was around 550. For a discussion of the date of the Year of the Elephant, see Lawrence I. Conrad, "Abraha and Muhammad: Some Observations Apropos

namely *Surat al-Fil* (Chapter 105: the Elephant) which reads: *Have you not considered what your Lord did to the People of the Elephant? Did He not turn their guile into futility? He sent against them feathered flocks, hurling at them stones from hell-fire, and left them like worm-eaten leaves.*[35]

The massacre of the Christians of Najran supposedly happened in 523 or 524 CE, and we have a contemporary letter in Syriac describing the event written by Simon of Beth Arsham in Najran to an abbot in Gabboula, southeast of Aleppo, also named Simon.[36] Yet, despite the massacre, Christianity remained there, as attested by the many accounts in Islamic and Nestorian sources. As noted earlier, we have stories about Christian delegations from Najran that came to the Prophet Muhammad in Medina in the late 620s. There is also the account of an accord signed in 284 H/897 CE between the Zaydi ruler of Yemen al-Hadi ila al-Haqq (r. 284 H–298 H/897–911 CE) and the Christians in Najran.[37] Christianity remained in Najran until the thirteenth century CE, according to the testimony of the Muslim traveler Ibn al-Mujawir (d. 690 H/1291 CE).[38] In this context, the fabled legend that caliph ʿUmar

---

of Chronology and Literary *Topoi* in the Early Arabic Historical Tradition", *Bulletin of the School of Oriental and African Studies* 50.2 (1987), 225-240.

[35] See Ibn Hisham, *al-Sira*, 1:32–47; Ibn Ishaq, *The Life of Muhammad*, 18–30; al-Tabari, *Ta'rikh*, 1:436–444; and idem, *History of al-Tabari*, 5:212–225. See also al-Baladhuri, *Ansab al-Ashraf*, ed. Muhammad Hamidullah (Cairo: Dar al-Maʿarif, 1987), 1:67–69.

[36] On the martyrs of Najran, see Joëlle Beaucamp, Françoise Briquel-Chatonnet and Christian Julie Robin, "La persécution des chrétiens de Nagrân et la chronologie himyarite", *Aram* 11–12 (1999–2000): 15–83; and Irfan Shahid, *The Martyrs of Najrân: New Documents* (Brussels: Société des Bollandistes, 1971).

[37] See Christian Robin, "Arabia, Christians and Jews in", in *Encyclopedia of the Middle Ages, Vol. 1 (A–J)*, eds. Andre Vauchez, Barrie Dobson and Michael Lapidge, trans. Adrian Walford (Chicago: Fitzroy Dearborn, 2000), 90.

[38] Ibn al-Mujawir estimated that the third of the population of Najran were Christians: see Ibn al-Mujawir, *Tarikh al-Mustabsir*, in *Arabische texte zur kenntnis der stadt Aden im mittelalter*, ed. Oscar Löfgren (Uppsala: Almqvist and Wiksells, 1936–1950), 209; and idem, *A Traveller in Thir-*

(r. 13–23/634–644 CE) expelled the Christians of Najran as part of his mission to liberate the Arabian Peninsula from all non-Muslims should not be given any historical validity whatsoever.[39]

B2. The Delegation of Christians from Najran in Medina

Shortly after the year 622 CE, a Christian delegation from Najran visited Medina to meet the Prophet Muhammad. It comprised 60 people, led by two chiefs named ʿAbd al-Masih and al-Ayham, and it also included the bishop of Najran, Abu Haritha. When they saw the Prophet, the bishop professed to his brother Kurz (or Kariz) that Muhammad was indeed the prophet they were awaiting. He also confided that he could not proclaim it in public for fear that the privileges and rewards his priestly position brought to him and his family would be taken away. Kurz converted to Islam at a later point.[40]

The delegation from Najran met with Muhammad in the mosque of Medina. Ibn Ishaq recorded that their Christian belief comprised of the following: "They uphold that Jesus is simultaneously God, Son of God, and part of the Trinity (*thalith thalatha*)". He added that they justified their saying "Jesus is God" on the basis that he used to raise the dead, cure the sick, foretell the future, and create birds from clay that became real after he breathed into them (Ibn Ishaq glossed that this was only possible because of God's command, for Jesus was made a sign (*aya*) to humanity, a reference to Qur'an 19.21). As for their belief that "Jesus is the Son of God", they justified it on the basis that no human is known to have fathered him, and that he talked while still an infant in the cradle which no child has ever done. As for their belief that "Jesus is part of the Trinity", they justified it on the basis that God used the first singular plural in scripture when saying "We have done", "We have commanded", "We have created", and "We have deter-

---

teenth-Century Arabia: Ibn al-Mujawir's Tarikh al-Mustabsir, trans. G. Rex Smith (London: the Hakluyt Society, 2008), 217.

[39] See, for instance, al-Baladhuri, *Futuh al-Buldan* (Beirut: Maktabat al-Hilal, 1988), 73–74.

[40] See Ibn Hisham, *al-Sira*, 2:162–163; Ibn Ishaq, *The Life of Muhammad*, 270–271.

mined". Had He been one, He would have used the first person singular "I have done", "I have determined", "I have commanded", and "I have created". This, according to Ibn Ishaq, proved in their view that God, Jesus and Mary form a Trinity.[41]

This legend reported by Ibn Ishaq offers a confusing understanding of Christianity in Najran in the early seventh century CE. This is especially the case given that it features glosses that reflect the Muslims' formulations of Christian belief. For instance, it was not the Christians of Najran who affirmed that their Trinity constituted of "God, Jesus and Mary". Rather it was Ibn Ishaq (or his informants) who made that claim, which was very likely based on Qur'an 5.116 (*Remember when God said to Jesus son of Mary: 'Did you really say to people: "Take me and my mother as Two gods, instead of God"?'*), which does not establish a trinity formed of God, Jesus and Mary, but rather condemns the worshiping of Jesus and Mary instead of God.

The encounter between the Prophet and the Christians of Najran also led to some theological debates and the subsequent revelation of verses of the Qur'an, such as the first eighty verses, or so, of *Surat Al 'Imran* (Chapter 3: The Family of Amram). These verses affirm the oneness and unity of God, recount the annunciation of Mary and Jesus, confirm the nature of Jesus, and challenge some of the beliefs that Christians uphold about him. There is no doubt a polemical tone in these verses, but the actual stories parallel canonical and extra canonical accounts that were in circulation among mainstream Christians in the Near East at the time.[42]

There was another alleged theological debate between Muhammad and the Christians of Najran that focused on the crucifixion and death of Jesus; though we do not know whether it occurred at the same time as the episode mentioned above, or at a different time. As a result of this debate, a part of *Surat al-Nisa'* (Chapter 4: the Women) was revealed, especially verses 157–158

---

41 See Ibn Hisham, *al-Sira*, 2:164; Ibn Ishaq, *The Life of Muhammad*, 271–272.

42 See Ibn Hisham, *al-Sira*, 2:165–170; Ibn Ishaq, *The Life of Muhammad*, 272–277. A much shorter version of this story is recorded in Ibn Sa'd, *al-Tabaqat*, 1:357–358.

(*And their saying: 'It is we who killed the Christ Jesus son of Mary, the messenger of God' – they killed him not, nor did they crucify him, but so it was made to appear to them. Those who disputed concerning him are in doubt over the matter; they have no knowledge thereof but only follow conjecture. Assuredly, they killed him not, but God raised him up to Him, and God is Almighty.*)[43] The Prophet contested the belief of the Christians of Najran, telling them that Jesus was not crucified and did not even die, and that his death is to occur in the future. But the alleged circumstances of this encounter, as reported in Islamic sources, do not fit with the language of verses 4.157–158. To assume so would imply that there were Christians who asserted in public that they killed Jesus, which is absurd to say the least. But more importantly, the direct context of verses 4.157–158 clearly blames the Jews for crucifying and killing Jesus: *by renouncing their covenant, by blaspheming against the revelations of God, by killing prophets unjustly ... they believe not, except a few* (Qur'an 4.155).[44] One cannot infer therefore that these verses were addressing Christians, or that the issue of Jesus's crucifixion and death was raised in an encounter between the Prophet Muhammad and some Christians. Again, such Qur'anic exegetical material helps us better understand Muslim polemics and formulations of Christian beliefs and not necessarily the forms of Christianity that flourished in Arabia at the time of Muhammad.

C. CHRISTIANITY IN EASTERN ARABIA AND BETH QATRAYE

The Islamic sources say very little about Christianity in eastern Arabia. We know of a letter sent by the Prophet Muhammad to al-Mundhir ibn Sawa (d. 632 CE), governor of Bahrain (the region of modern al-Hasa in Saudi Arabia), and to the Persian military leader

---

[43] See, for example, al-Tabari, *Jami' al-Bayan fi Tafsir al-Qur'an* (Beirut: Dar al-Kutub al-'Ilmiyya, 1992), 3:290.

[44] Such accusations parallel Christian denunciations of the Jews, as in Jerome's words "after they killed the servants of God, and finally his Son": Yoram Tsafrir, "70–638: The Temple-less Mountain", in *Where Heaven and Earth Meet: Jerusalem's Sacred Esplanade*, eds. Oleg Grabar and Benjamin Z. Kedar (Jerusalem: Yad Ben-Zvi, and Austin: Texas University Press, 2009), 86.

there. According to al-Baladhuri and Ibn al-Athir (d. 630 H/1233 CE), al-Mundhir converted to Islam upon the receipt of the letter along with all the Arabs in his region (al-Baladhuri added that some Zoroastrians converted as well). But the locals (called by al-Baladhuri *ahl al-ard*)—who were Jews, Christians, and Zoroastrians—did not convert and chose instead to pay the poll-tax (*jizya*).[45] There is something interesting in this report. It distinguishes between the Arabs and the locals in Bahrain, making it sound as if the locals (some of whom were Christians) were not Arabs, and that the Arabs were not locals. There is no doubt that the region was inhabited by Arabs and non-Arabs, and that several languages (varieties of Arabic, Syriac and Persian dialects) were spoken there.[46] But my point is about the distinction made by Ibn al-Athir between Arabs and *ahl al-ard*. The report makes it sound that before they accepted Muhammad's invitation to convert to Islam, the Arabs in eastern Arabia were not Christians. But from Christian sources as we will see below, the Arab tribe of ʿAbd al-Qays, to which al-Mundhir ibn Sawa belonged, was predominantly Christian. So the only way to make sense of this distinction (arab vs. *ahl al-ard*) is to understand it to mean bedouin people (*ʿarab*) verses settled people (*ahl al-ard*), and not as linguistic or religious division.

An earlier account of the conversion of al-Mundhir ibn Sawa is offered in al-Tabari's *Ta'rikh*. There, he is identified as al-Mundhir ibn Sawa al-ʿAbdi, so his identification with the tribe of ʿAbd al-Qays is made very clear. Moreover, al-Tabari did not say that al-Mundhir converted to Islam. Instead, the Prophet Muhammad made peace with him on the condition that the Zoroastrians in his area must pay *jizya* and "that their (Zoroastrians') sacrifices should not be eaten, and that one should not marry their women".[47]

---

[45] See Ibn al-Athir, *al-Kamil fi al-Tarikh*, ed. ʿAbd Allah al-Qadi (Beirut: Dar al-Kutub al-ʿIlmiyya, 2010), 2:98.

[46] On the languages spoken in Beth Qatraye, see Potts, *Arabian Gulf in Antiquity*, 244–245; and Kozah, "Syriac Writers of Qatar".

[47] See al-Tabari, *Ta'rikh*, 2:145; idem, *History of al-Tabari, Vol. 7*, trans. Michael Fishbein (Albany: SUNY Press, 1997), 142.

C1. Archaeological evidence for Christianity in Eastern Arabia

Archaeological evidence have shown an extensive presence of Christians in the region of Beth Qatraye, and even in what is today Oman (Beth Mazunaye). Coupled with evidence from correspondences between Nestorian centers in Iraq and Christian communities in eastern Arabia, they point to the fact that Christianity was introduced there as early as the fourth century CE and remained in existence until the ninth century CE or so. The region also produced some very influential Nestorian scholars such as Isaac of Nineveh (d. ca. 700 CE) and Dadishoᶜ (fl. late 7th century CE), both of whom came from Beth Qatraye. Let me briefly sum up some of the most important archaeological finds.

1. Two Nestorian churches (or remains of churches) have been excavated in modern Kuwait: one church in al-Qusur on the island of Failaka from around the eighth–ninth century CE, though some have dated it to the fifth–sixth century CE, and a second church on the old island of ᶜAkkaz (now known as al-Shuwaykh Island in Kuwait City) but with no verifiable date.
2. An extensive Nestorian monastic settlement from the middle of the seventh century CE (and possibly from the ninth century CE) was discovered on the island of Kharg (now annexed by Iran).
3. A church was unearthed in al-Jubail (modern Saudi Arabia), likely from around the seventh century CE. It is possible that this church was not Nestorian, but more likely Monophysite; the Syrian Monophysite Church had some followers in the region of al-Jubail.
4. Remains of a Christian settlement were found in Jabal Berri, near al-Jubayl.
5. Several Christian gravestones were discovered in al-Hinnah, near Thaj, which was a center of Christian presence, some 100 km west of al-Jubayl.[48]

---

[48] For more details on these sites, see Potts, *Arabian Gulf in Antiquity*; Bin Seray, "Christianity in East Arabia;" and Carter, "Christianity in the Gulf".

6. Two Nestorian monastic complexes were discovered on the islands of Sir Bani Yas and Marawah, off the western coast of the modern emirate of Abu Dhabi (UAE). They both likely date to the sixth century CE, and were abandoned by the mid-seventh century CE.[49]
7. And two months ago, a cross mold was discovered in Qatar; the first of its kind in Qatar.

Other archaeological finds in the Gulf area have been discovered as well. A few have been suggested as Christian, but they do not bear clear Christian identification.

C2. Textual evidence for Christianity in Eastern Arabia

Aside from archaeological evidence, we have textual evidence from a variety of Syriac sources, mostly Nestorian sources, about Christianity in eastern Arabia. They do not tell us how exactly Christianity spread into the eastern Arabian Peninsula. But we know of several factors that could have helped, chief among them the persecution of Christians in 339 CE in Iraq and Iran under Sapur II, as well as Christian traders who came to the region in search for pearls and other locally produced commodities, and who could have had a role in the spread of Christianity there.[50]

The documentary evidence points to a Christian presence in eastern Arabia starting in the fourth century CE.[51] For instance, *the Life of Jonah* speaks of a monastery on the boarders of the Black

---

[49] For more details on these two monasteries, see Joseph Elders, "The Lost Churches of the Arabian Gulf: Recent Discoveries on the Islands of Sir Bani Yas and Marawah, Abu Dhabi Emirate, United Arab Emirates", *Proceedings of the Seminar for Arabian Studies* 31 (2001): 47–57.

[50] Potts, *The Arabia Gulf*, 242; and Bin Seray, "Christianity in East Arabia", 317–319.

[51] *The Chronicle of Arbela* speaks of a bishopric in Beth Qatraye around the year 225, but this source is believed by most specialists to be a modern forgery: see Potts, *The Arabian Gulf*, 241. For a modern edition of this text, see Peter Kawerau (ed. & trans.), *Die Chronik von Arbela* (Louvain: Peeters, 1985). I will leave it out of my consideration due to its contested authenticity.

Island to the south of Beth Qatraye (somewhere between modern Qatar and Oman) built between 343 and 346 CE under the authority of a monk named Mar Zadoe.[52] *The Chronicle of Seert* mentions a monk named ʿAbdisho who came between 363 and 371 CE to the island of Ramath (somewhere off the coast between modern Kuwait and Qatar), where he Christianized the locals and built a monastery.[53] The island of Taloun (modern Bahrain Island) had a significant Christian presence, with the bishopric seat located in the town of Meshmahig (modern Samahij on al-Muharraq Island in Bahrain). Several bishoprics existed throughout the region of Beth Qatraye and Beth Mazunaye. All of these bishoprics were under the authority of the Metropolitan of Rev Ardashir (modern Bushehr in Iran), which in turn was under the authority of the Nestorian Patriarchate in Seleucia-Ctesiphon.

Moreover, records of Nestorian synods and correspondences also attest to the presence of bishoprics in several areas and towns in eastern Arabia. Names of bishops are included in the lists of attendees of several synods held in the fifth, sixth and seventh centuries CE.[54] For instance, the synod convened by the Nestorian Patriarch George I in Dairin in 676 CE was attended by a Metropolitan and several bishops from Beth Qatraye, several bishops from Beth Mazunaye, and bishops from the towns of Dairin (on Tarout Island opposite modern al-Qatif in Saudi Arabia), Hagar (possibly modern al-Hofuf in Saudi Arabia) and Hatta (modern al-Qatif). All of this information points to a widespread Christian presence along the coast of eastern Arabia and its islands from the fourth to the ninth century CE. Moreover, it seems that the majority of the Arab Christians in the region belonged to the ʿAbd al-Qays tribe.[55] Given that we also know of the existence of a local Syriac dialect and

---

[52] See Vööbus, *History of Asceticism*, 308–309; and Potts, *The Arabia Gulf*, 245 and 333.

[53] See *Histoire nestorienne inédite,* 1.2:311–312; and Potts, *The Arabia Gulf*, 245.

[54] See Jean-Baptiste Chabot (ed. & trans.), *Synodicon orientale ou Receuil de synodes nestoriens* (Paris: Imprimerie Nationale, 1902), 1–16.

[55] See Bin Seray, "Christianity in East Arabia", 325; and Potts, *Arabian Gulf in Antiquity*, 242.

of liturgical texts and hymns produced in Persian, the Christian presence in the region included a significant Syriac and Persian speaking communities.[56]

Christianity in eastern Arabia must have peeked in the sixth–seventh century CE as evidenced by two main features. The first is the appearance of a number of highly educated and influential Nestorian scholars who hailed from Beth Qatraye, such as Isaac of Nineveh, Dadishoʿ, Gabriel bar Lipeh, Abraham bar Lipeh, Gabriel Arya, and Ahob,[57] a point noted by Sebastian Brock in his seminal article on the Syriac authors of Beth Qatraye (some of these figures will be further discussed in papers in this volume). In Brock's opinion, it attests to a level of education comparable to that of the school of Nisibis (the see of Nestorian learning),[58] which indicates that we are not talking here about a marginal Christian existence. The second is the attempt in 647 CE, led by Abraham the Bishop of Meshmahig and other bishops in Beth Qatraye, to break away from the authority of the Nestorian Church in Seleucia-Ctesiphon; and they seem to have succeeded for some time, which testifies to the strength of the Christian communities there. Patriarch Ishoʿyahb III (647–659 CE) ineffectively tried to keep them in the fold through several letters that he sent.[59] It was only due to the visit of Patriarch George I (661–680 CE) and the synod that he

---

[56] On the languages spoken in Beth Qatraye and what they tell us about the ethnicities of Christians there, see Potts, *Arabian Gulf in Antiquity*, 244–245; and Kozah, "Syriac Writers of Qatar".

[57] On these authors, see Brock, "Syriac Writers;" and Kozah, "Syriac Writers of Qatar".

[58] Brock, "Syriac Writers".

[59] See *Išoʿyahb Patriarchae III, Liber Epistularum (CSCO Volumes 11–12)*, ed. and trans. Rubens Duval (Paris: Typographeo Reipublicae, 1904–1905), 201–202 and 260–283 (Syriac text). An English translation of the five letters that pertain to Beth Qatraye is forthcoming by Mario Kozah, "An Edition and Translation of the Syriac Text of Ishoyahb III's 'Letters to the Qataris'", in *The Syriac Writers of Qatar in the 7th Century CE - an Anthology* (Piscataway: Gorgias Press). An English summary of these letters is found in Healey, "The Christians of Qatar", 229–233.

convened in Dairin in 676 CE that ended the schism and brought the Christians of Beth Qatraye back under the control of the Nestorian Patriarchate.

Moreover, other documentary evidence suggests that in the sixth century CE, the Christians in eastern Arabia became so numerous that the local bishops sought Church instructions to organize the administration and liturgical customs of their communities, and even business practices. An important and interesting example of this trend comes from around 584 CE in the form of the request for instructions from Jacob, bishop of Dairin, to Patriarch Isho'yahb I, and the 20 canons that he received back from the Patriarch.[60]

A curious remark about the Christians of Beth Qatraye is worth noting here. It comes from *the Khuzistan Chronicle* (late seventh century CE). When the Sassanids besieged Alexandria in 619 CE, a Christian from Beth Qatraye named Peter, who was in Alexandria studying Philosophy, helped them breach the walls. Also, when the Arabs laid siege to Tustar in 640 CE, they were similarly helped breach the walls by a man from Beth Qatraye.[61] One wonders if the author of *the Khuzistan Chronicle*, writing in the late seventh century CE, had particular grudges against the Christians of Beth Qatraye. Possibly fueled by their attempt to split from the Church in Seleucia-Ctesiphon, he projected his biases in the way he treated them as traitors to Christianity (the capture of Alexandria, according to *the Khuzistan Chronicle*, led to many priceless Christian treasurers getting confiscated by the Sassanids and sent to Persia).

CONCLUSION

As seen in this presentation, we do possess a variety of evidence, both textual and archaeological, for the spread of Christianity in Arabia. They point to a Christian presence with varying degrees of significance in different parts of Arabia. Christianity in the Hijaz

---

[60] See *Synodicon orientale*, 424–451; and *Histoire nestorienne inédite*, 2.2:439.

[61] See *Chronicon anonymum* in *Chronica minora, part 1—CSCO Vol. 4* (Paris: Typographeo Reipublicae, 1903), 15–39.

existed in the form of a few individuals around the time of Muhammad, but it seems to have completely disappeared there by the year 630 CE. As for Najran, Christianity was introduced sometime in the mid to late fifth century CE and remained until the thirteenth century CE or a little later. Likely, the Christians of Najran were split into several denominations, including Nestorian and Monophysite. In Eastern Arabia, Christianity started there in the fourth century CE and remained until the ninth century CE with the majority being Nestorian, with some Monophysite presence.

Yet, one cannot emphasize enough the need for further study of Christianity in Arabia. This is especially the case given that we know little about the actual beliefs and practices of Arabian Christians aside from some very general statements (such as they were Nestorians or Monophysites). For instance, the study of Dadisho^c's *Commentary on the Paradise of the Egyptian Fathers* might help us understand the type of Christian monasticism practiced in eastern Arabia. The same applies to the works of other Christian authors from Beth Qatraye, such as Isaac of Nineveh, Ahob of Qatar and Rabban Gabriel. Such an undertaking will also guide us in better assessing the validity of the existing historical record.

THE QURANIC WORD *ḤANĪF* AND ITS EXPLANATION IN THE LIGHT OF THE SYRIAC ROOT

ABDUL RAHMAN CHAMSEDDINE
GEORGETOWN UNIVERSITY SFS, QATAR

ABSTRACT

The word ḥanīf *is used to describe Abraham in the Qur'an, where it appears twelve times in twelve different verses, seven of which are associated with Abraham. The term in most of these contexts can easily be understood as an adjective describing the righteousness of a pious Muslim. However, several accounts from pre-Islamic Arabian history show that there were some individuals who belonged to a special sect called the* ḥanīfiyya, *and that they had also claimed to be followers of Abraham. Furthermore, several ancient reports that use the term* ḥanīf *can be found in historical accounts originating from other Semitic languages, especially Syriac. This paper attempts to track the origins of the term in the Syriac language and tries to understand the Qur'anic term in the light of its origins.*

"Ibn Ishaq said: [...] One day when the Quraysh had assembled on a feast day to venerate and circumambulate the idol to which they offered sacrifices, this being a feast which they held annually, four men drew apart secretly and agree to keep their counsel in the bonds of friendship. They were: Waraqa b. Nawfal b. Asad b. ʿAbd al-ʿUzza, ʿUbaydullah b. Jahsh, Othman b. al-Huwayrith, and Zayd b. ʿAmro b. Nufayl, they were of the opinion that their people had corrupted the religion of their father Abraham, and that the stone they went around was

> of no account; it could neither hear, nor see, nor harm nor help. Hey people, "find yourselves a religion", they said; "for by god you have none". So they went their several ways in the lands, seeking the *ḥanifiyya*, the religion of Abraham…"[1]

What is this *ḥanifiyya* and what is the relation between this word and the Qur'anic word *ḥanif*? Western scholars, in general, agree on the Semitic origins of the word. The cognate Hebrew root *ḥ-n-f* is associated with heretics. Others have associated *ḥanif* with the Hebrew word *teḥinnoth* ("prayers"), or with *taḥannafa*, a word of Arabic origin, that is considered as a religious terminology. In Syriac documents the form *ḥanpa* denotes non-Christian "pagans".[2] Francois de Blois has pointed to the usage of *ḥanpa* in a Syriac context where it denotes a person that is not a Jew or a Christian but was nevertheless righteous.[3] Interestingly, in Syriac texts the term *ḥanif* is applied to the Sabi'a, who abandoned their original faith for a new one, and the word has the same meaning among the southern Arabs. It is also noted that the term is an Arabized version of a word of the Aramaic origin that spread in the Levant during the pre-Islamic period, indicating a pagan deviation. The Encyclopedia of Islam advises that *ḥanif*'s origins should be sought outside a Qur'anic context, and warns that terms such as these are subject to questions of authenticity and misinterpretation.[4]

The plural form of the term *hanif* in Arabic is *hunafa'* and it is mentioned twice in the Qur'an. The existence of this plural form led to the belief, at least among Muslims, that there was a group of people who held the same religious beliefs and formed a sect in pre-Islamic Arabia. Some Orientalists considered the *Ḥunafa'* as an

---

[1] رضوان السيد, مفاهيم الجماعات في الإسلام, دار المنتخب العربي, بيروت, 1993, ص. 9, نقلاً عن سيرة ابن هشام 1\222, و الروض الأنف 3\119-131.

[2] نبيه أمين فارس و هارولد و. جلدن, "تطور كلمة حنيف القرآنية", الأبحاث, 13 (1960): 25-42.

[3] "*Naṣrānī* (Ναζωραῖος) and *ḥanīf* (ἐθνικός): Studies on the Religious Vocabulary of Christianity and Islam", BSOAS 65 (2002): 16–25.

[4] (Encyclopedia of Islam) EI2 *hanif* article by Montgomery Watt.

Arab Christian sect, which was partially adopted by the so-called *Ḥunafa'* monks.[5]

In Arabic, the most common meaning of the word *ḥanif* is "inclination". In the dictionary *al-ʿAyn*, Al-Khalil b. Ahmad al-Farahidi writes, "*al-ḥanaf* is an inclination in the upper part of the foot, and a man could be *'aḥnaf* or a foot that can be *ḥanfa'* (patterns differ according to gender). It is also said that al-'Aḥnaf b. Qays (a name of a well-known *tabiʿi* [the one who met a companion of the Prophet but not the Prophet himself]) was given this name due to an inclination in his foot". The related verb form *taḥannafa* means to incline towards something. 'Ibn Qutayba writes, "*Ḥanif* means straight, and it was given for the crippled as a wish for him to get well (this is an old Arab habit.)"[6] The meaning of *ḥanaf* is therefore "inclination". As Al-Jawhari writes in his dictionary *al-Taj*, "*al-ḥanaf* is the curvature in the foot … and the man (who has this curvature) is called *aḥnaf*, and that's why al-Aḥnaf b. Qays was given this name". *Ḥanif* is also used to refer to "shoe", and its feminine pattern (*ḥanfa'*) refers to intrinsically curved objects such as "arch" and "penknife". 'Ibn Manzur, while defining this term in his *Lisan al-ʿArab*, writes, "*al-ḥanif* means the one who is leaning from good to bad or from bad to good".

Some scholars have come to believe that the word *ḥanif* was not Arabic at all, and was not clearly understood, but used loosely as a descriptive title without any clear meaning.[7] Most prominent among these scholars is Luxenberg, the author of *The Syro-Aramaic Reading of the Koran*,[8] where his interpretation of the word relies on the Syriac meaning—"pagan". Luxenberg uses this example to imply that the Arabs used terms that they did not properly understand

5 جواد علي المفصل في تاريخ العرب قبل الإسلام, ط. 2, دار العلم للملايين, بيروت, مكتبة النهضة, بغداد, ط. 3, 1970, ج 6, ص.456.

6 المعجم الجامع لغريب مفردات القرآن الكريم: ابن عباس، ابن قتيبة، مكي بن أبي طالب، أبو حيان، إعداد وترتيب الشيخ عبد العزيز عز الدين، بيروت: دار العلم للملايين، 1986م.

7 Hilmi Omar Bey, "Some considerations with regard to the Hanif question", *The Moslem World*, 22(1961): 72–75.

8 Christoph Luxenberg, *The Syro-Aramaic Reading of the Koran*, Schiller, Berlin, 2007.

(a position also taken by the renowned orientalist, Noldeke). Noldeke writes (as quoted by Luxenberg):

> "It is difficult to say, however, how the other meanings emerged from this original meaning. One must consider, though, that the naïve Arab heathens had no idea of the nature of other religions and thus could easily have misunderstood and falsely employed such expressions".[9]

Luxenberg follows this extraordinary statement by stating that the Qur'an repeatedly confirms that Abraham was not a polytheist, producing a bizarre linguistic explanation that Abraham was born as a *ḥanif*, i.e. pagan, but he believed in God at a later stage and then was no longer a polytheist.[10] If the Qur'an does in fact use the term in its "original" Syriac meaning—pagan—this means that Luxenberg has wrongly quoted Noldeke! It should also be noted that Luxenberg's knowledge of Arabic grammar is somewhat lacking. He deals with the *ḥal* (adverb) as if it was a *naʿt* (adjective), and also limits his work to the singular forms and neglects the plural forms of the term *ḥanif* (*ḥunafa'*) that are mentioned in the Qur'an.

ḤANIF IN THE QUR'AN

In Islamic literature, many Muslim commentators and collectors of tradition relate the Qur'anic word *ḥanif* to a group of people who lived in pre-Islamic Arabia, and separated themselves from pagan morals and customs, but who were never able to completely form an independent religious sect. These independent individuals were considered by some as the adherents of the Abrahamic *Ḥanifiyya* and were thus the predecessors of Muhammad.[11] Abraham is the most famous and important prophet to appear in the three monotheist religions: Judaism, Christianity, and Islam. Each group maintains that they are the true heirs of Abraham. "Surat Al-Imran"

---

[9] Theodor Noldeke, *Geschichte des Qorans* [History of the Koran], Gottingen, 1860, p. 163.

[10] Christoph Luxenberg, *The Syro-Aramaic Reading of the Koran*, Schiller, Berlin, 2007, p. 55–57.

[11] Hilmi Omar Bey, p. 73.

deals with this issue and tries to specify the religion of Abraham,[12] in order to legitimize the Muslim claim to Abraham.[13]

(ما كان ابراهيم يهودًيا ولا نصرانيًا و لكن كان حنيفًا مسلمًا و ما كان من المشركين)[14]

> Abraham was neither a Jew nor a Christian, but a man of pristine faith, a Muslim, nor was he an idolater.

One translator of the Qur'an translated *ḥanif* as "an upright man who had surrendered to Allah".[15] This verse has almost the same meaning as verse 135 of "Surat Al-Baqara":

(وقالوا كونوا هودًا أو نصارى تهتدوا قلْ بل ملة إبراهيم حنيفًا وما كان من المشركين)[16]

> And they say, be Jews or Christians, then you will be guided. Say to them we follow only the religion of Abraham *ḥanifa* and he was not of *Al-Mushrikun*.

This verse was revealed when the Jews of Medina and the Christians *(Naṣara)* of Najran quarreled with the Muslims, each group claiming that they had the best prophet, the best book, and the best religion; the Qur'an ended this quarrel by referring them to Abraham who was a *ḥanif* Muslim.[17]

It is clear from these two verses that the Qur'an is trying to give Abraham, the common prophet, an identity different from the

---

[12] Neal Robinson, "*Surat Al-Imran* and Those with the Greatest Claim to Abraham" *Journal of Qur'anic Studies*, 6 (2005): 7–8.

[13] Patricia Crone and Michael Cook, *Hagarism*, New York: Cambridge University Press, 1977, p. 32.

[14] "Surat Al-Imran" 67.

[15] Mohammed Marmaduke Pickthall, *The meaning of the Glorious Koran*, Mentor Book, Chicago, p. 67.

[16] "Surat Al-Baqara" 135.

[17] أسباب النزول, تحق. محمد عبدالقادر شاهين, دار الكتب العلمية, أبو الحس النيسابوري, بيروت, 2000,ص. 23.

other identities found in Arabia,[18] in other words a distinctive "Muslim" identity, employing the word *ḥanif*.

The word *ḥanif* appears in the Qur'an twelve times in twelve different verses; the first two verses are already translated above; the others are given below, translated according to the translation of Muhammad Taqi-ud-Din al-Hilai.[19]

البقرة 135:(وقالوا كونوا هودًا أو نصارى تهتدوا قل بل ملة إبراهيم حنيفًا وما كان من المشركين)

آل عمران 67:(ما كان إبراهيم يهوديًا ولا نصرانيًا ولكن كان حنيفًا مسلمًا وما كان من المشركين)

آل عمران95:(قل صدق الله فاتبعوا ملة ابراهيم حنيفًا وما كان من المشركين)

-Al-ʿImran 95: Say: Allah has spoken the truth; follow the religion of Abraham *Ḥanifa*, and he was not of *Al-Mushrikun.*

النساء 125:(ومن أحسن دينًا ممن أسلم وجهه لله وهو محسن واتبع ملة ابراهيم حنيفًا واتخذ الله ابراهيم خليلا)

-al-Nisaa' 125: And who can be better in religion than one who submits his face (himself) to Allah; and he is a good doer and follows the religion of Abraham *Ḥanifa.* And Allah did take Abraham as an intimate friend.

الأنعام 79:(إني وجهت وجهي للذي فطر السموات والأرض حنيفًا وما أنا من المشركين)

-al-Anaʿam 79: Verily, I have turned my face towards him who has created the heavens and the earth *Ḥanifa*, and I am not of *Al-Mushrikun.*

الأنعام 161:(قل إنني هداني ربي إلى صراط مستقيم دينًا قيمًا ملة إبراهيم حنيفًا وما كان من المشركين)

---

[18] G.R. Hawting, *The Idea of Idolatry and the Emergence of Islam*, Cambridge, 1992, p. 15.

[19] *Translation of the meanings of* THE NOBLE QUR'AN *in English Language*, King Fahd Complex For The Printing Of The Holy Qur'an.

-al-Anaʿam 161: Say: "truly, my Lord has guided me to a straight path, a right religion, the religion of Abraham, *Ḥanifa* and he was not of *Al-Mushrikun.*

يونس 105:(وأن أقم وجهك للدين حنيفًا ولا تكونن من المشركين)

-Younos 105: And direct your face entirely towards the religion *Ḥanif*, and never be one of the *Mushrikun.*

النحل 120:(إن إبراهيم كان أمة قانتا لله حنيفًا ولم يك من المشركين)

-al-Nahal 120: Verily, Abraham was an *Ummah* (a leader having all the good righteous qualities), or a nation, obedient to Allah, *Ḥanif* and he was not one of those who were *Al-Mushrikun.*

النحل 123:(ثم أوحينا إليك أن اتبع ملة ابراهيم حنيفًا وما كان من المشركين)

-al-Nahal 123: Then, we have sent the revelation to you: Follow the religion of Abraham *Ḥanif* and he was not of the *Mushrikun.*

الحج 31:(حنفاء لله غير مشركين به و من يشرك بالله فكأنما خرّ من السماء فتخطفه الطير أو تهوى به الريح في مكان سحيق)

-al-Haj 31: *Ḥunafaʾ Lillah,* not associating partners unto him; and whoever assigns partners to Allah, it is as if he had fallen from the sky, and the birds had snatched him, or the wind had thrown him to a far off place.

الروم 30: :(فأقم وجهك للدين حنيفًا فِطرت الله التي فطر الناس عليها لا تبديل لخلق الله ذلك الدين القيم ولكن أكثرالناس لا يعلمون)

-al-Rum: So set your face towards the religion *Ḥanif.* Allah's *Fiṭrah* with which he has created mankind. No change let there be in *Khalq-illah*: that is the straight religion, but most of men know not.

البينة 5: :(وما أمروا إلا ليعبدوا الله مخلصين له الدين حنفاء و يقيموا الصلاة ويؤتوا الزكاة وذلك دين القيمة)

-al-Bayyina: And they were commanded not, but that they should worship Allah, and worship none but him alone, and perform *As-Ṣalat* and give *Zakat*, and that is the right religion.

It is clear that the word *Ḥanif* always describes a Muslim or a believer who believes in a pure monotheism that is distinct from the practices of the *mushrikun* (who could be polytheists, idolaters, disbelievers in the oneness of Allah, and those who joined partners with Allah). It is attested ten times in the singular and twice in the plural. As Robinson notes, "In eight instances it refers explicitly to Abraham, and in seven of these it is followed by the assertion that he was not one of the associators"[20] [i.e. an idolater—one who associates another god with God].

Ibn Jarir al-Tabari (d.310/923) the first exegete whose work *Jami'al-bayan fi ta'wil al-Qur'an* was the first major work in the development of traditional Quranic sciences,[21] quotes a number of scholars who give different interpretations for *Ḥanif*. Most of these interpretations are associated with Islamic regulations, such as circumcision or pilgrimage, but these readings have been reasonably rejected by other scholars. If *Ḥanif* refers to the circumcised, then the Jews would also be considered *Ḥunafa'*, contradicting verse 67 of Al-Imran. And if *Ḥanif* refers to the pilgrim, then the Arab idolaters before Islam who also embarked on pilgrimages should also be considered *Ḥunafa'*, contradicting the same verse.[22] Since the Arabic root means "to incline", it could be understood as one who has abandoned the prevailing religions and has inclined to a religion of his own.[23] It is this latter connotation that is found in Arabic dictionaries.[24] In our case, however, there is no contradiction at all; Jews and Christians gave the title *ḥanif* to those who converted, and

[20]Neal Robinson, "Surat Al-Imran and Those with the Greatest Claim to Abraham", p. 7.

[21]Nadia Maria El Cheikh, "Surat Al-Rum: A Study of the Exegetical Literature", Journal of the American Oriental Society 118.3 (1998): 356–364.

[22] ابن جرير الطبري, جامع البيان في تأويل القرآن, مج. 1, دار الكتب العلمية, بيروت, 1992م, ص. 61.

[23] *Encyclopedia of the Qur'an*, ed. Jane Dammen McAuliffe, Brill, Leiden-Boston, 2002, v.2, p. 402.

[24] ابن منظور, لسان العرب, ج. 9, دار صادر, بيروت, 1992م, ص, 57.

the Qur'an gave this title to the same people who had abandoned their religions and became *Ḥunafa'*.

The Qur'an therefore uses the same negative title in a positive sense, since it appears in the Qur'an as the religion of Abraham and as a synonym for Muslim. However, it could also be applied to monotheists who lived prior to Islam and engaged in practices like pilgrimage and circumcision. However, some Arabic sources, for example al-Ya'koubi (d.292 A.H), use the term to refer to pagans who worship the stars *(al-sabi'un)*.[25] Al-Shahristani (d.54 A.H) differentiates between *al-sabi'a* and *Ḥunafa'* in his book al-Milal wa al-Nihal,[26] and considers them as two opposing groups. It is possible that al-Ya'koubi, al-Shahristani, and others relied on non-Arabic sources while talking about *Ḥanifs*.

We may then return to the anecdote narrated by Ibn Ishaq at the very beginning of this article. It is clear that these four individuals had actually denied the faith of their people and began to incline towards a new faith, and as a result they became in the eyes of their people *sabi'a* or *Ḥunafa'*.

---

25 Encyclopedia of the Qur'an, v.2, p. 403.

26 أبو الفتح الشهرستاني, الملل و النحل, المكتبة العصرية, صيدا-بيروت, ط2, 2001, ج 2, ص. 8.

THE MANUSCRIPT HERITAGE OF ISAAC OF NINEVEH: A SURVEY OF SYRIAC MANUSCRIPTS

GRIGORY KESSEL
MARBURG UNIVERSITY, GERMANY

ABSTRACT

The 20th century saw a growing renewed interest to the literary heritage of Isaac of Nineveh, but some issues, such as the transmission history of Isaac's works, have not been treated properly. This paper discusses the evidence provided by the extant Syriac manuscripts regarding dissemination and circulation of Isaac's corpus in three branches of the Syriac tradition: Church of the East, Syrian Orthodox, and Rum Orthodox. Attention is paid not only to the complete manuscripts but also to the monastic compilations that contain single treatises, fragments and excerpts from Isaac's corpus. Besides already well-known manuscripts that were used earlier for editions, this paper introduces a number of manuscripts that have become available (or were identified as containing Isaac's works) only recently. A comprehensive study of the actual manuscript witnesses and the manuscript transmission of Isaac's corpus will not only reveal some peculiarities of the corpus' history and filiations but will also help to clarify the individual character that the corpus received in different traditions.

The aim of this paper is to provide a brief introduction to the Syriac manuscripts containing the works of Isaac of Nineveh that have been preserved.[1] It should be noted that the survey covers only those works of Isaac of Nineveh upon which there is a scholarly consensus with regard to their authenticity. This concerns the so-called three *Parts* (or: collections), which make up a Syriac corpus of the works of Isaac. We shall leave aside a number of texts, which despite an explicit attribution to Isaac of Nineveh nevertheless at present are not considered to be authentic.[2]

The survey will consist of two unequal parts. In the main part I will introduce the main manuscript copies of each of the three collections while revealing their characteristic features within the manuscript tradition. In conclusion the importance of a comprehensive study of the manuscript tradition of the Syriac corpus of Isaac of Nineveh will be demonstrated and the principal tasks that are yet to be implemented will be indicated. The limits of the paper unfortunately do not allow me to deal with the proposed issues in great detail, and I rather see my task more as to point out the desiderata in this domain of research and thereby to stimulate prospective students to venture further.

In spite of the tremendous admiration which the works of Isaac have enjoyed throughout the centuries (and continue to be very popular also today), the original Syriac text of the *First Part* was published only in 1909 by Lazarist Paul Bedjan (1838–1920),[3] who became renowned in Europe as the publisher of a large number of Syriac texts, many of which—just as it is the case of the *First Part* of Isaac of Nineveh—became not only the *editio princeps* but also remain up to the present the only existing editions.

---

[1] The reader is kindly asked to refer to the Appendix that contains a list of the manuscripts in a table format.

[2] For a general bibliography on Isaac's œuvre see G. Kessel & K. Pinggéra, *A Bibliography of Syriac Ascetic and Mystical Literature* (Eastern Christian Studies, 11; Leuven: Peeters, 2011), pp. 103–122.

[3] H.L. Murre-van den Berg, 'Paul Bedjan, Missionary for Life (1838-1920),' in P. Bedjan, *Homilies of Mar Jacob of Sarug [Homiliae Selectae Mar-Jacobi Saurgensis]*, vol. VI (Piscataway, NJ: Gorgias Press, 2006, pp. 339-369).

In his introduction to the edition of the Syriac text Bedjan briefly describes the manuscripts he had used.[4] Apart from four manuscripts of the British and Vatican Libraries (descriptions of which are easily available in the catalogues of the relevant collections), the editor also made use of four other manuscripts coming from the Near Eastern collections of Mardin, Alqosh, Mosul and Siirt.

Researchers have continued to study the manuscript tradition and, in particular, have sought out new copies also after the appearance of Bedjan's edition. Moreover, it would be no exaggeration to say that in many ways this edition provided the impetus for further research of Isaac's *œuvre*.[5]

While putting together the available data we may say that at present twenty copies are known to exist (including the eight used by Bedjan) and they contain the text of the *First Part* in its most complete form.

In this connection it is important to note that treatises from the *First Part* are present also in the manuscripts of the other type, that is, compilations or monastic miscellanies, which contain se-

---

[4] P. Bedjan, (ed.), *Mar Isaacus Ninivita. De perfectione religiosa* (Parisiis-Lipsiæ: Otto Harrassowitz, 1909), pp. v–vi.

[5] A.J. Wensinck, *Mystic Treatises by Isaac of Nineveh* (Verhandelingen der Koninklijke Akademie van Wetenschappen te Amsterdam. Afdeeling Letterkunde. Nieuwe Reeks. Deel 23, Nr. 1; Amsterdam 1923), pp. xii–xvii; W. Thomson, *Isaac of Nineveh. A Study in Syrian Mysticism* (PhD thesis, Harvard University, 1924), pp. xxi–xxvii; É. Khalifé-Hachem, 'Issac de Ninive,' in *Dictionnaire de la Spiritualité* 7 (1971), col. 2053; A. Vööbus, *History of Asceticism in the Syrian Orient. A Contribution to the History of Culture in the Near East* (CSCO 500, Subsidia 181; Lovanii: Peeters, 1988), p. 339; S. Chialà, *Dall'ascesi eremitica alla misericordia infinita. Ricerche su Isacco di Ninive e la sua fortuna* (Biblioteca della Rivista di Storia e Letteratura Religiosa. Studi, 14; Firenze, 2002), pp. 66–68; G. Kessel, 'The manuscript tradition of the 'First Part' of Isaac of Nineveh. Preliminary observations,' in A. Muraviev (ed.), [*Mar Isḥaq Nineviyskiy. First Part. Treatises 1–6*] (Moscow, forthcoming).

lected treatises, as well as fragments.[6] The manuscripts of this type have yet not been systematically studied, but my preliminary research allows us to conclude that there are about thirty of them.[7] And, finally, we can also briefly point to the existence of small fragments (consisting just of a few pages) in regard to which it is impossible to determine whether they were a part of a complete copy of the *First Part* or if they belonged to a certain compilation. As an example we can refer to a fragment of a manuscript kept at Damascus that can be roughly dated back to the eleventh century.[8]

Thus, leaving aside compilations and fragments, let us move on to an overview of the copies of the *First Part* that (albeit in their original form) contained its text in its most complete form. All copies of the *First Part* may be divided into three groups depending on their ecclesiastical affiliation, that is, the Church of the East (to which Isaac of Nineveh himself belonged), the Syrian Orthodox Church and the Syro-Chalcedonian one. In contemporary scholarly usage it is customary to call them the East Syriac, Syrian Orthodox and Melkite. Similarly, in my survey I shall be providing the basic information on the manuscripts with an indication of their origin and ecclesiastical affiliation.[9]

---

[6] Some miscellanies contain not the selected treatises but the complete text of the *First Part*, e.g. Mar Mattai 27 and Sharfeh Raḥmani 310 (the former most probably served as its model).

[7] At the moment I am pursuing a project that aims to study all extant Syriac monastic miscellanies. The works attributed to Isaac of Nineveh constitute an essential element in the repertoire. The works attributed to Isaac of Nineveh constitute an essential element in the repertoire. For monastic collections see H. Teule, 'Les compilation monastiques syriaques,' in R. Lavenant (ed.), *Symposium Syriacum VII* (Roma, 1998), pp. 249–262; S.P. Brock, 'Crossing the Boundaries: An Ecumenical Role Played by Syriac Monastic Literature,' in M. Bielawski, D. Hombergen (eds), *Il monachesimo tra Eredità e Aperture* (Roma, 2004), pp. 221–238.

[8] S.P. Brock, 'Notulae syriacae: Some Miscellaneous Identifications,' *Le Muséon* 108 (1995), 69–78 [here p. 69]. Brock does not offer his opinion on the nature of the original manuscript.

[9] This distinction, however, does not account for the variation and difference in text form of the *First Part* (see below on the problem of two

Let us begin with the copies that represent the East Syriac tradition. Out of ten six were used by Bedjan for his edition.

The most ancient copies used by Bedjan are kept today in the British Library (Add. 14632 and Add. 14633),[10] whence they arrived in the nineteenth century from a monastery of the Syrians (Dayr al-Suryan) in the Nitrian Desert in Egypt. The manuscripts are in a fairly good condition, yet their connection to the Syrian Orthodox monastery (and some lacunae) compelled Bedjan to use for the base text of his edition a different, significantly later manuscript.

The Mardin copy was started by Rabban David in a north Mesopotamian village and completed sixteen years later by certain Paul in CE 1234/5. At the end of the nineteenth century the manuscript was kept in the library of the Chaldean diocese in Mardin (contemporary north east Turkey) under the number 46.[11] It is possible to trace the subsequent fate of this manuscript. Under not entirely clear circumstances (most likely for safety purposes at the outset of the First World War in 1914) the manuscript came to the Bibliothèque nationale de France where it is located today as BnF syr. 359. Only a couple of pages are missing in this copy that, as maintained by Bedjan, contains Isaac's text in its most complete and authentic form.

Regarding the manuscript from Siirt, Bedjan states merely that is was an 'old manuscript'. Recourse to the catalogue of the library of the Chaldean diocese in Siirt suggests that the manuscript, which Bedjan could have used, is likely to be identified with the one listed

---

redactions). Evidently, all three branches of the manuscript tradition are related to each other and also intersected, sometimes in a very curious manner. For instance, manuscript Berlin or. quart. 1159 is of East Syriac provenance whereas the text it provides is peculiar to the Syrian Orthodox tradition. Since the scribe used a Syrian Orthodox model I treat the manuscript as a witness to the Syrian Orthodox branch of the manuscript tradition.

[10] W. Wright, *Catalogue of Syriac Manuscripts in the British Museum, acquired since the year 1838*, vol. II (London, 1871), pp. 569–576 and 576–581.

[11] A. Scher, 'Notice sur les manuscrits syriaques et arabes conservés dans la bibliothèque de l'évêché chaldéen de Mardin,' in *Revue des bibliothèques* 18 (1908), p. 79.

under number 76.[12] The description shows that this is indeed an ancient manuscript (the author of the catalogue dates it to the 13th century) containing the *First Part* of Isaac. Unfortunately, the manuscript collection of Siirt was entirely destroyed during the First World War and so we do not have the opportunity to verify if the manuscript 76 was indeed the one used by Bedjan. Nevertheless, thanks to some secondary information such an identification can be considered to be a very plausible one.

Two other manuscripts of the East Syrian group of manuscripts were the copies from Mosul and Alqosh which were produced at Bedjan's behest in 1898. Subsequently, in 1915, the manuscripts were acquired by the Berlin State Library from Bedjan's private collection (now or.quart. 1159 and or.oct. 1258).[13] It deserves to be noted that the text of the Mosul manuscript was copied based on a Syrian Orthodox model.

Let us move on to the manuscripts that for whatever reason were not used by Bedjan.

In spite of the fact that the manuscript Vat.sir. 367 is one of the most ancient witnesses to the *First Part* of Isaac at the present time,[14] it has been generally neglected by scholarship, and this is most probably due to its poor physical condition. Based on the analysis of its ductus one can consider it as belonging to the manuscript production of the 8th – 9th c.

Apart from the manuscript of the British Library copied in Tell-Kepe in northern Iraq in 1898 (BL Or. 9362, belonged to E.A.W. Budge),[15] one more manuscript was not known to Bedjan. Moreover, it is safe to admit that it is the only copy of the *First Part*

---

[12] A. Scher, *Catalogue des manuscrits syriaques et arabes conservés dans la bibiothèque épiscopale de Séert (Kurdistan) avec notes bibliographiques* (Mossoul, 1905), pp. 57–58.

[13] J. Assfalg, *Syrische Handschriften. Syrische, Karšunische, Christlich-Palästinische, Neusyrische und Mandäische Handschriften* (Verzeichnis der orientalischen Handschriften in Deutschland, 5; Wiesbaden: Franz Steiner Verlag, 1963), pp. 40-42 and 42–43.

[14] A. Mai, *Scriptorum veterum nova collectio*, vol. 5 (Romae: Typis vaticanis, 1831), p. 42.

[15] Not yet catalogued.

concerning the very existence of which scholars knew practically nothing, since it was absolutely inaccessible until recently. It is the manuscript bearing the number 181 from the collection of the Syrian Orthodox Monastery of St. Mark in Jerusalem.[16] The manuscript was originally kept in the monastery of the Church of the East in Jerusalem. After its closure all of the manuscripts joined the library of the Greek Orthodox Patriarchate, whence under unknown circumstances part of this collection of manuscripts was moved to the library of the Syrian Orthodox Monastery of St. Mark where they remain to the present day.

Turning to the Syrian Orthodox manuscripts, we can notice that the earliest witnesses can be dated back to the 14th and 15th centuries (within monastic miscellanies the text is attested a couple centuries earlier). It is interesting to observe that during this period the copies of the *First Part* are not only present in the region of south-east Turkey (known as Ṭur ʿAbdin where the manuscripts Mardin Orth. 195,[17] Vat.sir. 562,[18] Mar Mattai 27[19] were copied), but also in Egypt (Vat.sir. 124)[20] where at that time there existed a number of Syrian Orthodox monasteries, one on the most famous of which was of course the monastery of the Syrians or Dayr al-Suryan. Bedjan had access to only one manuscript of that group and regarded them as inauthentic, the text having been altered in

[16] The manuscript collection was fully digitized by the Hill Museum & Manuscript Library (Collegeville, MN). For an earlier description see F. Dolabany, *Catalogue of Syriac Manuscripts in St. Mark's Monastery* (Syriac Patrimony, 8; Damascus: Sidawi Printing House, 1994), pp. 380–381.

[17] F. Dolabany, *Catalogue of Syriac Manuscripts in Zaʿfaran Monastery* (Syriac Patrimony, 9; Damascus, 1994), pp. 43–50.

[18] A. Van Lantschoot, *Inventaire des manuscrits syriaques des fonds Vatican (460-631), Barberini Oriental et Neofiti* (Studi e testi 243; Città del Vaticano, 1965), pp. 87–88.

[19] A. Vööbus, *Handschriftliche Überlieferung der Mēmrē-Dichtung des Jaʿqōb von Serūg. I. Sammlungen: die Handschriften* (CSCO 344, Subsidia 39; Louvain: Peeters, 1973), pp. 66–68.

[20] S.E. Assemanus, J.S. Assemanus, *Bibliothecae Apostolicae Vaticanae codicum manuscriptorum catalogus*, part I, t. 3. (Romae, 1759), pp. 143–151.

order to downplay the apparent theological elements peculiar to the East Syriac tradition.

We may note yet one more curious feature of the Syrian Orthodox group of manuscripts. Unlike the East Syriac manuscript witnesses that as a rule contain the text of the *First Part* only, examining the content of the Syrian Orthodox group of manuscripts it is easily apparent that by the 15th century there had been formed a peculiar Syrian Orthodox corpus of texts attributed to Isaac of Nineveh. It consisted of the *First Part* that was followed by the *Book of Grace* (the genuine author of which was a contemporary of Isaac of Nineveh who may have known him personally, Shemʿon d-Ṭaybuteh)[21] and the treatise *On Stillness* (the author of which may be yet another contemporary of Isaac of Nineveh, who, like Isaac, was a native of the province of Bet Qaṭraye – Dadishoʿ Qaṭraya).[22] In total this corpus is represented by eight copies, one of which—the Harvard one—is lost.

The third group of manuscript witnesses of the *First Part* comprises the manuscripts of Melkite origin. At present we know of only two such copies, both of which are very early witnesses to the text of the *First Part*: Sinai syr. 24 (8th–9th c.)[23] and Vat.sir. 125 (10th c.).[24] Only the latter manuscript was used by Bedjan who re-

---

[21] G. Kessel, 'La position de Simon de Ṭaibūteh dans l'éventail de la tradition mystique syriaque,' in A. Desreumaux (ed.), *Les mystiques syriaques* (Études syriaques, 8; Paris: Geuthner, 2011), pp. 129–158 [here pp. 124–125].

[22] G. Kessel, 'A manuscript tradition of Dadīšōʿ Qaṭrāyā's work 'On stillness' (ʿal šelyā) in Syrian Orthodox milieu,' in M. Tamcke & S. Grebenstein (eds), *Zu Sprache, Geschichte, Theologie und Gegenwartslage der syrischen Kirchen. Ausgewählte Beiträge zum 7. Deutschen Syrologen-Symposium in Göttingen (2011)* (Wiesbaden: Harrassowitz, forthcoming).

[23] A.S. Lewis, *Catalogue of the Syriac MSS. in the Convent of S. Catharine on Mount Sinai* (Studia Sinaitica, 1; London: C.J. Clay and Sons, 1894), p. 41; G. Kessel, 'Sinai syr. 24 as an Important Witness to the Reception History of Some Syriac Ascetic Texts,' in F. Briquel Chatonnet et M. Debie (eds), *Sur les pas des Araméens chrétiens. Mélanges offerts à Alain Desreumaux* (Cahiers d'études syriaques, 1; Paris: Geuthner, 2010), pp. 207–218.

[24] Assemanus, *Bibliothecae Apostolicae Vaticanae*, pp. 152–156.

garded it, similar to the Syrian Orthodox manuscripts, as presenting a deteriorated version of the text.

The two Melkite manuscripts are similar in content: apart from the *First Part* of Isaac of Nineveh, both also contain the *Letter to Patricius* by Philoxenus of Mabbug (d. CE 523) and the *Discourses* (*mēmrē*) of John of Dalyatha. These two manuscripts have a special significance for the history of the text of the *First Part*. In particular, they give us quite a clear idea of the manuscript used by Abramios and Patrikios, the translators of the *First Part* of Isaac into Greek around the end of the 9th century. These manuscripts, especially the Sinai copy, are not only close to the Greek translation in time, but also have interesting parallels with the Greek translation itself, which may explain the certain peculiarities of the latter. For example, it is worth recalling that the Greek translation of the *First Part* contains not only treatises by Isaac of Nineveh but also works by two other Syriac authors. The letter to Symeon the Wonder-worker is none other than an abridged version of *Letter to Patricius* by Philoxenus of Mabbug. Apart from this, four treatises forming part of the Greek translation belong to the pen of the 8th c. East Syriac mystical author John of Dalyatha. If one pays attention to the composition of the two Melkite copies of the *First Part*, then it is possible to see that they contain the very same *Letter* (in an abridged version) of Philoxenus of Mabbug as well the corpus of the *Discourses* of John of Dalyatha. However, apart from similarities in content, there is one more peculiar feature that offers an additional reason to bring together the Melkite copies to the *Vorlage* of the Greek translation. Namely, the Sinai manuscript (in that part which is kept at present in the Bibliothèque nationale de France) contains an indication as to where it was produced, viz. the Monastery of Mar Saba in Palestine. Thus in the case of the Sinai manuscript we are dealing not only with a copy close in content to the *Vorlage* of the Greek translation, but we can also regard it as a valuable document witnessing, firstly, to the type of manuscripts that included the works of Isaac of Nineveh that were available in the Monastery of Mar Saba and, secondly, to the connection which existed between the Syriac-speaking monks of Mar Saba Monastery and the Monastery of Sinai.

Summing up a survey of the manuscripts of the *First Part* one can say that there have come down to us quite a large number of copies, some of which must have been produced within a century after Isaac's life. The manuscripts of East Syriac provenance circulated mainly in the northern Mesopotamian region, were copied up until the 16th century (all the later copies were commissioned by European scholars) and usually contained only the text of the *First Part*. Moreover, by the 12th–13th c. the East Syriac copies had reached the Syrian Orthodox milieu, in particular in northern Mesopotamia and Egypt. Acquaintance with the works of Isaac of Nineveh lead to the formation of a Syrian Orthodox corpus containing, apart from the treatises of the *First Part*, several other works by two different authors which were explicitly attributed to Isaac. It is in the form of that corpus that the *First Part* circulated in the Syrian Orthodox communities. Finally, the Melkite copies are important for a study of the *Vorlage* of the Greek translation and unanimously testify to the active use of the *First Part* of Isaac in Melkite circles in Palestine and Sinai in the period of 8th through 10th c.

THE SECOND PART

In spite of the obvious loss of a large number of manuscript copies of the corpus of Isaac, the extant copies of each collection is certainly a fair reflection of the degree of how popular and widespread each of them used to be.

Thus in contrast to the twenty manuscript copies of the *First Part*, we know today of only four copies containing (or originally containing) the *Second Part* and one of these is lost to boot. When Bedjan published the text of the *First Part* he included in the same volume as an appendix selected fragments from the *Chapters of Knowledge* (that, as we know today, belong to the *Second Part*), using the manuscript that he had discovered in Urmia. The manuscript disappeared in the Near East (along with hundreds of others) during the upheaval of the First World War. Since Bedjan only says a few words about that manuscript we have no detailed information about it.

Due to the loss of the Urmia manuscripts the text of the *Second Part* was believed to be lost until 1983 when Sebastian Brock recognized it in one of the uncatalogued manuscripts of the Bodleian Library in Oxford. Twelve years later there appeared an edition of chapters 4 through 41 which make up approximately half of the total content of the *Second Part*. The *Chapters of Knowledge* remain unedited except for some fragments which were published by Bedjan.[25] At present the Italian scholar Paolo Bettiolo is preparing an edition of the remaining chapters of the *Second Part*.

Which manuscripts were used by Brock in his edition? Apart from the Bodleian manuscripts, he managed to find three other copies containing the complete text and seven manuscripts with selected treatises and fragments.

The appearance of an edition of the *Second Part* (albeit in incomplete form) provided the impulse for further research of the heritage of Isaac of Nineveh and, particularly, of the manuscript witnesses to his corpus.[26] Bringing together all the available data, we can state that, similar to the *First Part*, the text of the *Second Part* was known and circulated in the same three branches of Syriac Christianity.

The principal manuscript containing the complete text is Bodleian Library syr. e. 7 dated approximately to 10th–11th c.[27] There is also its apograph preserved today in Tehran, yet it is of little value as it is a recent copy of the Bodleian manuscript. Nevertheless, the Tehran manuscript testifies to the fact that the Bodleian manuscript was located in the region of northern Mesopotamia up until it was transferred to Great Britain at the beginning of the 20th c. Two other manuscripts (BnF syr. 298[28] and Houghton syr. 57[29])

---

[25] S.P. Brock, *Isaac of Nineveh (Isaac the Syrian). 'The Second Part', Chapters IV-XLI* (CSCO 554/5, Syr. 224/5; Louvain: Peeters, 1995).

[26] Chialà, *Dall'ascesi eremitica*, pp. 68–70; G. Kessel, 'New Manuscript Witnesses to the Second Part of Isaac of Nineveh,' in Markus Vinzent (ed.), *Papers presented at the Sixteenth International Conference on Patristic Studies held in Oxford 2011* (Studia Patristica LXIV; Leuven: Peeters, 2013), pp. 245–257.

[27] The manuscript remains uncatalogued.

[28] J.B. Chabot, 'Notice sur les manuscrits syriaques de la Bibliothèque Nationale acquis depuis 1874,' *Journal asiatique* IX, 8 (1896), 234–290 [here pp. 237–8]; twenty-four folios that once belonged to that codex are preserved today in the Cambridge University Library, Or. 1144 (Kessel, 'New Manuscript Witnesses,' pp. 247–252).

[29] M.H. Goshen-Gottstein, *Syriac Manuscripts in the Harvard College Library: A Catalogue* (Harvard Semitic Studies 23; Missoula, Montana: Scholars Press, 1979), p. 61.

although significantly damaged yet nonetheless are important for the further study and publication of the text of the *Second Part*. It is difficult to say anything concrete in relation to their origin but they are most likely from northern Mesopotamia.

Unlike the *First Part*, the manuscripts containing the selected chapters, as well as fragments from the *Second Part* have been relatively well studied and it enables us to include the evidence they provide in the survey.

The eight treatises from the *Second Part* can be found in a very important East Syriac monastic miscellany (Baghdad Chaldean Monastery, syr. 680)[30] of ascetical and mystical texts, which was copied in the thirteenth century at the famous Monastery of Rabban Hormizd in northern Mesopotamia. This manuscript served as a model for the three manuscripts which were copied from it in the first half of the twentieth century (Baghdad Chaldean Monastery, syr. 681, Vat.sir. 509 and Mingana syr. 601).

Despite the insignificant number of East Syriac witnesses to the text of the *Second Part*, it is important to note that its text was well known beyond the borders of the communities of the Church of the East already beginning from the 12th–13th c. Thus, the treatises from the *Second Part* were identified in five Syrian Orthodox manuscripts copied between the 12th–13th and 18th c. With maybe only one exception (manuscript BL Add. 14729 is of uncertain provenance, perhaps from Dayr al-Suryan),[31] all of them most probably come from the region of Ṭur ʿAbdin.

An analysis of the text preserved in the Syrian Orthodox witnesses allows us to draw the following conclusions. Firstly, all the Syrian Orthodox manuscripts seem to represent one particular type of the text. Secondly, there are grounds to admit that it was quite early (approximately in the 12th/13th c. century) when a selection of certain treatises and fragments from the *Second Part* was made. In the course of further usage and copying that original selection of texts was subjected to further editing, rearranging and handling.

---

[30] J.-M., Vosté, 'Recueil d'auteurs ascétiques nestoriens du VIIe et VIIIe siècle,' *Angelicum* 6 (1929), pp. 143–206.

[31] Wright, *Catalogue of Syriac Manuscripts*, pp. 874–876.

The third group of witnesses to the text of the *Second Part* are the manuscripts of Melkite origin. Like the Melkite copies of the *First Part*, in this case we can observe a very early acquaintance of the Melkite communities with the text of the *Second Part*. Regrettably, we know for sure the time and place of origin of only one of these three manuscripts. The so-called *Codex Syriacus Secundus* was produced in 882 CE near Beirut and belongs to the genre of monastic miscellanies.[32] The other two manuscripts (also miscellanies) are of roughly the same date and might well have been copied in the Melkite milieu of Palestine and Sinai. All this documents the availability and popularity of the *Second Part* during the 9th–10th c. in the Melkite circles.

Since all extant Syrian Orthodox and Melkite witnesses are miscellanies that contain only selected texts, it remains unclear if the *Second Part* was ever available in the respective milieu in a complete form.

THE THIRD PART

It is only recently that the *Third Part* has become known and, thanks to the assiduous endeavors of Sabino Chialà we have today a complete edition accompanied by an Italian translation.[33] The *Third Part* consists of seventeen treatises, three of which are also included in the *First Part* (chs. 22 and 40) and one is present in the *Second Part* (ch. 25). The text has been preserved in the unique manuscript preserved today in the Chaldean church in Tehran. The manuscript itself was copied between 1900 and 1903 CE in the Urmia region. Unfortunately, nothing is known of the manuscript that served as its model and it is indeed a miracle that it had survived until the beginning of the 20th c. Nevertheless, some traits of the Tehran manuscript suggest that its model must have been of

---

[32] Edited in facsimile W. Strothmann, *Codex syriacus secundus. Bibel-Palimpsest aus dem 6./7. Jh. (Katalog Hiersemann 500/3)* (GOF.S., 13; Wiesbaden: Otto Harrassowitz, 1978).

[33] S. Chialà, *Isacco di Ninive. Terza Collezione* (CSCO 637/638, Syr. 246/247; Leuven: Peeters, 2011).

East Syriac origin and likely to be of an old age, being copied perhaps before 14th/15th c.

The availability of the complete text of the *Third Part* has enabled the identification of some of its treatises scattered in various monastic miscellanies. Chialà discovered two treatises from the *Third Part* in the aforementioned East Syriac monastic miscellany of the thirteenth century (Baghdad Chaldean Monastery, syr. 680). An earlier mentioned Syrian Orthodox manuscript BL Add. 14729 containing fragments from the two treatises can also be dated to the same period. Moreover, excerpts from various treatises of the *Third Part* were discovered in a Syrian Orthodox prayer book (BnF syr. 178)[34] that was copied in 1490 CE at Dayr al-Suryan in Egypt.[35] Besides this Syrian Orthodox prayer book, Chialà has discovered similar prayers in the ninth-century Melkite manuscript *Codex syriacus primus*. It is worth stressing that the given manuscript is a fine illustration of the fact that by the 9th c. at least some texts of all three parts known today were available in the Syro-Chalcedonian milieu.

A faint trace of the *Third Part* in the Syrian Orthodox and Melkite traditions does not make it possible to suggest that its complete text was available, rather, it is more likely that both traditions were familiar with only a few such selections.

CONCLUSIONS

It seems quite easy to get lost among the numerous manuscripts containing either the complete text of a particular part or selected

---

[34] H. Zotenberg, *Catalogues des manuscrits syriaques et sabéens (mandaïtes) de la Bibliothèque Nationale* (Paris: Imprimerie nationale, 1874), pp. 124–126.

[35] Here we must make a slight digression and highlight the fact that one regularly comes across various prayers attributed to Isaac of Nineveh in the Syriac manuscripts and a study of some of those makes clear that they often turn out to be excerpts from certain treatises of Isaac. However, this type of manuscript witnesses has not been thoroughly studied and therefore I have not included in present survey manuscripts containing prayers.

treatises or, finally, fragments and excerpts from the treatises.[36] Moreover, an impression may arise that the text of the three *Parts* has been published in full and no more work related to the manuscripts is required. Why then is it still important to explore the manuscript tradition of Isaac's corpus? Let me express some considerations regarding the consecutive order of the parts.

After the appearance of Bedjan's edition of the *First Part*, researchers adopted a now widespread view of its satisfactory or even fine quality, primarily due the use of the ancient East Syriac copy that Bedjan had selected as the basis for his edition. It is only this *a priori* trust[37] that can explain the lack of attention paid to the particularities of the manuscript tradition of the Syriac text and the absence of special studies devoted to the manuscript tradition and textual criticism of the *First Part*. In reality, my preliminary analysis of the edition (against the actual manuscript, BnF syr. 359) demonstrates that (on a par with other editions by Bedjan) the underlying principles followed by the editor fall short of current conventional standards.[38] By way of an example, we may notice that the text contains emendations that were introduced by Bedjan without any indication or that the codices within two couples of manuscripts from London and Vatican are not distinguished in the apparatus (signified merely by sigla L and V). Moreover, if we take into account a substantial number of witnesses that come from the 8th and 9th c. the necessity to produce a critical edition becomes fundamental for any proper study of Isaac's thought. I should also underline that some of the ancient witnesses have never been studied and therefore an evaluation of their significance for the establishment of a critical edition remains an important desideratum for future research.

One cannot but regret that up to this day a whole set of questions related to the manuscript transmission of the *First Part* has

---

[36] Here it is once again essential to note that in the case of the *First Part* I have left aside the so-called monastic miscellanies, or collections containing selected treatises or fragments from treatises.

[37] A general underdevelopment in Syriac philology is not to be dismissed too.

[38] Kessel, 'The manuscript tradition of the 'First Part'.

not been settled. Firstly, there is no complete list of all the manuscript witnesses to the *First Part* in their different types (complete copies, manuscripts with selected treatises, fragments and excerpts).[39] The extant witnesses were not compared to each other, although there is a remarkable degree of variation both on the level of the ordering and in the textual form. We do not know the circumstances of the origins of the extant witnesses. Monastic miscellanies are yet to be explored for the treatises from Isaac's corpus. We should also not overlook the titles and rubrics that feature in the treatises in different form.

Next, a major problem of two redactions (first mentioned by Bedjan) requires urgent revision.[40] In short, it is accepted by scholarship that there are two different text forms of the *First Part*: an authentic, East Syriac form and a reworked, Syrian Orthodox one, where all unacceptable theological and dogmatic elements were leveled. However, an examination of the manuscripts shows that the actual situation is much more complex. For instance, the witnesses of Melkite provenance exhibit some variants that make it difficult to assign them straightforwardly to the Syrian Orthodox redaction of the text and hence their position in the manuscript transmission of the *First Part* is yet to be pinpointed. Equally, one cannot observe a uniformity and stability in the witnesses of East Syriac provenance (that at times agree with the text provided by the Syrian Orthodox witnesses) and a critical assessment of their authenticity has not yet been implemented.

In addition, I should stress the fact that there are numerous explanatory comments on the margins of some manuscripts (e.g. the Mardin and Jerusalem ones). Although these scholia remain unpublished (only roughly one third was included by Bedjan in his edition) and unexplored, they are without a doubt very important

---

39 One should by no means exclude (however faint it would be) a possibility that new and previously unknown witnesses will be unearthed in the Middle Eastern libraries.

40 Bedjan, *Mar Isaacus Ninivita*, pp. iv-v; [D. Miller], *The Ascetical Homilies of Saint Isaac the Syrian, translated by the Holy Transfiguration Monastery* (Boston, 1984), pp. lxxvii-lxxix; Chialà, *Dall'ascesi eremitica*, p. 67; Kessel, 'The manuscript tradition of the 'First Part'.

for a study of the reception of Isaac's thought. One cannot exclude the possibility that they are not mere *ad hoc* notes jotted down by a reader but were borrowed by a scribe from a commentary.

To sum up, it is the strong certitude of the present author that the very first task of the prospective study of the *First Part* should be a revision of Bedjan's edition. It must be implemented while taking into account the evidence of as many manuscript witnesses as possible. A sorting out of the manuscript witnesses should be a precondition for the preparation of the critical edition. A need for the critical edition is also supported by the very fact of the broad expansion of the manuscript tradition of the text. Undoubtedly, all these ramifications require adequate documentation.

The *Second Part* is critically edited but only partially so and, therefore, an editor of what remains cannot manage without a thorough study of the manuscript tradition. It is worth highlighting that a quest for additional witnesses (especially those that contain selected treatises and fragments) may prove successful. While talking about the *First Part* I mentioned the presence of explanatory comments in some of the manuscripts. Interestingly enough, a similar set of scholia may also be found in the manuscripts that contain the *Second Part* and definitely deserve to be explored.

In the case of the *Third Part*, the situation is much better, because the editor, Sabino Chialà, produced an edition of the text in full and used all the manuscript witnesses that he had been able to find. Nevertheless since the unique complete copy of the text is very recent an evaluation of the evidence provided by other witnesses may play a crucial role for researching into the history of the *Third Part* and for a clarification of the authenticity of some of the treatises it contains (it is worth recalling that Chialà has already conceded that there are a couple of problematic texts).

A comprehensive study of the manuscript tradition of all the three collections will provide a necessary foundation for further inquiry concerning the history of the formation and development of the collections as we know them today. The presence of identical treatises may serve as a reliable indication that their present composition is an outcome of later editorial work, whereas initially there was no division into separate *Parts*. Another proof for this, as it seems, is offered by the Arabic tradition of the works of Isaac that has a remarkably different composition of the corpus. Having mentioned the Arabic version (but it would be of course more precise to call it 'versions' for the works of Isaac were translated into Arabic more than once and not only from Syriac but also from Arabic) one should say that the texts preserved in Arabic with an attribution to Isaac of Nineveh have been barely studied and we cannot exclude that a full-scale research of the many dozens of extant manuscripts may bring about discoveries of authentic works of Isaac that are not preserved in Syriac.

Concluding this survey, I would like to point out that besides textual criticism there is one more aspect that makes us to consider a study of the manuscript tradition of Isaac's *œuvre* as having an immense significance for the Syriac tradition. I am talking about a history of Isaac's corpus from the point of view of its penetration, circulation and impact within different branches of Syriac Christianity, first in Syriac and later in Arabic, each with its own distinctive profile and trajectory. To comprehend the actual significance of Isaac's thought one cannot but avail oneself of painstaking research into the manuscript transmission of his corpus.

APPENDIX: THE MANUSCRIPT TRADITION OF THE PARTS I–III OF ISAAC OF NINEVEH

FIRST PART (* – used by Bedjan) – 82 chapters

Complete (or originally complete) mss:

	East Syriac mss			**Syrian Orthodox mss**			**Melkite mss**	
1	Vat. sir. 367	VIII c.		*Vat. sir. 124	XIV c.		Sinai syr. 24 [+ BnF syr. 378, ff. 61-68 + Milan Chabot 35]	VIII-IX c. St. Saba monas-tery
2	*BL Add. 14632	X c.		Mar Mattai 27	XV c.		*Vat. sir. 125	X c.
3	*BL Add. 14633	XI-XII c.		Mardin Orth. 195	CE 1469 Mardin			
4	*Mardin/ Scher 46 (= BnF syr. 359)	CE 1234/5 Walṭō		Vat. sir. 562	CE 1487			
5	*Siirt/Scher 76	XIII c. (the ms is lost)		Sharfeh Raḥmani 103	CE 1897 Mosul			
6	St Mark's Monastery in Jerusalem, MS 181	CE 1561/2		Harvard Semitic Museum 4058	CE 1901 (the ms is lost)			
7	BL Or. 9362	CE 1898 Tell Kepe		Sharfeh Raḥmani 310	CE 1904-1906 Mosul			
8	*Berlin or. quart. 1159	CE 1898 Mosul		Mingana syr. 151	CE 1906 Mosul			
9	*Berlin or. oct. 1258	CE 1898 Alqosh						
10	Siirt/Scher 77	??? (the ms is lost)						

Selections and fragments:
Not properly investigated. According to my preliminary research there are about 30 mss of different origin (East Syriac, Syrian Orthodox and Melkite). Some of those contain also text from other *Parts*: e.g. Baghdad Chaldean Monastery, syr. 680, Mingana syr. 86, Berlin, Sachau 203, Codex Syriacus Primus, Codex Syriacus Secundus, Sinai syr. 14.

SECOND PART – 41 chapters

Complete (or originally complete) manuscripts – only East Syriac ones
Ms from Urmia – lost

Bodleian Library, syr. e. 7 (X–XI c.)

BnF syr. 298 + Cambridge Or. 1144 (XII–XIII c.)

Harvard, Houghton Library syr. 57 (XIII–XIV c.)

Teheran Issayi Collection, ms. 4 (CE 1895) [copy of Oxford's ms]

Selections and fragments
[to be added: a) the mss of the *First Part* that contain chs 16–17 (= chs 54-55 of the *First Part*) and b) a copy of the *Third Part* that contains ch. 25]:

	East Syriac mss			**Syrian Orthodox mss**			**Melkite mss**	
1	Baghdad Chaldean Monastery, syr. 680	CE 1288/9 monastery Rabban Hormizd		BL Add. 14729	XII-XIII c.		Codex Syriacus Secundus	CE 882 Beirut
2	Baghdad Chaldean Monastery, syr. 681	CE 1909 (copy of Baghdad ms)		Mingana syr. 86	XIII c.		Codex Syriacus Primus	IX c. (lost)
3	Vat. sir. 509	CE 1928 (copy of Baghdad ms)		Mardin Orth. 420	CE 1471/2 Ṭur ʿAbdin region		Sinai syr. 14	X c.
4	Mingana syr. 601	CE 1932 (copy of Baghdad ms)		Berlin, Sachau 203	after CE 1493			
5				Sharfeh Raḥmani 181	XV-XVI c.			
6				Vat. sir. 543	CE 1782			

THIRD PART

Seventeen texts, out of which two appear already in the *First Part* (chs 20 and 40) and one in the *Second Part* (ch. 25).

Complete

Teheran, Issayi collection, ms. 5 (Urmia region, between CE 1900 and 1903)

Selections and fragments

[additional witnesses for a disputable ch. 10 are not taken into account]

	East Syriac mss			**Syrian Orthodox mss**			**Melkite mss**	
1	Baghdad Chaldean Monastery, syr. 680	CE 1288/9 monastery Rabban Hormizd		BL Add. 14729	XII-XIII c.		Codex Syriacus Primus	IX c. (lost)
2	Baghdad Chaldean Monastery, syr. 681	CE 1909 (copy of Baghdad ms)		Paris syr. 178	CE 1490 Dayr al-Suryan			
3	Vat. sir. 509	CE 1928 (copy of Baghdad ms)						
4	Mingana syr. 601	CE 1932 (copy of Baghdad ms)						

NB: quite a large number of Syriac manuscripts contain different prayers attributed to Isaac that can be identified with particular passages from each of the three *Parts*.

REMEMBRANCE OF GOD AND ITS RELATION TO SCRIPTURE IN ISAAC III INCLUDING INSIGHTS FROM ISLAMIC AND JEWISH TRADITIONS

MARY HANSBURY
USA

According to S. Brock the theme of divine love (*ḥubbâ alâhâyâ*) is central throughout Syriac tradition, from Ephrem to Isaac the Syrian. And according to T. Bou Mansour, the centrality of divine love in Jacob of Serug, for example, is understudied and he considers it to be the most profound intuition of Jacob's work. But the high point of the tradition comes in Isaac with his insight that the Incarnation did not occur because of sin but only because God loves humanity:

> If zeal had been appropriate for putting humanity right why did God the Word clothe himself in the body in order to bring the world back to his Father using gentleness and humility? And why was he stretched out on the Cross for the sake of sinners, handing over his sacred body to suffering on behalf of the world? I myself say that God did all this for no other reason except to make known to the world the love that he has, his aim being that we, as a result of our increased love resulting from an awareness of this, might be captivated by his love when he provided the occasion of this manifesta-

> tion of the power of the Kingdom of Heaven—which consists in love—by means of the death of his Son.[1]

In Isaac III, particularly in ch. 5, 6 and 11, there are sublime passages illustrating this love: "O infinite love of God for His work <of creation>! Let us look at this mystery with wordless insight so as to know that He has united creation to His essence, not because He needed to, but to draw creation to Him that it might share in His riches so as to give it what is His and make known to it the eternal goodness of His nature" (Is. III V.14).

This language reflects realities of transformation and *theosis* in a wonderful way. So transcendent and determinative is this love that it leaves mankind with little alternative but to remember God always and that *ʿuhdânâ d-alâhâ* flows from this love. The remembrance of God has deep roots in Syriac tradition. To better understand its meaning in Isaac, it is helpful to look at this historical development.[2]

In the works of Evagrius, a major influence on Isaac, there is little mention of *ʿuhdânâ* as noted by H. Teule.[3] He says that it does

---

[1] *Keph.* IV 78; the Kephalaia are found in P. Bettiolo, *Discorsi Spirituali* (Bose, Magnano: Edizioni Qiqajon, 1985). Translation of this passage, S. Brock, *Spirituality in Syriac Tradition* (Kottayam: SEERI, 1989) 84–85. For commentary on this insight of Isaac see I. Hausherr, "Un Précurseur de la Théorie Scotiste sur la Fin de l'Incarnation", *Recherches de Sciences Religieuses* 22 (1932) 316–20. And see A. Louf, "Pourquoi Dieu se manifesta selon Isaac le Syrien", *Connaissance des Pères de l'Église* 80 (2000) 37–56. Louf says that for Isaac the Incarnation "ne faut que reprendre le fil d'une Histoire d'amour que la chute d'Adam avait brutalement interrompue", p. 40. On divine love in Isaac, see H. Alfeyev, *The Spiritual World of Isaac the Syrian* (Kalamazoo, MI: Cistercian Publications, 2000) 35–61, esp. p.50: "The Incarnation took place, then, because of the love of both the Father and of the Son for human beings, and because of the Incarnation a human person is able to attain such a state of love when he becomes like God".

[2] See the article on remembrance of God in *Dictionnaire de Spiritualité*, MNÈMÈ THEOU, H.J. Sieben, 10(1980)1407–14.

[3] H. Teule, "An Important Concept in Muslim and Christian Mysticism: the Remembrance of God, *dhikr Allah – ʿuhdōnō d-Alōhō*" in M.

occur in *On Fasting*. And from *On Instruction*, Teule quotes: "Remembrance of God cannot establish itself in the soul which is occupied with the necessities of living in society but is promoted by a virtuous life and a number of ascetical practices, such as spiritual reading, prayer, and *aksnoyuto* (*xeniteia*)". From this Teule concludes that *ʿuhdânâ* is a spiritual attitude and not just an ascetical exercise, for Evagrius. Later, however, Evagrius seems to contradict this. It is a distinction which may be made about subsequent Syriac authors, including Isaac.

Philoxenus (+523) was born in the vicinity of modern day Kirkuq. He has an important place not only in Christology but also in asceticism. Having been influenced by Evagrius, he carries forward the Greek-Syriac synthesis. His influence on Isaac does not appear as significant as that of Theodore of Mopsuestia, Evagrius or John the Solitary. But the occurrences of *ʿuhdânâ* are very numerous. One could profitably write about *Remembrance of God* in Philoxenus. In his Discourses one finds many occurrences. For him the soul is dead without the remembrance (*ʿuhdânâ*) of God and the understanding (*madʿâ*) is no longer even able to "hear the cries of the divine voices".[4] Most often mention is made concerning the relation of remembrance of God to fear of God and to repentance. Throughout Disc.VI, occurrences are very numerous. I paraphrase: often linked to judgment, remembrance (*ʿuhdânâ*) of the judgment of God (p.163); therefore the remembrance (*ʿuhdânâ*) of God is the life of the soul (p.166); remembrance (*ʿuhdânâ*) of God is the light which shows the things which are to come (p.170); wakefulness of the remembrance (*ʿuhdânâ*) of God... sleep of contempt... abyss of carelessness (p.175); the remembrance (*ʿuhdânâ*)

Tamcke (ed.) *Gotteserlebnis und Gotteslehre. Christliche und islamische Mystik im Orient* GOF.S., 38 (Wiesbaden: Harrassowitz, 2010) 11–23.

[4] See Disc.I.5 in E.A. Wallis Budge (ed.) *The Discourses of Philoxenus Bishop of Mabbôgh* (London: Asher & C0., 1894). Implied here for 'divine voices' are the words of Scripture, understood in the context of treading and hearing the Word. See also R. Kitchen (tr.) *The Discourses of Philoxenus of Mabbug*, Cistercian Publications (Kalamazoo MI: Liturgical Press, 2013), p.3. On the importance of Scripture in Philoxenus see Kitchen, p. LVI–LXIV, where he says there are 1300 biblical references in the Discourses.

of God is true knowledge (*îdaʿtâ*) (p.176); the remembrance (*ʿuhdânâ*) of God together with the fear of Him makes one new (p. 177). Also in Disc.VII *ʿuhdânâ* occurs not infrequently, concluding with #29: "By the recollection (*ʿuhdânâ*) of his awesome and venerated <N>ame, let us maintain our lives in complete vigilance and let us raise up praise at all times to the Father and to the Son and to the Holy Spirit forever".[5] While not a formulaic expression, this seems to go beyond a spiritual attitude and be almost an ascetical exercise, reflecting the distinction Teule noted in his article concerning Evagrius.[6]

Sahdona was also from the vicinity of Kirkuk, modern Iraq, born towards the end of the 6th cent. His writings are deeply rooted in Scripture. His use of *ʿuhdânâ* is much closer to the spiritual density that one sees in Isaac. Here are some beautiful sections from his *Book of Perfection*:[7]

> 57. If we take great trouble over this, then maybe the air we feel around us will not be as close to our exterior senses as is the Spirit of God who is continuously in our hearts. Through him the memory (*dukrânâ*) of him is clear at every moment, and in this way He dwells all the more in us and is seen by us. He also nourishes our souls just as the air nourishes our bodies, for the soul at every moment depicts in itself the thought of God and the praise of his name: it becomes a hidden church[8] where the Godhead is ministered to in an excellent way.
>
> 58. … For the soul in which no thought of God is to be found, and whose intellect is deprived of the recollection (*ʿuhdânâ*) of him, is in very truth dead as far as the life of the Spirit is concerned. For just as the body dies and its life departs

---

[5] Kitchen, *Discourses*, p. 175.

[6] See Teule, "An Important Concept".

[7] Translation as found in S. Brock, *The Syriac Fathers on Prayer and the Spiritual Life* (Kalamazoo MI, Cistercian Publications, 1987) 225–27. See also A. Halleux, *Martyrius (Sahdona): Oeurvres spirituelles III* CSCO 252 SS 110 (1965) 1–27.

[8] *Book of Steps*, Discourse XII.

> when it is prevented from breathing, so too when the soul's mental faculty is held back from the recollection (*ʿuhdânâ*) of God, the soul dies as far as the life of righteousness is concerned, and the Holy Spirit, whose grace it had breathed in at baptism, departs from it.
>
> 59. Accordingly we ought to open our mouths at all times to God, and breathe in the breath of his grace that nourishes our souls with the recollection (*ʿuhdânâ*) of him. We should be even more assiduous in this than we are with external breathing. As one of the saints said: 'Let the recollection (*ʿuhdânâ*) of God be even more continuous than your breathing,' … or again, 'You should remember God at every moment; then your mind will become heaven.

In Sahdona, the literalness and moral tone of Philoxenus concerning *ʿuhdânâ*, begin to look more like the mysticism of Isaac.

Perhaps the most ample comparison can be made with John of Dalyatha (690–780), born in Beit Nuhadra, northwest Iraq near the mountains of Kurdistan. The term *ʿuhdânâ d-alâhâ* occurs often in his writings, especially Letter 50.[9] For John, remembrance of God is a directing of the intellect (*hawnâ*) to God present in the heart.[10] In his use of heart there is Macarian influence: a sense of the heart as the spiritual center of a person, including intelligence as well as feelings. It is the place where the Holy Spirit dwells and where one meets God. One must work hard to cultivate its "earth" (Letter 50.19) and to guard it carefully. Guarding is done by "remembrance of God", thus penetrating within and remaining mo-

---

[9] See M. Hansbury (tr.) *The Letters of John of Dalyatha*, (Piscataway, NJ: Gorgias Press, 2006) 232–43. See also R.Beulay, OCD (ed.) *La Collection des Lettres de Jean de Dalyatha.* Patrologia Orientalis 180 (Belgium: Brepols, 1978).

[10] Beulay says that his writings are not Messalian and he points to many times John insists that the soul sees God's glory and never His Nature, see R. Beulay, *L'Enseignement Spirtituel de Jean de Dalyatha: Mystique syro-oriental du VIII siècle.* Théologie historique 83 (Paris: Beauchesne, 1990) 423–64.

tionless before the depth. John describes this at length in Discourse 20.[11]

John's writings evoke later Byzantine Hesychast experience without reflecting any of their technique. A possible allusion to technique may be found in Letter 36.6 where the invocation of 'Father' is used to help direct the intellect (*hawnâ*) within the heart.

More study may also reveal parallels with Islamic tradition and the Muslim mystical use of *dhikr*,[12] particularly in the work of Kalabadi (995).[13]

Isaac does not reach the degree of complexity as shown in John of Dalyatha concerning *ʿuhdânâ*. Actually Beulay attributes this to a tendency in Isaac to misinterpret Evagrius[14] and also to

---

[11] As found in Beulay, *Enseignement Spirituel* in the section on remembrance of God, 124–42. See also N. Khayyat (ed.), *Jean de Dalyatha, Les Homélies I–XV* Sources Syriaques (Lebanon: CERO/UPA, 2007) 51–57.

[12] "The Qur'an employs the term *dhikr Allah*, 'the remembrance of God,' twenty-six times". "The Qur'an refers to itself as a remembrance (*dhikr*) or reminder more than forty times". If the Qur'an is a remembrance so also is the human response to it". "To be human is to remember: to acknowledge and confirm the obvious". "Why should God be remembered? Because human beings are commanded to remember him by his revelations to the prophets and because ultimate human felicity depends upon this remembrance". Quotes as found in *Encyclopedia of Religion* Vol.4, article of W.C. Chittick, 341–44.

[13] See R.Beulay, "Formes de Lumière et Lumière sans Forme: Le thème de la Lumière dans la Mystique de Jean de Dalyatha", in *Mélanges Antoine Guillaumont: Contributions a l'étude des christianismes orientaux*: Cahiers d'orientalisme 20 (Geneva, 1988) 134. See also his "Quelques axes de l'enseignement de Denys l'Aréopagite chez les mystiques syro-orientaux, et leur continuité possible en mystique musulmane", Actes du colloque-Patrimoine Syriaque IX: *Les Syriaques, transmetteurs de civilisations* (Lebanon, 2005) 97–107.

[14] For a discussion of this see É. Khalifé-Hachem, "La prière pure et la prière spirituelle selon Isaac de Ninive", *Mémorial Mgr Gabriel Khouri-Sarkis,* ed. F.Graffin (Louvain,1969) 157–72. And see P. Bettiolo, "Prigionieri dello Spirito", Annali di Scienze Religiose 4 (1999) 343–63.

conflate prayer with *tehrâ*.[15] But perhaps Beulay did not see all the implications of *tehrâ* in Isaac and its relation to revelation.[16] Often *tehrâ* is awestruck wonder while reading Scripture, e.g. salvation history. While *temhâ* is stillness (*šelyâ*).[17] But according to Alfeyev 'stillness of the mind is not a synonym for unconscious and insensible oblivion…<rather> the capture of the mind by God…a state of extremely intense activity of the mind, which finds itself entirely under the power of God.'[18]

Teule concludes his comments on *ʿudhânâ* in Isaac by saying that it is a constant state of awareness of and not an ascetical practice, a distinction Teule also suggests concerning Evagrius. But he says that *ʿuhdana* in Isaac is not easy to study because of relatively short passages, allusions rather than systematic elaborations, scattered over different homilies.[19] This is true. Actually in all of Bedjan

---

[15] See Beulay, *La Lumière sans forme* (Belgium: Éditions de Chevetogne, 1987) 52–53. See Is.III XVI and the ample comments of Chialà on the distinction between pure prayer and spiritual prayer.

[16] See my "'Insight without Sight': Wonder as an Aspect of Revelation in the Discourses of Isaac the Syrian", *Journal of Canadian Society for Syriac Studies* 8 (2008). See also A.Louf, "Temha-stupore et tahra-meraviglia negli scritti di Isacco il Siro", *La grande stagione della mistica Siro-orientale (VI–VIII sec.),* ed. E.Vergani and S.Chialà (Milan: Biblioteca Ambrosiano, 2009) 93–119. Louf cautions about a tendency to see *temhâ/tehrâ* as synonyms, p.93, citing the work of S. Chiala, *Dall'ascesi eremitica alla misericrdia infinita. Ricerche su Isacco di Ninive e la sua fortuna.* (Florence, 2002) 141. And see S. Seppälä, *In Speechless Ecstasy*: expression and interpretation of mystical experience in classical Syriac and Sufi literature; Appendix, A Case Study: semantic history of the words temhâ and tahrâ. (Helsincki, 2003). Beulay looks at *temhâ/tehrâ* in relation to Islamic literature, see R. Beulay, "De l'émerveillement à l'extase: Jean de Dalyatha et Abou Sa'id al-Kharraz", in *Youakim Moubarac: dossier dirigè pour Jean Stassinet*, (L'Ange d'Homme: Paris 2005) 333–43.

[17] In *Keph.* IV 95, Isaac explains the close relationship between stillness and wonder: at Gen.2.21 and 15.12 the Greek has *temhâ* (ἐκστάσις) and the Syriac Peshitta has *šelyâ.*

[18] See Alfeyev, 220–21.

[19] See Teule, "An Important Concept", 17–18.

there are only six occurrences of *ʿuhdânâ d-alâhâ*. And in Is.II, two.[20] Whereas now in Is.III, though a shorter text, there are eighteen occurrences, twelve in ch.8.

3.23 sets the tone:

> Because He governs all and without Him nothing is possible—He whose glory is from His Nature, and His kingdom is above all, and His power holds all the frontiers—He had willed that by using the form of prayer[21] with which we attend to these realities that concern Him, the remembrance of Him may be with us always.

> 6.45: For on account of our continual remembrance of Him, He dwells in us continually.

> 8.1 The temple of God is a *house of prayer*. The soul, then, is a house of prayer in which the memory (*dukrânâ*) of God is celebrated continually. If all the saints are sanctified by the Spirit to be temples of the adorable Trinity: the Holy Spirit sanctifies them by means of the constant remembrance of His divinity. Constant prayer, then, is the continual remembrance of God (*ʿuhdânâ ammînâ d-alâhâ*). Therefore, by means of continual prayer (*ammînûtâ da-ṣlôtâ*), the saints are sanctified, becoming a dwelling for the action of the Holy Spirit.[22] As one of the

---

[20] See Is. I, 258, 260, 261–62, 493, 512, 547. And see Is.II VIII.15; XXX.4.

[21] Form of prayer (*eskêmâ da-ṣlôtâ*): Chialà suggests that this expression which recurs in Is.III ch.3 (5,7,8,23,24,29) and ch.4 (12,14,15), refers to 'materiality and exteriorization' of prayer, their elements. Here it refers to the words of the Our Father, in the context of ch.3. It does not seem to reflect any formulaic reference to *ʿuhdânâ*. Seppälä says he has not found a prayer formula linked to *ʿuhdânâ* in Is.I or Is.II. See Seppälä, *Speechless Ecstasy*, 25.

[22] Action of the Holy Spirit (*maʿbdânûtâ d-ruḥâ d-qudšâ*): as noted by Chialà, Isaac frequently emphasizes the relationship between prayer, remembrance/memory of God and the indwelling of God or the Holy Spirit. And that continual prayer is possible only because the Holy Spirit dwelling in a person, prays in him and for him. See Chialà, Is.III (CSCO) p.83.

saints said: "Be mindful of God always and your intelligence will be heaven".[23] (Nilus, *Perle* 2).

8.2 Prayer (*ṣlôtâ*), then is the definition of the remembrance of God, removing the occasions of error which cause all the evils we suffer.

8.3 So then, let us persevere in prayer which is the luminous form (*ṣûrtâ*) of the remembrance of our Lord God: all temptations will be removed from us which are sent providentially for this – to set in us the remembrance of God by means of persistent intercession and the crucifixion of the intellect (*zqîfûtâ d-hawnâ*).

8.4 All evil things give way, somehow, to the remembrance of God which is in us; shouting, they flee from before the Lord.

8.5 The continual remembrance of God is in fact an altar which is established in the heart,[24] from it all the mysteries ascend to the sanctuary of the Lord; one finds there not one of the contrary events we have set forth.

8.6 But sometimes, even when we are diligent about <prayer>, some of these realities are allowed to remain and show their impudence to vex us, because we have not begun in a right way this continual remembrance of the Lord.

8.13 It is the power and energy <of God> that sanctifies and sets apart from the other souls that soul in which the Lord is sanctified, by means of the remembrance of Him: by the manifestation of a revelation and the knowledge of the mysteries revealed in it, and not by an inhabiting of the divine Nature <in us>.

---

[23] Nilus, *Perle* 2 in P. Bettiolo (ed.), *Gli scritti siriaci di Nilo il Solitario* (Louvain-la-Neuve, 1983).

[24] On the "liturgy of the heart", see S. Brock, "Spirituality of the Heart in Syrian Tradition", *The Harp* I (1988) 93–115. He discusses the various aspects of it in the *Book of Steps*: "The liturgy of the heart, properly conducted, thus has a revelatory effect: in its course the church on high will be revealed". Other Syriac writers on the topic are included.

8.14 Let us sanctify ourselves by the continual remembrance of Him which we call to mind by means of prayer. We become holy temples by prayer, to receive within ourselves the adorable action of the Spirit. As the Apostle says: *Everything is purified and sanctified by the word of God and by prayer* (1 Tim.4:4-5).

8.15 Let us continually remember God and our mouth will be blessed, as one of the saints once said to some seculars: "Stand and greet the solitaries that you might be blessed! Because their mouths are holy since they continually speak with God".[25]

8.17 "Always remember God and your intelligence (*tar'ītâ*) will be a heaven".[26]

8.18 "Pure prayer[27] is what causes the continual remembrance of God in the soul. Thus we will be temples for God in that He dwells in us by the continual remembrance with which we call Him to mind".[28] ...And the temple in which the continual memory (*dukrânâ*) of the Lord dwells, gives light such that the rays from it shine forth and <are visible> even from afar.

8.19 The continual remembrance of God is the mystery of the future world: there we receive fully all the grace of the Spirit.[29]

---

[25] E.A.W. Budge (tr.), *Paradise of the Holy Fathers*, 2 vols. (London: 1907; repr. Blanco, Texas: New Sarov Press, 1994) vol.2, p.148, #634.

[26] Nilus, *Perle* 2.

[27] On pure prayer (*ṣlôtâ dakyâ*), see Is.III XVI and the comments of Chialà. And see É. Khalifé-Hachem, "La prière pure et la prière spirituelle".

[28] Basil: Letter II, 4 in M. Forlin Patrucco (ed.) *Basilio di Cesarea. Le lettere I* (Turin, 1983).

[29] Future world (*'âlmâ da'tîd*) He. 2.5; 6.5: occurs very frequently in Isaac. Chialà gives all the references in his footnote to Is.III ch.1. An alternative form is New World (*'âlmâ ḥadtâ*), especially common in John the Solitary who interprets the whole history of salvation and the nature of the spiritual life according to this hope in the New World, influenced by Theodore of Mopsuestia. If after baptism, one remains in a state of spiritual growth, one is already in the new life of the New World. There is of

And the remembrance of God there, will no more depart from us because we will be wholly His temple.

9.6, 11: memory of God (*dukrânâ*) occurs twice.

10.65 Sanctify our hearts, my Lord, and fill <them> with the Spirit of Your glory, and by means of the holy remembrance of You may they receive the Spirit of joy.

11.2 But we ought to look beyond the flesh with the insight of divine Scripture. We have risen by a virtuous way of life; we have risen by faith in the future realities; we have risen in the knowledge concerning the divine Nature, in the perception of His Essence, in the glory of His greatness, in the height of His Nature, in the hope for the good things kept for us, in the knowledge of the mysteries of the *New World*,[30] in faith in the marvelous transformation which is prepared for creation.

11.3 Rightly, then, does the Apostle proclaim to us a true resurrection in Christ, as a reality in which we already exist. That is to say, we have risen by the renewal of the mind. In the former generations, there was no remembrance of God; indeed remembrance of Him was completely dead. As to the intermediate generations, even while knowing Him, they knew Him in a limited way.

11.4 We, indeed, have been renewed in our mind by a new knowledge which was not revealed to them. For we have known this Being who has no beginning nor end.[31]

---

course the sense of pledge in what Isaac says in 8.19, but also participation and fulfillment by means of *'uhdânâ.*

[30] New World (*'âlmâ ḥadtâ*), Mt.19.28.

[31] This section, 11.2–4, is the most complex of the entries concerning *'uhdânâ*. Here Isaac indirectly links it to resurrection and renewal of the mind. In #2 having described the aspects of transformation implied in resurrection, in #3 he says that in fact we have risen *by the renewal of the mind* (*ḥuddâtâ d-mad'â*). See also Evagrius Cent.V 19,22, 25 where he speaks of the resurrection of the body, the soul and the *nous*. And see Evagrius, *On the Faith* 7/23: "For what does he say in the Gospel? 'And I will resur-

Going forward to a better understanding of *ʿuhdânâ* in Isaac, following the suggestions of R. Beulay[32] and N. Khayyat,[33] it might be helpful not to isolate Isaac from his historical context. Khayyat is quite clear that she does not intend derivation but symbiosis and possibly to indicate where the Syriac tradition has influenced Islam. Beulay said it was his deepest desire to pursue this.

I am grateful to Khayyat for her informative article in which she quotes from the work of the following author, offering him as a possible area of research.[34]

Jaʿfar al-Sadiq was born in Medina in 702 and died there in 765. He was the sixth imam of the Shiʿites and guided both Sunnis and Sufis. What is quoted here is from his commentary on the Qur'an:[35]

---

rect him in the last day' (Jn 6.40) meaning by 'resurrection' the transformation from material knowledge to immaterial contemplation, and calling 'the last day' that knowledge beyond which there is no other. Our mind has been resurrected and roused to the height of blessedness only when it shall contemplate the Word's being One and Only". As found in A.M. Casiday, *Evagrius Ponticus* (London: Routledge, 2006) 52.

32 See Beulay, "Quelques axes".

33 N.Khayyat, "L'approfondissement mystique du "souvenir de Dieu", du Pseudo-Macaire à la mystique musulmane, à travers le prisme de l'expérience spirituelle syriaque", Actes du colloque – Patrimoine Syriaque IX: *Les Syriaques, transmetteurs de civilisations* (Lebanon, 2005) 109–24.

34 She quotes from P. Nwiya, *Le Tafsir mystîque attribué à Jaʿfar Sadiq* (Beirut, 1968). In her article, Khayyat uses slightly different quotes from the ones I have chosen from the English translation of Jaʿfar's commentary.

35 As found in *Spiritual Gems.The Mystical Qur'an Commentary Ascribed to Jaʿfar al-Sādiq as contained in Sulamī's Haqā'iq al-Tafsīr from the text of Paul Nwyia,* trans. and annotated by F. Mayer (Louisville KY: Fons Vitae, 2011).

p.13 ...and so the veils of forgetfulness are drawn back from them and thus they witness His beneficence and kindness; nay rather they witness the Beneficent, the Kind [Himself].[36]

p.64 He (God) effaces forgetfulness and establishes the remembrance of God.

p.80 When you have forgotten others, then draw close to Me with remembrance.[37]

p. 146 Whoever remembers God, most high, but then forgets His remembrance, was untouched by His remembrance. The remembrance of God, most high, is His oneness, His prior eternity, His will, His power, and His knowledge – never does any forgetfulness or unawareness befall Him for they are among human qualities. Whoever, then, remembers God, most high, remembers Him through His remembrance of him.[38]

p. 190 When the fires of love ignite in the heart of the believer, they burn up every eagerness for (what is) other than God, and every remembrance other than His remembrance.

There is no proof that the earliest Muslim mystics read texts of Syrian mystical writings. This is why Khayyat uses the term symbiosis, living together in the same milieu given to mysticism and with

---

[36] Notes as found in *Spiritual Gems*, tr. F. Mayer, n.31: In Sufism, *ghaflah* (forgetfulness or negligence) is the opposite of *dhikr* (the remembrance or recollection of God, especially through the invocation of His name(s) and existentially through harmony with his qualities.

[37] Mayer, n.146: ...includes meditative prayers, repetitions of holy formulae and Qur'anic phrases, and monologic prayer, involving the invocation of the divine name(s).

[38] Mayer, n.238: True *dhikr* is only through absorption into the divine *dhikr*. n.239: The true remembrance of God then, is His own eternal, uninterrupted Self-awareness, and from the human point of view it is an uninterrupted participation in this through the constant receptivity in the heart, of God's gaze which conveys His Presence and qualities, and in the extension of these through the soul. The ceaseless remembrance of God is literally a state of being—that of harmony with the divine qualities.

verbal contacts more than reading of texts.[39] Reading Jaʿfar for example, as noted by Khayyat, one senses a Macarian atmosphere. And about Isaac she explains how for Isaac the remembrance of God continues on its own, based on the prayer of the Holy Spirit present unceasingly in a person. For Jaʿfar the remembrance of God is based on the remembrance that God has of a person.[40] In both cases even if one ceases to remember God, the basis of remembering cannot cease.

I conclude with remarks of Beulay. In his article he is very convinced of the need for more research concerning Syriac and Muslim interaction. Like Khayyat, he is always careful to speak of symbiosis and not derivation. Of course his focus is not Isaac but John of Dalyatha. In John, Beulay gives the example of the loss of human attributes in ecstasy, and sees it as common to both Syriac and Islamic traditions. He suggests this comparison with Jaʿfar quoted here. It is not about *ʿuhdânâ* but it is stunning. He also uses Jaʿfar to show other remarkable similarities. This is about Moses:

> p.37 He heard a speech extrinsic to his human state. He <God> made the speech rest upon him and spoke to him through Moses inner disposition and his slavehood and Moses disappeared from his soul and was effaced from his qualities and Moses heard, from his Lord, the description of Moses.

Beulay mentions that even if mystical Islam comes from an "*interiorisation spirituelle*" of the Qur'an,[41] one ought not exclude that exterior factors such as Syriac mystical literature may have influenced

---

[39] But see P. Sbath (ed.) *Traités religieux, philosophiques et moraux, extraits des oeuvres d'Isaac de Ninive (VII siècle) par Ibn as-Salt (IX siècle)*, Cairo, 1934. Khayyat does not cite this material as it does not include anything on *ʿudhânâ*.

[40] From previous quote, see above, Jaʿfar, p.146.

[41] See Beulay, "Quelques axes", 102–103. He attributes this to Massignon, see L.Massignon, *Essai sur les origines du lexique technique de la mystique musulmane* (Paris: Cerf, 1999). See also L. Massignon, *Essay on the Origins of the Technical Language of Islamic Mysticism,* tr. B.Clark (Notre Dame, IN: University of Notre Dame Press, 1997). Beulay also mentions the research of P. Nwyia in this regard, without citing the work.

its development, if not textually, verbally. He feels that though more research is necessary, even now more discussion could occur. Beulay was profoundly interested in this and considers it to be as an occasion of 'sincere and cordial dialogue beyond the complexity of dogmatic dialogue'.[42]

"READING SOWS IN THE SOUL CONSTANT RECOLLECTION OF GOD" (IS.I 135)

Perhaps the most striking influence on Isaac, at least in this manuscript, is Scripture. From reading (*qeryânâ*), limitless prayer (*ṣlôtâ*) is generated (9.12) and of course it is the reading of Scripture which is intended. Reading is for prayer (9.3). Reading is meditation (*hergâ*) and prayer (9.11). Prayer without reading is weak (9.15). In addition there are very many citations and allusions to Scripture in this manuscript making it seem almost like a sub-text.

As mentioned there is Evagrian influence in Isaac. And according to Columba Stewart, exegesis was everything for Evagrius: "it was not about finding suitable garnish for his theological speculations or merely an aspect of monastic pedagogy. It was a mode of being, a keying himself into texts recited by heart day in and day out. He wrote that monastic life means 'knocking on the doors of Scripture with the hands of the virtues'" (*Thoughts* 43).[43] While

---

[42] In the Avant-Propos of Beulay's *Enseignement Spirituel*, Guillaumont gives a lengthy encouragement to pursue Syriac-Muslim research. And Wensinck in his introduction to *Mystic Treatises by Isaac of Nineveh* encourages consideration of Isaac in relation to Muslim mystics. He also explores some points that seem to have influenced Muslim mysticism and concludes by saying: "… it is in his whole set of ideas that Isaac appears to be one of those Christian thinkers such as have determined the general character of sufism". LIV–LVI. See the comments of S. Seppälä, *In Speechless Ecstasy*, 20–22. And see S.Brock: "Syriac Views of Emergent Islam", *Syriac Perspectives on Late Antiquity* (London: Variorum Reprints, 1984) Ch. VIII, 9–21.

[43] Columba Stewart, "Imageless Prayer in Evagrius Ponticus", *Journal of Early Christian Studies* 9 (2001) 199–201.

Evagrius is notable for his use of Scripture, Isaac surpasses him at least in his later works.[44]

Citations of *qeryânâ* occur in Is.I and Is. II, especially in Is. II where mention of it is spread over 3 chapters. But in Is.III it seems less diffuse and more concentrated which Chialà has noticed about other topics as well. As to recitation (*tenyâ*), it does not occur in Is.III but several times in Is.II, usually about the Psalms. I have not found it in Is.I. Interestingly, the chapter in Is.III with the most occurrences of *qeryânâ* comes right after the chapter on *ʿuhdânâ* as if Isaac understood the remembrance of God in the context of Scripture.

> 9.3 That which the power of prayer is to the way of life, reading (*qeryânâ*) is for prayer (*ṣlôtâ*). Every prayer, then, which is not sustained by the light of Scriptures is offered with bodily understanding (*îdaʿtâ*).
>
> 9.5 These realities receive power from reading regarding knowledge (*îdaʿtâ*) – its deepening and progression from insight (*sukkâlâ*) to what follows which is more amazing and more luminous.
>
> 9.7 The reading of a portion <of Scripture> brings to perfection this work of meditation (*hergâ*), and it is the <reading> which assists with marvelous realities, so as to last. See to the order of reading because it is useful for this labor.
>
> 9.8 One who is wise, then, who wishes to grow strong in spiritual realities, let him read the lesson according to the understanding which the meditation generates. Not just any reading is suitable for growth in the Spirit, but only that which tells about divine realities. This enriches the mind regarding spiritual mysteries, and instructs about the hope which is above the body. It transfers the thought (*ḥuššâbâ*) from earth to the world above, so as to raise it to that way of life of immortality.
>
> 9.9 The <reading> moves the senses of the soul to look into the hidden mystery of divine wisdom. It brings one to the un-

[44] Cf. Is. III and Is. V (forthcoming).

derstanding of its incomprehensibility and the truth about its nature. It makes one marvel at the hidden Essence and direct one's thoughts (*ḥuššâbê*) to the mysteries of the future hope (*sabrâ da-ʿtîd*). It brings forth the riches of His love, revealed to all and ready, indeed, to be spread abroad. These realities are the root of spiritual meditation, to which reading, by means of insight, continually lifts the mind making it wander about and delight in the divine virtues which are above all, and in the hope for humanity preserved near God.

9.10 When, then, this labor <of meditation> grows strong and is consolidated in the soul, at that time there is not much need for reading. Not that one may be entirely without it but there is not much need for extensive reading. Which is to say that a continual meditation on the Scriptures is not necessary, although Scripture ought not to leave one's hands. In that, even when one is occupied with a small matter in these things, by means of the power that one draws out of a few verses, one is captivated with the Lord in contemplation.

9.11 … reading…is meditation and it is prayer. It is meditation in that it is not just part of the tongue, but it's only intention is to bring the mind (*hawnâ*) to discernment. And it is prayer in that by the memory (*dukrânâ*) of God, it always captivates and fills within and without, with the desire and the meditation of heavenly realities.

9.12 From this reading, limitless prayer is generated, whose meditation arises secretly in the mind (*madʿâ*) and continually fills the intellect (*hawnâ*) with God, and as I said, it always captivates and attracts the mind (*reʿyânâ*) with the realities of the Lord.

9.15 Prayer, however of itself, without meditation and reading is <too> weak and obscure to make the intellect ascend and come together with the heavenly realities.

Dadisho, a contemporary of Isaac, also originated from Qatar and later lived in the monastery of Rabban Shabur as did Isaac. P. Bettiolo examines the anthropological dimension of *qeryânâ* and how it leads to purity of heart and to the vision of the spiritual meaning hidden in Scripture and in nature. Bettiolo alludes to Evagrian influence as he sketches this itinerary in Dadisho of how one is led by *qeryânâ* to personal integrity and to the light of the Trinity.[45]

One might inquire where this influence of Scripture on the spiritual life originated. In his comprehensive study of Isaac, S. Chialà describes the dependence of Syriac monks on Scripture.[46] The Syriac Church of the East early on developed schools of exegesis not only for clergy and monks but also for the laity in village schools where learning to read and write was done through biblical texts and the psalms. In addition to the psalms and biblical material in their liturgical office, canonical monks, at least as novices, spent most of the morning in biblical study.[47] Even in the School of Nisibis, with its semi-monastic framework, the first year was dedicated to the book of Psalms and the second year to Old and New Testaments, with heavy emphasis on the commentaries of Ephrem and Theodore of Mopsuestia. Their writings were thus major components in the development of East-Syrian exegesis.

A. Becker looks at monastic writing in the context of East-Syrian schools and dedicates several pages to Isaac.[48] The relationship between school and monastery was complex and could at times lead to tension. Becker gives the example of a story preserved in the *Book of Governors* about a dispute between Īšōʿyabh III and the monks of Bēt'Ābē over his wanting to build a school in the place of his cell, to provide a 'monastery of instruction'. Whereas the monks said one should "not teach the other chanting or how to read a manuscript" but sit in the cell for the solitary reading of scripture.[49] In Isaac, Becker sees a view of monastic life which dif-

---

[45] P. Bettiolo, "Esegesi e purezza di cuore. La testimonianza di Dadišo' Qatraya (VII sec.), nestoriano e solitario", *Annali di Storia dell' Esegesi* 3 (1986) 201–13.

[46] Chialà, *Dall'ascesi eremitica*, 89–92.

[47] See J.M.Fiey "La Bible dans la vie de l'église Syrienne Orientale", *Bible et Vie Chrétienne* 67 (1966) 35–42.

[48] A.Becker, *Fear of God and the Beginning of Wisdom* (Philadelphia: University of Pennsylvania Press, 2006) 184–88.

[49] Ibid., 169–72. And as noted by Becker, according to a canon from the rule of Dadīšōʿ, brothers were only permitted to enter the monastery

fers from a scholastic understanding of Christianity. He considers the work of Isaac as a high point in literature of East-Syrian monasticism and quotes from Is.II XXII.1–3 to describe the spiritual labor of the ascetic, consisting of three levels:

> The initial stage involved laboring with a great deal of recitation (*tenyâ*), and just the treading out of the body by means of laborious fasting. The intermediate culminating point lessens the amount of (all) these, exchanging persistence in these for persistence in other things, laboring on (spiritual) reading (*qeryânâ*) and especially on kneeling. The culminating point of the third (stage) lessens persistence along the lines of the previous stage, laboring (instead) on meditation (*hergâ*) and on prayer of the heart.

As noted in the passages quoted above from Is.III IX on *qeryânâ*: "reading is for prayer (*ṣlôtâ*)" 9.3; "reading is meditation (*hergâ*) and it is prayer" 9.11. Monastic writers, according to Becker, "were opposed to the school practice of lingering on the words and debating the meaning (*sukkâlâ*) of the text".[50] And Isaac even says if "someone is very learned and highly educated in the habit of ordinary reading and in the exact rendering of words" he may not be permitted "to perceive the full sense of what he is reading".[51] Reading also requires ascetic practice. Becker concludes: 'Ultimately, access to the divine is a grace and can occur whenever God permits it and that the goal of Isaac's whole monastic practice is the revelation of the divine.'[52]

There is yet another attempt to come to terms with the Sasanian context in the work of M. Vidas.[53] He refers to the research of Becker concerning Jewish and Christian institutions of learning in

---

if they could already read since "the monastery served solely the perfection of a brother's spiritual life". See Becker, 181.

[50] Ibid., 185.

[51] Is. II XXXI.1.

[52] Becker, 186.

[53] M. Vidas, *Tradition and the Formation of the Talmud* (Princeton NJ: Princeton University Press, 2014).

late antique Mesopotamia.[54] According to Vidas: "Recent scholarship has focused on the extent to which Jews, Christians, Zoroastrians and others in that region shared spaces, practices and ideas".[55] He shows, for example, how both Jews and Christians were concerned about Zoroastrian recitation of sacred texts. Both groups present it as "performative murmuring and contrast it with intellectual engagement". From the Christian perspective, Vidas cites the *Life of Īšōʿsabran* by Īšōʿyabh III.[56] In the *Life*, Īšōʿsabran, a Zoroastrian, is baptized a Christian and must leave his hometown due to persecution … eventually he decides that as a Christian he needs to learn to read Scripture. When he asks about how to learn he is told:

> A person first learns the alphabet, then its pronunciation, and after that he repeats (*tenyâ*) the psalms. Little by little he reads from all of the scriptures. When he is trained in the reading (*qeryânâ*) of the scriptures, then he proceeds to their interpretation.

Vidas sees here a similarity to the process of learning in the Talmud of reading, reciting and interpretation and he says it suggests common schooling practices. In the *Life*, Īšōʿsabran prefers recitation to reading or interpretation and Īšōʿyahb explains that this is a shocking position and is because he is Zoroastrian and oral recitation was the exclusive mode of study.[57] Vidas suggests that Īšōʿyahb's criticism of Īšōʿsabran is also directed against certain Christian monastic practices.[58]

---

[54] See Becker, 169–203, esp. 184–88.

[55] Vidas, 196–97.

[56] See J-B Chabot, "Histoire de Jésus-Sabran: écrite par Jésus-yab d'Adiabène", Nouvelles archives des missions scientifiques et littéraires 7 (1897) 485–584. Quoted in Vidas, 211–13 and in Becker, *Fear of God*, 205–06.

[57] Sacred Zoroastrian texts were transmitted in a language which the majority of Zoroastrians did not understand, hence the necessity of memorization and recitation.

[58] Vidas, 213. See the story quoted above of Īšōʿyahb wanting to build a school next to the monastery.

In his conclusion,[59] Vidas reflects on the comments of Becker in relation to recitation in Jewish life: "If there were, as the Talmud suggests, Sasanian Jewish 'masters of tradition' or 'reciters' who found in the memorization and recitation of tradition the ultimate expression of their Judaism; if there were Sasanian Christian monks who read "just for the sake of recitation" which took the form of a meticulous bodily performance, as we hear from Isaac of Nineveh—then these Sasanian Jews and Christians simply approached religion and religious textuality like the practitioners of the state religion of the empire in which they lived". Perhaps it is right as Vidas suggests that "against this background we should see the polemical references to Zoroastrian recitation by the two "scholastic" movements, the Talmudic academies and the East Syrian schools". At the very least it shows how both Jews and Christians struggled with similar issues without implying influence.[60]

In a subsequent article, coming to terms with the problem of "influence" Becker says "...I do not think it is a coincidence that the Jewish and Christian communities had parallel institutions of learning, Jews and Christians in Mesopotamia spoke essentially the same language, were subjects of the same state, and shared a common imaginary world, which included notions of magic, mysticism, eschatology, revelation, and the need for inquiry into the meaning of that revelation".[61] He even uses the same term as Khayyat used in her description of relations with Islam, *symbiosis*: Becker says "... two distinct entities mutually interacting over time, responding to each other, critiquing and sharing".[62] To give one example of a par-

---

[59] Vidas, 216–17.

[60] Unfortunately, it goes beyond the scope of this paper to say much about the rabbinic aspects of recitation and its place within Hekhalot literature as discussed by Vidas, particularly in relation to the *Sar ha –Torah* or Prince of Torah. Prince is a common term in Hekhalot literature for angels.Vidas mentions one Hekhalot fragment which "...assimilates the recitation of rabbinic literature to the angelic liturgy..." See Vidas, 248.

[61] A. Becker, "The Comparative Study of Scholasticism in Late Antique Mesopotamia: Rabbis and East Syrians", *AJS Review* 34:1 (April 2010) 98–99.

[62] Ibid., 99.

allel between East Syrians and the rabbis, he cites the work of Neusner comparing, amoraic *yeshivot* and Syrian schools and monasteries:[63]

> What is most striking about the schools is the conception that in them lived holy men, who more accurately than anyone else conformed to the image of God conveyed by divine revelation through the Torah of Moses "our rabbi".[64]

As noted by Becker, without the word Torah the statement could be about East Syrians. He closes the article with a reminder of S. Brock's article[65] which speaks of the 4th century as the end of living Jewish traditions being employed by Syriac authors. However in a subsequent article,[66] commenting on Brock's article, Becker suggests if movement of material came to an end, might there still be evidence of interaction? If not, how to explain anti-Jewish literature, for example?[67] And as a long range goal Becker suggests going beyond the issue of influence to a better understanding of the Sasanian context making it less important, even unnecessary to prove

---

[63] Neusner, *History of the Jews in Babylonia*, 3: 195–200. See the critique of Neusner's research, at least in this aspect in Becker, "Comparative Study", 105. Becker does not question this comparison but he cautions that Neusner relies on outdated work of Võõbus and that Võõbus and Neusner then tend to employ sources that project much later institutions onto an earlier period.

[64] Neusner, 4: 283.

[65] S. Brock, "Jewish Traditions in Syriac Sources", *Journal of Jewish Studies* 30 (1979) 212–32.

[66] A. Becker, "Polishing the Mirror, Some Thoughts on Syriac Sources and Early Judaism", in *Envisioning Judaism: Studies in Honor of Peter Schäfer on the Occasion of his Seventieth Birthday* (Tübingen: Mohr Siebeck, 2013) 897–915.

[67] The reality of anti-Jewish literature is now understood to be more complex than once assumed. See the research of Shepardson where she examines its anti-Arian and anti-Christian aspects while not excluding all anti-Judaism. See C. Shepardson, "Anti-Jewish Rhetoric and Intra-Christian Conflict in the Sermons of Ephrem Syrus", *Studia Patristica* XXXV (Peeters, 2001) 502–07. See also her subsequent publications.

influence. He concludes the article saying: "I do not think the study of Syriac literature will revolutionize the study of early Judaism, or that many individual passages from Syriac literature will radically alter scholars' readings of rabbinic texts. But I do think that a patient engagement with the Syriac corpus and an awareness of Syriac Christian history will shed some light on, and help to clarify some points in, the history of the Jews in Late Antiquity and the early Islamic period".[68] Might the same not be said concerning a light to be shed by Judaism on Syriac literature?

MYSTIC ASCENT

Encouraged by Becker's remarks and the fact that symbiosis may have occurred, I offer the following comparisons: Isaac's use of ladder/ ascent with the same motif in *Hekhalot Rabbati*. In Is. III IX, just after the section on *qeryânâ* there are interesting passages:

> 9.12 From this reading (*qeryânâ*), limitless prayer (*ṣlôtâ*) is generated, whose meditation (*hergâ*) arises secretly in the mind (*madʿâ*) and continually fills the intellect (*hawnâ*) with God, and as I said, it always captivates and attracts the mind with the realities of the Lord. This order of prayer is sublime, more than all ways of life, and is incomparable with the ways of life, in that it is <prayer> which gives life to them with the life which is in God. <Prayer> is the <means of ascent> which lifts up to heaven as far as the order of revelation, in the place of a ladder (*sebeltâ*). This is its work, lifting up to whatever high place requested.
>
> 9.13 When however, one has ascended to that place, then prayer will have another use there: at once the use for which it went up on the roof has arisen for it, and until it descends again to earth, its function of ladder (*sebeltâ*) is no longer needed. But if prayer is a figure of a raised ladder which lifts up to heaven, by which the intellect ascends continually – prayer satisfies the purpose of a ladder for the intellect – therefore as long as we are on earth, we always need this ladder which is

[68] Ibid., 915.

> prayer, by which we ascend at all times to God, so as to be made worthy by it of the heavenly light.
>
> 9.14 Meditation also strengthens, refines and grants victory to the prayer of the heart. It shows the intellect the way of heavenly and mysterious realities, for it is moved toward them at the time of prayer. Then this prayer rises up like a ladder (*sebeltâ*) and makes the intellect ascend.

Ladder (*sebeltâ*) appears in Is.I.[69] Again *sebeltâ* is briefly mentioned in Is.II XXXV.7, 13. and *Keph.* IV 31. These occurrences are mostly statements of fact, whereas in Is. III it is a pattern of ascent and descent: ladder combined with language of ascent and descent, much like the language of the *Hekhalot Rabbati* where the ladder which the mystic uses for his ascension recurs frequently. The Merkabah mystic is like "a man who has a ladder in his home which he ascends and descends, and nobody can interfere with what he does" (xiii,2; xx,3). And again there is the "heavenly ladder which stands on earth and reaches up to the right leg of the Throne of Glory" (xiv,1). Gruenwald mentions that what seems to be behind this is Jacob's ladder (Gen. xxviii, 12) but with angels climbing up and down.[70] "What is the technique of the Merkavah mystic like? It is like having a ladder in one's house and being able to go up and down at will. This may be done by anyone who is pure of idolatry, sexual offenses, bloodshed, slander, vain oaths, profanation of the Name, impertinence, and unjustified enmity, and who keeps every positive and negative commandment".[71]

---

[69] See Is.I 156: just one brief mention of the ladder of Jacob in a chapter on revelation based on Theodore of Mopsuestia.

[70] Philoxenus has an extended use of 'ladder' (*sebeltâ*) at the beginning of Disc. VII, with humans ascending and angels descending. And the first step of the 'ladder' is faith, the second simplicity, perhaps in keeping with the order of the Discourses. The commandments are also referred to as steps. See Kitchen, 152–54.

[71] Quotes as found in I.Gruenwald, *Apocalyptic and Merkavah Mysticism* (Leiden: Brill, 1980)120–21; 160–61. See also M. Himmelfarb, "The Practice of Ascent in the Ancient Mediterranean World", in *Death, Ecstasy and Other Worldly Journeys*, J. Collins and M. Fishbane (eds.), (Albany NY:

ANGELIC MEDIATION[72]

Throughout the writings of Isaac, angels are constantly mentioned and their primary function seems to be the mediation (*mesʿâyûṯâ*) of divine revelations.[73] Alfeyev notes[74] how Isaac was influenced by Dionysius in the understanding that divine revelations are transmitted from God to the angels through the mediation of Jesus, and then from the angels to human beings:

> We have them as teachers, as they have each other, namely those who are lower <are taught> by those who are more instructed and enlightened than themselves...up to the one who has as teacher the Holy Trinity. And even he <does not receive instruction> of his own, but he has as teacher Jesus the Mediator (*mesʿâyâ*) through whom he receives instruction and transmits it to those who are at the same level and lower. (Is.I 197-98)

Alfeyev concludes by saying that according to Isaac: "In the age to come, the saints will contemplate God face to face, while in this present life contemplation is possible only through the mediation of angels".[75]

In the *Kephalaia* there are three main sections relevant to this discussion. In *Keph.* II 69-76, #72 stresses communion with the angels in the revelations of one's mind; #76 stresses becoming worthy of the mystery of angelic revelations and worthy to receive

---

SUNY, 1995) 123–37. In her conclusion she suggests "...while techniques for ascent were not unknown, the dominant understanding of ascent in ancient Jewish and Christian literature is of a process initiated not by the visionary but by God. Further, the idea of ascent was so powerful that in some times and places reciting accounts of ascents was believed to offer tangible benefits... that simply reading about ascent had a kind of power as well".

[72] Excerpted from my "Insight without Sight", where additional references concerning angelic mediation may be found, 68–70.

[73] See the comments of Bettiolo in his "Prigionieri dello Spirito", 359–65.

[74] Alfeyev, *Spiritual World*, 227–232.

[75] Ibid., 228.

revelations of incomprehensible realities. In *Keph.* III 55-60, #55 speaks of movements of revelations produced in us by the angels and those which are from the Holy Spirit. In #59 Isaac specifies how revelations manifested by angels are, as noted in Scripture, either during sleep in dreams or through the senses in a vision or a voice: Jacob, Joshua, Isaiah, Daniel, the minor prophets, Zechariah the priest and other saints. Whereas in #60 he says that revelation from the Holy Spirit arises apart from the senses as occurred to Samuel, Elisha, Peter (Acts 10.10). In *Keph.* III 91-92, he makes another important distinction that angelic revelations purify whereas the Holy Spirit sanctifies with its revelations. Isaac quotes Evagrius (*Praktikos* 76) that the angels fill us with spiritual visions of every kind while according to Isaac the order (*ṭeksa*) and the manner (*ẓna*) of the Holy Spirit's revelation are one (*ḥaḏ*).

Is. II XVIII has the most references to the role of angels. #19 "...wonder (*temhâ*) at the insights...set in motion from the proximity of the angels (*metqarbânûṯâ d-mal'âkê*)". #20 "insights which do not (come) as a result of investigation or will, but ...through the mediation (*mes'âyûṯâ*) of the holy angels". #22 "...thoughts that originate from the angels...", which Brock refers to Evagrius, *Praktikos* 24, 80.

In Isaac III there are two significant passages. Ch. 8.11 concludes a previous discussion of revelation and Scripture by saying that all revelations (*gelyânê*) come by means of angels until one arrives at the divine vision (*ḥzâṯâ alâhâyâ*). He then reminds that angelic revelations precede divine revelations which are the work of the Holy Spirit. In Ch. 9.18-31 right after the mention of ladder, ascent/descent, Isaac continues to speak about the role of angels. He distinguishes again between angelic revelations and those of the Holy Spirit. He mentions OT interventions, e.g. Moses, Exod. 3:12. As proof text he gives Heb. 2:2 and Acts 7:35-37. All the OT *economia* (*mdabbrânûtâ*), concerning the people of Israel and the glorious realities that were revealed in their midst, was entrusted to an angel. In Ch. 9.25, as to Sinai, all the commandments given to Moses that are narrated in the Law are as coming from God while the words of the Law given to the people are angelic revelations. Finally, the OT *economia* had been revealed by the angel at the Lord's command, and only after Pentecost (Acts 3) and the Holy Spirit's descent on the Apostles, came the fullness of the grace of the Spirit.

This distinction between angelic revelations and those of the Holy Spirit seems important and may in fact reflect Theodore of Mopsuestia. In Isaac *Keph.* III 55, he had spoken about distinctions between angelic revelations and those of the Spirit. But in Is.III he says that in the OT all revelation was by mediation (*mesʿâyûṯâ*) of the angels.[76]

ANGELS OF REVELATION

P. Schäfer gives an overview of all the macroforms[77] in the Hekhalot material: *Hekhalot Rabbati*; *Hekhalot Zutarti*; *Maʿaseh Merkavah*; *Merkavah Rabbah*; *3 Enoch*.[78] According to Schäfer, the Hekhalot literature revolves around the relationship between God, the angels and man. The relationship between man and God and man and the angels is determined almost exclusively by the transmission of a mystery and the mystery consists of the knowledge of the divine names.[79] He outlines each macroform according to God, Angels and Man. And within the category of Angels in each macroform, he lists their functions: Bearers of the Throne; Heavenly Praise; Individual Angels: Gatekeepers; Intercessors of Israel; Prince of the Torah (*sar ha-torah*);[80] Angels of Revelation; Guardians and Examiners; Metatron.[81]

---

[76] This may derive from Theodore directly or indirectly, who did not accept awareness of a separate *hypostasis* of the Holy Spirit in the OT. See Robert C. Hill, trans. *Theodore of Mopsuestia: Commentary on the Twelve Prophets* (Washington: Catholic University of America Press, 2004) 117, 313–14. And see R. Greer, *Theodore of Mopsuestia, Exegete and Theologian* (Westminster: The Faith Press, 1961) 29, 107.

[77] Schäfer uses 'macroform' to describe a literary unit instead of the term 'writing' or 'word' because these texts fluctuate in Hekhalot literature and often have different manifestations in the various manuscripts.

[78] P. Schäfer, *The Hidden and Manifest God. Some Major Themes in Early Jewish Mysticism* (New York: SUNY Press, 1992).

[79] Ibid., 107–08.

[80] Individual angels also mentioned in *Hekhalot Rabbati*: *Angel of the Countenance*, *Metatron*, *ʿAnafiʾel*, *Dumiʾel* and *Qaspiʾiel*, see Schäfer, 28–33.

[81] *Metatron*, an angelic prince, is a central figure featured in 3 Enoch, though he does appear elsewhere in Hekhalot literature. See P. Alexander,

Concerning Angels of Revelation, in *Hekhalot Rabbati* many of their names are given.[82] In *Maʿseh Merkavah*, according to Schäfer, the most dominant task of the angels is the transmission of revelation.[83] In *Merkavah Rabbah* other functions are given up and the conveyance of revelation becomes the dominant task.[84]

A new translation of Hekhalot material[85] has only now become available to enable further reflection on Angels of Revelation. Perhaps this work of Davila will encourage further exploration of symbiotic situations in Sasanian times and shed light on angelic mediation and its relation to revelation and other aspects in Syriac literature including in the work of Isaac the Syrian. In his Introduction, Davila comments: "Broadly speaking, the Hekhalot literature focuses on two main themes. The first is how a practitioner may ascend (or, frequently and paradoxically, "descend") to heaven in order to be transformed, at least temporarily into a being of fire; to join in the angelic liturgy in the divine throne room; and to sit enthroned, sometimes on God's lap, and be granted theurgic power. The second is how the practitioner may gain control over angels, especially the Sar Torah or Prince of Torah who can grant expertise in rabbinic Torah lore without the need for the normal arduous study".[86]

---

3 (Hebrew Apocalypse of) Enoch (fifth-sixth century A.D.) as found in *The Old Testament Pseudepigrapha* ed. J.H. Charlseworth 2 vols. (New York: Doubleday, 1983) vol.1: 223–315. At the end of his introductory remarks Alexander suggests: "it would be worth investigating the possibility of Jewish Merkabah speculation having had some influence on Syriac Christian writers. And interestingly he also, though denying possible Islamic influence on Merkabah doctrine, says: "it is possible that the influence worked in the other direction, and that the Islamic *mushabbiha* thinkers drew on Jewish Merkabah traditions". See p. 253.

82 As cited in Schäfer, 36.

83 Ibid., 84–86.

84 Ibid., 106–107.

85 J. Davila, (tr.) *Hekhalot Literature in Translation: major texts of Merkavah mysticism* (Leiden: Brill, 2013).

86 Ibid., 5. See also J. Davila, *Descenders to the Chariot: The People Behind the Hekahalot Literature* (Leiden: Brill, 2001).

In fact there is a growing interest in this area of research. M. Bar-Asher Siegal comments that her purpose is: "… to illustrate the closeness of the two worlds—the rabbinic and the monastic—as manifested in their respective literatures. Thanks to the anthological nature of both corpora, it is possible to find a range of statements and opinions on, and usages of, a given topic, idea, or even literary image. Among these statements, opinions and usages are intriguing analogues suggesting that monks and rabbis both viewed the world around them in a similar fashion and phrased these observations of it in similar literary forms".[87]

[87] M. Bar-Asher Siegal, "Shared Worlds: Rabbinic and Monastic Literature", *Harvard Theological Review* 105:4 (2012) 423–56. See also her "Literary Analogies in Rabbinic and Christian Monastic Sources" (Ph.D. diss., Yale University, 2010) and her *Early Christian Monastic Literature and the Babylonian Talmud* (Cambridge University Press, 2013).

TWO DISCOURSES OF THE "FIFTH PART" OF ISAAC THE SYRIAN'S WRITINGS: PROLEGOMENA FOR APOKATASTASIS?

SABINO CHIALÀ
ITALY

ABSTRACT

Biographical sources for Isaac the Syrian are not very clear about how much he wrote, speaking generally about various "tomes" or "parts". In one case, however, we have an interesting indication: a certain Daniel Bar Tubanita is supposed to have written a rebuttal to the "Fifth volume" of Isaac the Syrian. The manuscript tradition has transmitted to us a First, a Second and a Third Collection, as well as two discourses of a "Fifth Part" by the same author. These last are preserved in four recent manuscripts, one in the Vatican Library, one in the Sharfet Library (Lebanon), and two in the collection of the Chaldean Monastery formerly in Baghdad and now in northern Iraq. Having prepared a critical edition of these two discourses for the Orientalia Christiana Periodica, in this paper I return to the question about the authenticity of the texts, which is not by any means certain, as well as the idea of apokatastasis.

1. ISAAC'S LITERARY LEGACY

In the past century many studies have been dedicated to Isaac the Syrian and his works. Besides clarifying important points of his biography, these studies have served to establish the extent of his literary production.[1] To the *First collection*, translated in antiquity into a dozen or so eastern and western languages, it has been possible to add a *Second collection*, rediscovered and published in part by Sebastian Brock, and a *Third collection*, edited by me.[2]

In spite of this praiseworthy and careful work, the search for and study of Isaac's literary heritage cannot be considered ended. Various Syriac and Arabic manuscripts attribute to him discourses that are not included in the three known collections. In some instances it may be a case of spurious works, that is, works erroneously attributed to Isaac, as I was able to demonstrate for the Arabic tradition, in a recent conference held in Moscow.[3] In other cases, only further, deeper studies can determine whether a text is genuine or not.

Among the writings that do not belong to any one of the three Collections are two discourses that are the subject of this paper. These two discourses are presented unanimously by the manuscript tradition as "taken from the fifth part of Mar Isaac, bishop of Nineveh". I have recently published a critical edition of these texts,

---

[1] For a general introduction, see Chialà, S. (2002), *Dall'ascesi eremitica alla misericordia infinita. Ricerche su Isacco di Ninive e la sua fortuna*. Firenze: Olschki.

[2] For the edition of the *First collection*, see Bedjan, P. (ed.) (1909), *Mar Isaacus Ninivita. De perfectione religiosa*. Parisiis-Lipsiae: Harrassowitz. On the translations of the *Collection*, see especially Brock, S. (1999–2000), From Qatar to Tokyo, by Way of Mar Saba: The translations of Isaac of Beth Qatraye (Isaac the Syrian). *Aram* 11–12, pp. 475–484. See the edition and English translation of the second part of the *Second collection* in Brock, S. (ed.) (1995), *Isaac of Nineveh (Isaac the Syrian). 'The Second Part', Chapters IV–XLI*. Lovanii: Peeters (CSCO 554–555, Script. Syr. 224–225). The first part of this collection remains unedited. For the edition and Italian translation of the *Third collection*, see Chialà, S. (ed.) (2011), *Isacco di Ninive. Terza collezione*. Lovanii: Peeters (CSCO 637–638, Script. Syr. 246–247).

[3] See Chialà, S., The Arabic Version of Saint Isaac the Syrian: A Channel of Transmission of Syriac Literature (to be published soon).

based on the entire manuscript tradition known to me.[4] Here I wish to return to the question of their authenticity, a question still open, by proposing a possible solution.

2. THE FIFTH PART ACCORDING TO THE ANCIENT SOURCES AND MANUSCRIPTS

I will begin with a rapid exposition of what is known concerning the existence of a "Fifth part" or "Fifth collection" of the discourses of Isaac the Syrian, that is to say, ancient sources and the manuscript tradition.[5]

Preliminary evaluations are given by certain ancient sources, which I will briefly summarize here:

- in one of the two anonymous biographies of Isaac, we read that Isaac is supposed to have composed "five volumes of instruction for monks";
- the *Catalogue of ecclesiastical writers* of ʿAbdishoʿ Bar Berika, bishop of Nisibe (d. 1318), reports that Isaac "composed seven volumes on the conduct of the spirit, on the divine mysteries, on judgments, and on the [divine] dispensation";
- another note in the same *Catalogue of ecclesiastical writers*, dedicated to Daniel Bar Tubanita, bishop of Tahal, attributes to him a work with the title "Solution of the questions of the fifth theological volume of Mar Isaac of Nineveh";
- the *Poem on the [divine] economy from the beginning to the end* of Isaac Shebadnaya (d. 1480) contains a quote introduced by the words "thus Mar Isaac has written in his fifth part".

These statements show that Isaac, directly or through one of his disciples, edited a "Fifth part", referred to as "theological" by ʿAbdishoʿ of Nisibe.

The Syriac manuscript tradition provides a second avenue for investigation. As mentioned above, four different manuscripts contain two discourses presented as taken from the "Fifth part" of Isaac.

---

[4] Chialà, S. (2013), Due discorsi ritrovati della Quinta parte di Isacco di Ninive?. *Orientalia Christiana Periodica* 79, pp. 61–112.

[5] For further details, see ibid., pp. 61–64.

I here summarize the salient points:

- *Sharfet, Rahmani 80 (Sony 797)*: a manuscript miscellany in Eastern Syriac script, copied by a scribe identified only as Michael, undated, but for which dates have been proposed ranging from the seventeenth to the twentieth century;
- *Baghdad, Dawra sir. 694 (olim Alqosh, Scher 116 e Vosté 247)*: an undated manuscript miscellany, probably from the nineteenth century, in a sufficiently correct Eastern Syriac script;
- *Baghdad, Dawra sir. 938 (olim Alqosh, Vosté 329)*: a manuscript miscellany, copied in 1894 in an elegant Eastern Syriac script by the monk Michael of the monastery of Our Lady of the Sowings at Alqosh;
- *Vaticano, sir. 592*: a manuscript miscellany written, differently from the above, in a Western Syriac script, even though it is clearly Eastern Syriac (Chaldean to be precise), as can be deduced from the name of the catholicos mentioned twice by the copyist, Joseph Emmanuel II, patriarch 1900–1946; the codex was written by the deacon Matthew, son of Paul, at Mosul in 1908, for Maruta Hakim, son of Peter, of Amida.

To these witnesses should be added other codices that appear in catalogues as containing extracts from the "Fifth part" of Isaac, probably the same two discourses as in the manuscripts listed above, but these codices are at present lost.[6]

As is clearly evident from the list given above, all the witnesses come from relatively recent manuscripts. This, however, is not a problem in establishing authenticity. The late date of manuscripts is a common trait in the Eastern Syriac tradition, which can be explained by historical reasons that cannot be gone into here. An analogous example is provided by the *Third collection* of Isaac's writings, attested by a single manuscript from 1900, but there are no serious reasons to doubt its authenticity.

---

[6] For this too, see ibid. pp. 68–74.

3. STYLE, CONTENTS AND AUTHENTICITY OF THE TWO DISCOURSES

We have, therefore, sources that inform us about the existence of the "Fifth part" and four manuscripts that transmit two discourses of a work that bears the same title. It now remains to examine whether these discourses are really parts of the work by Isaac mentioned in the sources.

To ascertain the authenticity of the discourses, their style and contents must be analyzed in close comparison with the rest of Isaac's known works.

Concerning their style, the results obtained seemingly testify against their authenticity. These two discourses, in fact, are collections of biblical passages marshaled to support an idea that the author intends to affirm. They are two long series of quotes, mostly from the Old Testament, but some from the New, often simply ranged one after another, followed at certain intervals by only a few explanations. This stylistic trait leaves the habitual reader of Isaac perplexed. It is not rare for Isaac to furnish biblical proofs for his statements, but not in such a systematic and protracted way. From a stylistic point of view, therefore, there are evident differences from the rest of Isaac's opus. As for the vocabulary, it is difficult to express a judgment, since for the main part the biblical passages are faithfully quoted and passages of original composition, from which something about the author's own style can be gleaned, are rare.

An analysis of the contents, on the other hand, leads to contrasting evaluations. The two discourses appear as texts defending a precise theological thesis. The first has the title "Examples of confirmation [taken] from the Scriptures, against those who assert that the world proceeds fortuitously, without a guide", while the second is titled "Other examples with another intent". Here a habitual reader of Isaac cannot but note a certain dissimilarity with Isaac's usual themes, such as the spiritual life, asceticism, prayer, and others of this kind. Although theology is by no means extraneous to his topics, it is rare to see Isaac engaged in closely argued theological topics, although there are exceptions, especially in some discourses of the *Second collection*.

We must consider, however, that according to what the ancient sources say, this "Fifth part" is distinguished from the rest of Isaac's opus by its peculiar character. In fact, in the note of the

Catalogue of ecclesiastical writers of 'Abdisho' about Daniel Bar Tubanita, the "fifth volume" is referred to as "theological", thus resolving the difficulties with the work's content.

4. PROLEGOMENA FOR THE AFFIRMATION OF THE FINAL UNIVERSAL SALVATION?

As the title of the first discourse proclaims, the author opposes the idea that the world "proceeds fortuitously, without a guide" (I, title). God, thus, is not extraneous to what occurs, whether good or evil (I,1). Then, after a first long series of biblical quotes, he affirms that rational beings are "tools" in the artisan's hand for realizing the divine economy. It is God who grants the power of acting to those who act (I,31).

A little further, however, the author seems to balance what he has just said, which risks ending in an absolute predeterminism. He says, in fact, that this does not mean that God is the executor of every single action done by men. He only allows these actions to happen, a reason for not being able to assert that things happen by chance and without God's assent (I,34). The first discourse concludes then with the following words:

> It is not [God] who sets in motion the actions of correction and punishment, not is it he who operates in those who act. He only consents, allowing them [to happen] when he wants them to happen. And it is not he who brings about such wishes and ideas in good or bad events through those who carry them out. Nor is it he who provokes the way in which a corrective action occurs and cases suffering.

God is like the space in which everything occurs. It is not he who provokes evil, but for evil actions to occur, he has to allow them to happen.

The author is aware that he is moving on an extremely delicate and thin ice, so he hastens to add: "But how little is [our] knowledge about these things and how weak [as regards] the truth!" (I,34), which are the very last words of the first discourse and which seem to echo various passages of Isaac's indubitably authentic *Centuries*, where he comments in the same way.[7]

The second discourse opens with the affirmation that the Scriptures show that the impulse to carry out actions that bring joy or suffering to men, even though it comes from God, is carried out by those who bring it to be (II,1–2). Here again is evident the author's intention to prove that it is God who moves and operates, for the realization of his economy, but exactly "who" will act and "when" and "how" "depend on the occasion" (II,18–19).

God's will does not annul man's freedom. In quoting Psalm 135,6 (*All that he wills, the Lord fulfills*), the author specifies: "This too is said in human terms! Not that the Lord operates all that he wills", but everything that happens does not happen outside his space (II,23). In fact, he continues, "God's will is action" (II,24). The Lord has always, that is, before time, but things then happened in time (II,25). His will is equal to action; for him it is enough to will (II,27–31).

The discourse then concludes with two rhetorical questions:

> Who, then, is [so] infantile in heart and so lacking in knowledge about all these things as to say that benefits and straits come to man independently of God? Or that even one movement of his creature lacks [divine] support?

The assertion that opened the first discourse, thus, is taken up again; according to this, everything that affects man, good or evil, happens because God made it possible. The author concludes:

> Nevertheless, it must not be said that being consigned [to evil] is [the work] of God, but the custody that [comes] from him is to be confessed above all. These things will be [sufficient] for the useful persuasion of those who ask (II,34).

---

[7] See especially Isaac of Nineveh, *Centuries* I, 51; II, 102; IV, 83; see Bettiolo, P. (ed.) (1990), *Isacco di Ninive, Discorsi spirituali*. Magnano: Qiqajon, pp. 63, 114–115, 185, where he refers to the inscrutability of the divine judgments concerning his providence and economy regarding his creatures, which are contemplated only as through fog.

All this, the author affirms, is not the fruit of personal elaboration, but is proposed "on the basis of well-known testimonies, of experience, and of study" (II,34), a statement that seems to echo a passage of the *First collection* of Isaac's works.[8]

The idea that is defended, hence, in spite of difficult articulation, is sufficiently clear: nothing of what happens can be said to be outside of God's plan, outside his economy. God, then, takes care of creation, as the author hastens to affirm at the end of the second discourse. There he appears to be not so much concerned about repeating that God is the cause of the evil that affects the creature, but rather that "the custody that [comes] from him be confessed", that is, the care he has for creation.

At this point I propose to find a possible application for what has been said so far on the theme of "universal salvation". By this I mean the particular theological affirmation according to which at the end of history God will find a way to reintegrate every fragment of creation into his design of salvation, hence the sufferings of sinners in hell do not have a definitive character, but only cathartic. This idea, expressed in different ways by the authors in whom it occurs and known as "apokatastasis", was condemned as heretical in Origen and Theodore of Mopsuestia. It occurs, however, with particular accents also in orthodox fathers, such as Gregory of Nyssa, Maximus the Confessor, and also Isaac.[9]

God's infinite love, which embraces every fragment of creation and even the demons, is one of the aspects of Isaac's thought that has most fascinated his readers in every age and every place, even beyond the frontiers of Christianity. We know that Isaac was read by Muslim authors.[10] In one case he is explicitly mentioned as a witness to this very idea under discussion. The author who men-

---

[8] Where Isaac appeals for the confirmation of is thought to the testimony of truthful men and of experience, see *First collection* 14; see Bedjan (1909), p. 127.

[9] For details, see Chialà (2002), pp. 269–276.

[10] For instance, al-Muḥāsibī (d. 857); see Van Ess, J. (1961), *Die Gedankenwelt des Ḥārit al-Muḥāsibī anhand von Übersetzungen aus seinen Schriften*. Bonn: Selbstverlag des Orientalischen Seminars der Universität.

tions him is Shahrastani (d. 548/1153), who calls him by the Syriac expression "Mar Isaac".[11]

Certainly, the connection between the statement that nothing happens without God willing it and the idea of a final recapitulation in which God finds a way to bring back to himself every fragment of creation, without violating its liberty, may not appear as immediate. We must not forget, however, that we have only a part of a more substantial work. We may suppose that we have the initial discourses, hence scriptural prolegomena to an explicit statement in further discourses.

All this is hypothetical and can only be confirmed if other fragments or parts of the work are eventually found. The hypothesis, however, deserves to be formulated. It may find confirmation in a further issue that can be adduced in favor of my reconstruction.

I begin by summarizing what has been said so far:

- Isaac wrote a *Fifth part*, or his writings were arranged in at least five parts by his disciples;
- this *Fifth part* had a "theological" character, according to what is stated in the *Catalogue of ecclesiastical writers* of 'Abdisho', in the information about Daniel Bar Tubanita;
- according to the same information, this text aroused Daniel's opposition, who wrote a "solution" for it.

Now, from other sources we know that what Daniel questioned in Isaac was God's infinite mercy for creation and his design of universal salvation. We are informed about this by an Arabic author of the ninth century, Ibn as-Salt.[12]

Here, then, is a confirmation that the "theological" argument defended in the *Fifth part* regards God's infinite mercy. Our two discourses may support this thesis, and it is possible that they are an authentic part of this collection.

---

[11] See Pagani, S., Ibn 'Arabī and Political Hell. In: Lange, Ch. (ed.), *Locating Hell in Islamic Tradition*, Leiden (in print). On the possible relation between Shahrastani and Isaac's writings and thought, see also Thomas, D. (2008), *Christian Doctrines in Islamic Theology*. Leiden: Brill, p. 53, fn. 29.

[12] Here again, see Chialà (2002), pp. 60–63.

SYRIAC BIBLICAL INTERPRETATION FROM QATAR: AHOB OF QATAR

BAS TER HAAR ROMENY
VU UNIVERSITY AMSTERDAM

ABSTRACT

Biblical interpretation plays a large role in the various Syriac Christian traditions, and the interpretation of the Scriptures was a major battle ground in the controversy between the Church of the East and the Syriac Orthodox. The Christians in Beth Qatraye, belonging to the Church of the East, contributed to the vast corpus of exegetical writings. This paper examines some of the writings of Ahob of Qatar. Their textual tradition will be discussed, as well as their place within the East Syriac tradition of biblical interpretation. On the one hand their relationship to earlier Syriac exegetes and the works of Theodore of Mopsuestia is important, on the other hand also the way later authors incorporated the material from Qatar. We shall also examine the role of glosses translating Syriac words into the language of Qatar.

INTRODUCTION

Biblical interpretation plays a large role in the various Syriac Christian traditions. Exegesis is found not only in biblical commentaries, but also in sermons, poetical works, and chronicles. The interpretation of the Scriptures was a major battle ground in the controversy between the Church of the East and the Syriac Orthodox. Therefore it does not surprise that the Christians in *Bet Qaṭraye*, belonging to the Church of the East, also contributed to the vast corpus of exegetical writings. Interestingly, in addition to interpretations in the tradition of the East Syriac schools, we find glosses translating Syriac words into the language of Qatar.

This paper will examine some of the writings of one of the main authors: Aḥob of Qaṭar. Editions of *The Cause of the Psalms* by Ahob of Qatar and of a number of quotations preserved in the so-called *Anonymous Commentary* and the *Commentary on the Psalms attributed to Denha or Gregory* are being prepared as part of the Qatar Foundation project on the Syriac Writers from Bet Qatraye. Their textual tradition will be discussed, as well as their place within the East Syriac tradition of biblical interpretation. On the one hand their relationship to earlier Syriac exegetes and the works of Theodore of Mopsuestia is important, and on the other hand also the way later authors incorporated the material from Qatar is significant. In addition, we shall go into the role of the glosses in the language of Qatar.

WHO WAS AHOB OF QATAR?

According to Assemani's edition of his famous tenth-century catalogue, ʿAbdishoʿ bar Brika mentions the name of Ayyub of Qatar.[1] Chabot has already argued on good grounds that the correct spelling of the name is Ahob.[2] The latter spelling is corroborated by a number of manuscripts. It would seem natural to assume that those authorities who read Ayyub, that is, Job, have adapted the lesser known name Ahob to the biblical name Job. ʿAbdishoʿ credits Ahob with an 'Elucidation of the whole New (Testament), of the Pentateuch, and all Prophets, in addition to (or: except for) an elucidation of the Bet Mawtbe'.

---

[1] J.S. Assemani, 'Carmen Ebedjesu metropolitae Sobae et Armeniae continens catalogum librorum omnium ecclesiasticorum', in *idem* (ed.), *Bibliotheca Orientalis Clementino-Vaticana* 3.1 (Rome: Sancta Congregatio de Propaganda Fide, 1725; reprint Piscataway: Gorgias Press, 2002), pp. 3–362, esp. p. 175 n. 4.

[2] J.B. Chabot, 'Ahob de Qatar', *Journal Asiatique* 10.8 (1906), pp. 273–74.

In a footnote Assemani states without further substantiation that Ahob lived around AD 990.[3] Anton Baumstark has already cast doubt on this on the basis of Ahob's quotations of Persian words, which in his opinion could very well point to pre-Islamic times.[4] It was Roger Cowley who noted that the Chronicle of Sʿert mentions an Ayyub, 'the interpreter of Seleucia', who was a candidate for election to the Catholicosate in 581, when Ishoʿyahb I eventually got the position.[5] He suggests identifying Ahob of Qatar with this Ayyub of Seleucia. He would then have been born in Qatar, from where he moved to Seleucia. His main argument is that Ishoʿdad of Merv (9th. cent.) would have quoted Ahob. We shall come back to this point.

An additional argument for an early dating of Ahob is the fact that according to Jean Maurice Fiey Christianity had already disappeared from Bet Qatraye by the beginning of the tenth century.[6] I have therefore suggested in an earlier publication that he should not be dated much later than other important scholars from Bet Qatraye such as Isaac of Nineveh, Dadishoʿ, and Gabriel of Qatar.[7] Sebastian Brock also seems to think along these lines, as he does not rule out the possibility of equating the Ahob of ʿAbdishoʿ's catalogue with 'the monk at the monastery of Rab Kennare (in Bet Huzzaye) who requested Dadishoʿ Qaṭraya to write his Commen-

---

[3] Assemani, 'Carmen Ebedjesu', p. 175 n. 4.

[4] Anton Baumstark, *Geschichte der syrischen Literatur mit Ausschluß der christlich-palästinensischen Texte* (Berlin: W. de Gruyter, 1968 [1922]), p. 132 n. 1.

[5] Roger W. Cowley, 'Scholia of Aḥob of Qaṭar on St John's Gospel and the Pauline Epistles', *Muséon* 93 (1980), pp. 329–43.

[6] See Jean Maurice Fiey, 'Diocèses syriens orientaux du Golfe Persique', in F. Graffin (ed.), *Memorial Mgr Gabriel Khouri-Sarkis (1898-1968)* (Leuven: Imprimerie Orientaliste, 1969), pp. 177–219 (211–12).

[7] See my 'The Hebrew and the Greek as Alternatives to the Syriac Version in Išoʿdad's Commentary on the Psalms', in A. Rapoport-Albert and G. Greenberg, *Biblical Hebrew, Biblical Texts: Essays in Memory of Michael P. Weitzman* (JSOT Supplement Series 333; Sheffield: Academic Press), pp. 431–56, esp. p. 451.

tary on the Asceticon of Abba Isaiah'.[8] On the other hand, in another footnote to the same *Aram* article on the Syriac writers from Bet Qatraye, Brock states that Cowley made 'the wrong choice in identifying this Aḥob with Ayyub, the Interpreter of Seleucia'.[9] It is not clear to me why he rejects Cowley's proposal; perhaps it is the fact that we do not have more at our disposal than the title *mpaššqana* 'interpreter', and the—imperfect—agreement of the names (the interpreter of Seleucia is called Ayyub or Job, whereas we have just seen that the exegete mentioned by ʿAbdishoʿ should probably be called Ahob).

So far, we have seen a reference to an exegete named Ahob of Qatar, dated for unclear reasons to the tenth century by Assemani, but probably to be assigned to the sixth or seventh centuries, and perhaps to be identified with Ayyub, the Interpreter of Seleucia. Until new evidence presents itself, the latter identification will indeed remain tentative. It is, however, possible to obtain slightly more certainty with regard to the dating. For this issue we should look at fragments attributed to Ahob quoted in some of the East Syrian exegetical collections.

Ahob's Works

As we have seen above, ʿAbdishoʿ credits Ahob with an 'Elucidation of the whole New (Testament), of the Pentateuch, and all Prophets, in addition to (or: except for) an elucidation of the Bet Mawtbe (i.e. Joshua, Judges, Samuel, Kings, Ruth, and wisdom books)'. None of these works has survived in full. There used to be a New Testament commentary which Baumstark suggested attributing to Ahob, but the only known manuscript, MS Sʿert 27, did not survive the First World War. We do have quotations in later authors, however.

Roger Cowley's starting-point were the scholia attributed to one 'Agob' in the Gəʿəz translation of Ibn at-Tayyib's *Commentary on the Four Gospels* and in the commentary on the Pauline epistles

---

[8] Sebastian P. Brock, 'Syriac Writers from Beth Qaṭraye', *Aram* 11–12 (1999–2000), pp. 85–96, quotation on p. 92 n. 37.

[9] Brock, 'Syriac Writers', p. 93 n. 39.

known as *tərgwame pawlos*. Ibn at-Tayyib lived and worked in Baghdad in the 11th century, and wrote extensive commentaries on the Bible in Arabic, using the ninth-century Syriac author Ishoʿdad of Merv as one of his main sources. Now Cowley notes that out of the 22 comments attributed to Agob/Ahob, 16 also appear in more or less the same wording in Ishoʿdad. This would support the idea that Ahob was working earlier than Ishoʿdad, that is, earlier than *c.*850 CE.[10] There is a problem, however. Ishoʿdad never gives Ahob's name. Even though it is well known that Ishoʿdad is not consistent in mentioning names, this does leave the possibility open, at least in theory, that it was Ahob who used Ishoʿdad rather than the other way round. For this reason we should have a look at the more extensive evidence for Genesis—already mentioned by Cowley—and Psalms.

Let me first introduce the sources. Ishoʿdad and Ibn at-Tayyib are quite well known,[11] and I have already mentioned them above. For Genesis, both texts have been edited and translated, by Vosté and Van den Eynde and by Sanders, respectively.[12] The tradition of the *Diyarbakır Commentary* and the so-called *Anonymous Commentary* probably need some more extensive introduction.

1. The Anonymous Commentary and the Diyarbakır Commentary

The so-called *Anonymous Commentary* is, in its most extended form, a commentary on the Old and New Testaments. Most manuscripts,

---

[10] Cowley, 'Scholia of Aḥob of Qaṭar', p. 339.

[11] See, for example, the recent articles on them in Sebastian P. Brock *et al.* (eds.), *Gorgias Encyclopedic Dictionary of the Syriac Heritage* (Piscataway: Gorgias Press, 2011): Lucas Van Rompay, 'Ishoʿdad of Merv', pp. 216–17; Aaron M. Butts, 'Ibn al-Ṭayyib', pp. 206–207.

[12] Ceslas Van den Eynde, *Išoʿdad de Merv: Commentaire sur l'Ancien Testament* (CSCO 126, 156, 176, 179, 229, 230, 303, 304, 328, 329, 433, 434 / Syr. 67, 75, 80, 81, 96, 97, 128, 129, 146, 147, 185, 186 ; Leuven : Peeters, 1950–81) [first volume with J.-M. Vosté]. For the New Testament, see Margaret Dunlop Gibson, *The Commentaries of Ishoʿdad of Merv, Bishop of Hadatha (c. 850 A.D.)* (Horae Semiticae 5–7, 10–11; Cambridge: University Press, 1911–16 = Piscataway: Gorgias Press, 2003). J.C.J. Sanders, *Ibn aṭ-Ṭaiyib. Commentaire sur la Genèse* (CSCO 274–275; Leuven, 1967).

however, contain only the Old Testament part, or even only the Pentateuch section. A facsimile edition with English translation of the *Anonymous Commentary* on Gen 1:1–28:6 was published by Abraham Levene.[13] This facsimile is from MS Mingana 553, a very late copy. Levene does not discuss the rest of the manuscript tradition, as Taeke Jansma pointed out.[14] The latter gave the first survey of the manuscript tradition. Some additions can be found in an article by Lucas Van Rompay.[15] The situation is as follows.

The oldest and most complete manuscript is MS (olim) Diyarbakır 22, containing 530 folios, written before 1605 (14th c.?). After the First World War it travelled from Diyarbakır to the library of the Chaldean Patriarchate in Mosul. By 1961 this library had been moved to Baghdad, where it received the new shelf mark 21.9. I do hope it is still there, or better still, brought to a safer place, and I would be interested in any further information, as the pages on the microfilm which I have, based on images probably made by the Dominican Father A. du Boullay in the 1950s, are not always very easily readable. This may be due to the fact that the collection had spent some time in a collapsed house before it was brought to Mosul.

MS (olim) Diyarbakır 22 contains a commentary on the whole Bible, and on the basis of earlier indications I had hoped that at least two manuscripts would contain the whole Old Testament. However, it appears that the two manuscripts in question contain only part of the Old Testament. MS Mosul 11.1–3, dated to 1684–1701, also went to the library of the Chaldean Patriarchate in Baghdad. Mosul 11 consists in fact, as the shelf mark suggests, of three volumes: the Pentateuch, the Bet Mawtbe, and the Prophets.

---

[13] Abraham Levene, *The Early Syrian Fathers on Genesis from a Syriac Ms. on the Pentateuch in the Mingana Collection* (London: Taylor's Foreign Press, 1951).

[14] Taeke Jansma, 'Investigations into the Early Syrian Fathers on Genesis', in P.A.H. de Boer (ed.), *Studies on the Book of Genesis* (OTS 12; Leiden: Brill, 1958), pp. 69–181, esp. 71–74.

[15] Lucas Van Rompay, 'A Hitherto Unknown Nestorian Commentary on Genesis and Exodus 1–9, 32 in the Syriac Manuscript (olim) Dijarbekr 22', *Orientalia Lovaniensia Periodica* 5 (1974), pp. 53–78, esp. 55–57.

Of these it gives the full text of the Peshitta as well as the *Anonymous Commentary*. MS Vat. sir. 578, dated to 1917, is related to this tradition. These manuscripts do not give the Psalms, Song of Songs, or Job. Ezra, Nehemiah, and Chronicles are not present in any of the witnesses, as was perhaps to be expected.

Finally there are a number of manuscripts containing the Pentateuch only:

MS Sʿert 21, dated to 1605. Lost in the First World War, but accessible through copies:

- MS Alqosh 34 (olim 22), dated to 1887. Whereabouts uncertain, but accessible through two copies:
    - MS Vat. sir. 502, dated to 1926.
    - MS Mingana 553, dated to 1930—the manuscript used by Levene.
- MS Ayn Qawa. Whereabouts unknown to me.

MS Sʿert 22, 17th c. Lost in the First World War; no known copies.

MS Kirkuk 8, dated to 1706. Whereabouts uncertain, but accessible through a microfilm.

MS Leningrad, Diettrich 2, of unknown date (but certainly not very early, as it is written on paper).

MS Louvain, CSCO, syr. 13, dated to 1902. A copy of a MS from Selok = Kirkuk dated to A.G. 2027 = 1715/16 CE. Given the fact that the title is identical to the title of MS Kirkuk 8 mentioned above,[16] one wonders whether this is not simply a copy of the latter (in which case there is a mistake in the dating: 1716 should be 1706, if the indications regarding Kirkuk 8 are correct).

---

[16] 'Elucidation of difficult words in the Pentateuch which are drawn from the commentaries of the blessed Mar Theodore and the traditions of the Syrians Mar Ephrem, John and Abraham of Bet Rabban, Mar Michael, and other teachers.' The Sʿert MSS have the same title, but give John and Abraham in the opposite order.

From the above, it appears that for the New Testament and the Psalms, we have only MS (olim) Diyarbakır 22. It is clear that for the Pentateuch, we cannot limit ourselves to MS Mingana 553, as Levene did, as this is a copy of a copy. One should at least use the readily accessible witnesses, that is: Diyarbakır 22, Mosul 11.1–3, Vat. sir. 578, Diettrich 2, as well as Vat. sir. 502 and Mingana 553 as representatives of Sʿert 21.

One further point should be noted, and this brings me to the *Diyarbakır Commentary*. This is the name, for want of anything better, given to the first section, from Genesis to Exod 9:32 in the MS (olim) Diyarbakır 22. This section replaces the original folios, which must have been lost at some stage. However, the text used as a replacement does not represent the *Anonymous Commentary* known from the other manuscripts (part of which was edited by Levene), but a slightly longer commentary. The editor of this longer commentary, Lucas Van Rompay, has been able to reconstruct the relationship between this text, the *Anonymous Commentary*, and Ishoʿdad.[17]

Let me first clarify that the *Diyarbakır Commentary* is a collection of material containing the common stock of East Syriac exegesis. Theodore of Mopsuestia was of course *the* Interpreter for the East Syrians, but he was soon deemed too difficult to read, and his style had to be simplified. Objections to his exegesis also had to be dealt with. The *Diyarbakır Commentary* therefore quotes, and where necessary summarizes and simplifies, Theodore's words, while adding comments and observations from other Greek and Syriac authors. Names are mentioned only now and then, but it is clear that one Rabban Gabriel, probably Gabriel of Qatar, takes pride of place. The place accorded to him and the fact that he is introduced several times as 'our Rabban' is an important key to the dating of the commentary, according to Van Rompay. He assigns the work to the early eighth century, when the School of Seleucia, where

[17] Lucas Van Rompay, *Le commentaire sur Genèse–Exode 9,32 du manuscrit (olim) Diyarbakır 22* (CSCO 483–484, Syr. 205–206 ; Leuven: Peeters, 1986).

Rabban had worked, was flowering, and Christians from the Bet Qatraye region contributed to East Syrian culture.[18]

Van Rompay's studies have also made it clear that the *Anonymous Commentary*, at least in the section where we can compare the two, represents an abridgement of the *Diyarbakır Commentary*.[19] The anonymous editor has, for instance, omitted introductory and connecting phrases, making the work into a collection of scholia which all start with a lemma quoting the biblical text. Digressions and theological developments of certain texts have also been removed. On the other hand, the editor has also added material. Here the interest for our purpose today becomes clear: not only has he added a fragment of Ephrem and quite a few by Ishoʿdad, he has also given two references to Ahob, and we may assume that this is Ahob of Qatar. In addition, it appears that the editor has not only preserved the four references to the language of Qatar found in the *Diyarbakır Commentary*, but added eight more. This circumstance made Van Rompay suggest that the editor, who may have worked around the year 900, had contacts with southern Mesopotamia or worked in one of the schools where Christians from the Gulf region were numerous. There is one other option, though: Van Rompay also mentions the fact that Ahob of Qatar was known for his quotations of the language of Qatar. Could these eight additional references in the *Anonymous Commentary* not go back to Ahob himself?

Let us have a closer look at the two explicit references to Ahob in the *Anonymous Commentary*. They occur in Gen. 15:9–10 and Gen. 50:10. Interestingly, for Gen. 15:9–10 the *Diyarbakır Commentary* and the *Anonymous Commentary* give almost word for word the same text.[20] It is only in the latter (and not even in all the manuscripts) that the name Ahob appears. For Gen. 50:10, both commentaries present an identical gloss (the word Aṭar would be Egyptian for 'grave'). This time all the witnesses to the *Anonymous Commentary* give the name Ahob. The simplest explanation for this is a procedure which we often see in East Syrian exegetical collec-

[18] Van Rompay, *Le commentaire* [version], pp. lii–liii.

[19] Van Rompay, *Le commentaire* [version], pp. xl–xliv.

[20] See Cowley, 'Scholia of Aḥob of Qaṭar', p. 339.

tions: they tend to work on the basis of an earlier core, to which they add new material. When they come across parallel material, that is, material from their additional sources which is already present in some form in the earlier core, they often give a fuller reading or they add further information. Thus in this case we may assume that in addition to the *Diyarbakır Commentary* (the core collection which he presented in an abridged form), the editor of the *Anonymous Commentary* had direct access to Ahob. In two instances he must have added Ahob's name on this basis. We can only guess at the extent of his further use of Ahob, as names were given only now and then, and we have no way of knowing what belonged to Ahob and what did not—apart from, perhaps, the eight additional references to the language of Qatar.

In theory, there is indeed the option that Ahob used the *Diyarbakır Commentary* or one of its sources, and took over this material in his own commentary, which was then quoted by the *Anonymous Commentary*, but this clearly is not the simplest solution, given the known close connection between the *Diyarbakır Commentary* and the *Anonymous Commentary*. The material is representative of what we know about Ahob. The note on Gen. 50 gives an interpretation on the basis of Egyptian. Though it is unlikely that he knew Coptic himself, the appeal to other languages is one of the hallmarks of his work. The note on Gen. 15 is a simplified version of a comment which we know from the Greek *Collectio Coisliniana*, a collection of exegetical fragments centred on Theodoret of Cyrrhus's *Quaestiones*.[21] The authorship of the fragment is uncertain, but arguments have been brought forward to attribute it to Theodore of Mopsuestia.[22]

Now what about Ishoʿdad of Merv? Van Rompay's studies have shown that this author, who must have worked around the year 850, had access to a larger array of sources, including a copy of the Syro-Hexapla—probably the copy made on behalf of the Ca-

---

[21] Françoise Petit, *Catenae Graecae in Genesim et in Exodum: Collectio Coisliniana in Genesim* (Turnhout: Brepols, 1986), *Csl.* 186.

[22] See now, in addition to the note in Petit's edition (preceding footnote), Augusto Guida, *Teodoro di Mopsuestia. Replica a Giuliano Imperatore* (Florence: Nardini editore, 1994), pp. 123–26.

tholicos-Patriarch Timothy I earlier during the ninth century.[23] But he must also have used a work identical or nearly identical to the *Diyarbakır Commentary*, which he used as a basic collection of material. Thus he takes over nearly all the quotations of Rabban Gabriel from this work, but without mentioning his name and often in abridged form.[24] Interestingly, Ahob's comment on Gen. 15 is quoted in the same form as in the *Diyarbakır Commentary* and the *Anonymous Commentary*, but Ishoʿdad explicitly rejects Ahob's explanation of Aṭar on the basis of Egyptian in Gen. 50, adopting a different interpretation instead. This makes it clear that for the Ahob material Ishoʿdad could be dependent on *Diyarbakır* in the same way as he depended on this collection for Rabban Gabriel. It is also clear that the *Anonymous Commentary*, whose author knew and quoted Ishoʿdad, did not follow the latter in his rejection of the Egyptian gloss. The fact that in addition to the material from the *Diyarbakır Commentary*, he had direct access to Ahob material might have caused him to appreciate Ahob more.

On the basis of the observations just made regarding the position of Ahob in the *Anonymous Commentary*, I had hoped to find some considerable amount of Ahob material in its Psalms section as well. The study of this section was disappointing in this respect, however. The Psalms section is relatively short: some six folios. It is placed between the Prophets and the Bet Mawtbe in the MS (olim) Diyarbakır 22, but as we have seen, it is missing from the two manuscripts that contain the Old Testament commentary. Scholars have already expressed uncertainty with regard to the question of whether the Bet Mawtbe and Prophets sections were written by the same author as the Pentateuch section. Given the situation in the manuscripts, we should now also express the same uncertainty with regard to the authorship of the Psalms section: was it written by the one who compiled the Bet Mawtbe and Prophets sections, or was it added later on? Ceslas Van den

---

[23] Bas ter Haar Romeny, 'Biblical Studies in the Church of the East: The Case of Catholicos Timothy I', in M.F. Wiles and E.J. Yarnold (eds.), *Studia Patristica* 34. *Papers Presented at the Thirteenth International Conference on Patristic Studies held in Oxford 1999* (Leuven: Peeters, 2001), pp. 503–510.

[24] Van Rompay, *Le commentaire* [version], pp. l–li.

Eynde's statement on this section could be read in the latter sense: 'On a l'impression qu'il a été composé uniquement parce qu'on voulait un commentaire complet sur l'A.T.'[25]

The Psalms section of the *Anonymous Commentary* contains some 250 very short scholia which explain words or expressions, but it appears that it does so without the use of other languages which is characteristic of Ahob. For the very limited agreement with Ishoʿdad it is hardly necessary to assume that the author had access to Ishoʿdad's Psalter commentary. However, he did quote, also explicitly, Ishoʿ bar Nun's *Selected Questions*,[26] and he must have had access in one form or the other to a work which, at least in its later tradition, is very important for our study of Ahob of Qatar.[27] Let us move on to that work, therefore: the *Denha-Gregory Commentary on the Psalms.*

2. The Denha-Gregory Commentary on the Psalms

Willem Bloemendaal gave the first survey of the manuscript tradition of the *Denha-Gregory Commentary*.[28] Some additions and corrections were given by Van Rompay.[29] In the textual tradition, four stages can be discerned as follows.

1. Stage 1 is represented by the MS Berlin Sachau 215. This is a commentary on the Psalms attributed to Theodore of Mopsuestia. The text commented on is the Peshitta rather than the Greek text of the Psalter, however. The work is probably best described as a commentary on the Peshitta

---

[25] Van den Eynde, *Commentaire d'Išoʿdad de Merv* 6. *Psaumes* [version], p. xxxviii.

[26] Corrie Molenberg, *The Interpreter Interpreted. Išoʿ bar Nun's Selected Questions on the Old Testament* (doctoral thesis; Groningen: Rijksuniversiteit, 1990), p. 22–23.

[27] Van den Eynde, *Psaumes* [version], p. xxxvii–xxxviii.

[28] Willem Bloemendaal, *The Headings of the Psalms in the East Syrian Church* (Leiden: Brill, 1960), p. 16.

[29] Lucas Van Rompay, *Théodore de Mopsueste: Fragments syriaques du Commentaire des Psaumes* [version] (CSCO 436 / Syr. 190 ; Leuven: Peeters, 1982), pp. ix–xiv.

in the spirit of Theodore and using mainly material deriving from him.

2. Stage 2 is represented by MS Paris, BnF syr. 367 (olim Sʿert 29), dated to 1252, and MS Paris, BnF syr. 351, probably to be dated to the 16th or 17th century.[30] This text is a commentary on the Psalms attributed, according to the MSS, by some to Rabban Denha and by others to Rabban Gregory, a monk from Gamre. The latter is unknown; the former might be identified with a student of Ishoʿ bar Nun of this name, who lived in the first half of the ninth century (which would make the author a contemporary of Ishoʿdad).[31] This text is, as Robert Devreesse already stated, 'a revised and augmented edition' of the commentary of Stage 1.[32] The additional material is of a different provenance; it contains more Christological explanations. Bernhard Vandenhoff has suggested that he might have been a follower of Hnana of Adiabene,[33] but this is no more than a hypothesis, probably based on the fact that Hnana's works were later suppressed in the East Syrian tradition.
3. Stage 3 is represented by a number of nineteenth-century manuscripts, two of which are accessible: MS London, British Library, Or. 9354, and MS Mingana 58, both dated to 1895.[34] A third manuscript, of which the whereabouts

---

[30] The whereabouts of MS Urmia 217, dated to 1682/3, and MS Urmia 151, to be dated to *c.*1880–90, are not known. It is therefore difficult to establish whether they belong to this stage or the next.

[31] Van den Eynde, *Psaumes* [version], p. xxxvi.

[32] Robert Devreesse, *Le Commentaire de Théodore de Mopsueste sur les Psaumes (I–LXXX)* (Studi e testi 93; Vatican City: Biblioteca Apostolica Vaticana, 1939), pp. xxviii-xxix.

[33] Bernhard Vandenhoff, *Exegesis Psalmorum imprimis messianicorum apud Syros Nestorianos e codice adhuc inedito illustrata* (Rheine: Altmeppen, 1899), pp. 12–14.

[34] The following manuscripts are not accessible to me: MS Mosul 20, dated to 1875; MS Alqosh 35 (olim 28), partly dated to 1710, partly to 1893; MS Alqosh 36 (olim 20), dated to 1884; MS Alqosh olim 21, dated

are now not known, was used by Vandenhoff, who edited a number of sections on its basis.[35] For our purpose this stage and the next are the most important, because it is here that we find material attributed to Ahob of Qatar. The manuscripts of this stage comprise three main parts:

a. The *Book of the Aims of the Psalms*, which is a collection of introductory treatises to the Psalms, the first of which is attributed to Ahob of Qatar.
b. The *Denha-Gregory Commentary*, to the main text of which five passages from Ahob have been added within frames. At least fourteen additional fragments of Ahob are found in the margins.
c. A commentary on the canticles of the Old Testament.

4. Stage 4 is known from only one manuscript, MS Cambridge, University Library, Or. 1318, which must be dated to the end of the nineteenth century. This manuscript gives all the material known from the Stage 3 manuscripts, but the order of the treatises in the *Book of the Aims of the Psalms* is slightly different, and several additional texts have been added: an extract from the *Scholion* of Theodore bar Koni, an extract from John bar Penkaye's *Book of the Main Points of the History of the Temporary World* (twice!), an extract from Theodore of Mopsuestia's *Commentary on the Psalms*, and some hymns on Mary by Giwargis Warda.

---

to 1893 (became part of Vosté's personal collection; whereabouts unknown); MS of Octčanes, mentioned by Vandenhoff. MS Alqosh 35 belonged to Stage 2, but has been 'updated' to Stage 3 in 1893, it seems (see Van Rompay, *Théodore de Mopsueste* [version], p. xiii n. 44 and 45). This makes the Mosul MS of 1875 the oldest witness to this group.

[35] Vandenhoff, *Exegesis Psalmorum*. The manuscript was copied in Alqosh, as Vandenhoff states (*Exegesis Psalmorum*, p. 3), which makes it likely that it was based on one of the Alqosh MSS mentioned in the preceding footnote. See Van Rompay, *Théodore de Mopsueste* [version], p. xii n. 42.

It is clear that for our study of Ahob, Stages 3 and 4 are the most important, as it is here that we find an introductory treatise on the Psalms written by him, as well as at least nineteen fragments. The composition of the Stage 3 manuscripts made Vandenhoff suggest that it was Ahob who compiled the collection in this form. After all, the collection begins with his introduction, and it is at Stage 3 that the Ahob fragments were added to the *Denha-Gregory Commentary*. However, there are no further indications for this, and it is not impossible that the collection came to be copied in this form only in the nineteenth century (the oldest witness to Stage 3 being dated to 1875; but see below).[36] It would seem that both the introductory treatise and the fragments were taken from a full commentary on the Psalms written by Ahob—even though ʿAbdishoʿ bar Brika does not mention one.

Let us first have a look at the fragments.[37] There are points of agreement between Ishoʿdad on the one hand and Denha-Gregory and Ahob on the other. Van den Eynde suggested the possibilities of interdependence and a common source as the possible origins of this agreement, but did not choose between them.[38] Corrie Molenberg argues that the only conclusion to be drawn from the agreement is that Ishoʿdad had at his disposal the same material as that which has been preserved in the Stage 3 manuscripts.[39] This could imply that neither Denha–Gregory nor Ahob borrowed from Ishoʿdad, but because of the uncertainty attached to the dating of these authors, this possibility is hard to exclude from the outset. However, what we have seen above with regard to Genesis suggests that Ishoʿdad must have had access through some other collection to Ahob, rather than the other way round. This lends further support to Molenberg's point of view.

Another clue can be found within the fragments on the Psalms attributed to Ahob themselves. My first soundings show that some of the notes clearly present the exegesis of Theodore of

---

[36] See note 34 above.

[37] The following resumes pp. 449-52 of my 'The Hebrew and the Greek' (see note 7 above).

[38] Van den Eynde, *Psaumes* [version], xxiii.

[39] Molenberg, *The Interpreter Interpreted*, p. 219.

Mopsuestia. Where Ishoʿdad has a parallel comment, it can be seen that both authors give the same reworked version of Theodore's exegesis,[40] and that this version is sometimes developed further by Ishoʿdad. For instance, for Ps. 5:4 Theodore offers three explanations of the word 'morning'. Ahob quotes only these three, whereas Ishoʿdad adds a fourth.[41] These parallels between Ahob and Ishoʿdad can be explained by assuming that Ishoʿdad used Ahob, but not the other way round. As I have shown elsewhere, Ahob was also an important source for Ishoʿdad's alternative readings of the biblical text, especially the readings attributed to 'the Hebrew'.[42]

An interesting detail which may also suggest that the Ahob material was added to Ishoʿdad's commentary, possibly even at a later stage, is the fact that some of Ahob's notes and readings appear at different places in the three manuscripts of Ishoʿdad: they appear to have been added as marginal notes by Ishoʿdad himself or by a later author.[43]

Finally we come to the *Book of the Aims of the Psalms* by Ahob, which is the first treatise of the collection of introductory treatises of the same name, which was added before the *Denha-Gregory Commentary* in the Stage 3 and Stage 4 manuscripts. Mingana and Vosté's attribution to Ahob of yet another treatise, a classification of

---

[40] Compare for example the Greek text of Theodore, ed. Devreesse, *Le Commentaire*, p. 261,5–12, with Ahob, MS Mingana 58, fol. 60v boxed, and Ishoʿdad, ed. Van den Eynde, *Psaumes* [texte], p. 64,3–9; idem [version], p. 74,39.

[41] Latin text of Theodore: ed. Luc De Coninck, *Theodori Mopsuesteni Expositionis in Psalmos Iuliano Aeclanensi interprete in latinum versae quae supersunt* (CCSL 88A; Turnhout: Brepols, 1977), p. 26,44–47. Ahob: MS Mingana 58, fol. 20v margin. Ishoʿdad: ed. Van den Eynde, *Psaumes* [texte], p. 24,15–18; idem [version], pp. 28,25–29,2. Cf. also a case relating to the introduction to Ps. 45(44): Greek text of Theodore, ed. Devreesse, *Le Commentaire*, p. 277,19–21. Ahob: MS Mingana 58, fol. 63v margin. Ishoʿdad: ed. Van den Eynde, *Psaumes* [texte], p. 66,15–16; idem [version], p. 76,22–23.

[42] See the article mentioned in note 7 above.

[43] See for example Van den Eynde, *Psaumes* [version], pp. 69 n. 3, 113 n. 16, and 115 n. 28 (ed., p. 104 n. 54).

the Psalms,[44] is probably incorrect, however. This attribution was based on the fact that neither this treatise, which is the third one in the Stage 3 manuscripts, nor the second treatise bear the name of an author. However, Vandenhoff had already shown that the second treatise was taken from the so-called *Expositio Officiorum*.[45] The third treatise can therefore no longer be connected to the first.

In the *Book of the Aims of the Psalms* Ahob explains the extraordinary usefulness of the book of Psalms, which is 'more than all other books excellent and abundant in benefits'. According to Ahob it is like the head to the body of Scripture. Whereas most books contain prophecy or history or legislation or wisdom, the Psalter contains all of these. It is the most accurate guide to divine knowledge, inspiring us to serve God. Ahob then goes on to explain why the Psalms are set to music: this is because music ensures that we will never be satisfied and always want to hear more of them. Finally, Ahob praises David, who was 'humbler than all other prophets, whereas there is in him request, fasting, prayer, repentance, imploring, worship, love, faith, clemency, hope, goodness, grace, understanding, knowledge, life, healing, and remission of sins.' The Fathers made us chant from the Psalter more than from all other books: 'first, because Christ is from (David's) seed; second, because he prophesied about (Christ's) divinity and humanity, about the passion, the martyrdom, the resurrection, and the ascension.'

Now the first section of the work, on the extraordinary usefulness of the book of Psalms, agrees to a large extent with the fifth treatise added to the *Denha-Gregory Commentary*. The thoughts that are expressed are the same, and a few sentences even match word for word. This fifth treatise is also on the aim of the Psalter, but it is ascribed to Nathniel of Shirzor (or Shahrzur, in the north-east of

---

[44] Jacques-Marie Vosté, 'Sur les titres des Psaumes dans la Pešitto, surtout d'après la recension orientale', *Biblica* 25 (1944), pp. 210–35, esp. 228–33, and Alphonse Mingana, *Catalogue of the Mingana Collection of Manuscripts, Now in the Possession of the Trustees of the Woodbroke Settlement, Selly Oak, Birmingham* 1. *Syriac and Garshūni Manuscripts* (Cambridge: Heffer, 1933), col. 158.

[45] Vandenhoff, *Exegesis Psalmorum*, p. 6.

present-day Iraq). Nathniel studied at the School of Nisibis. As bishop of Shirzor he signed the acts of the East Syrian synods of 585 and 605. He was put to death by the Persian king Khosrau because of his opposition to a Persian commander who had destroyed churches.[46] Interestingly, ʿAbdishoʿ bar Brika does credit him with a commentary on the Psalms, as well as a number of polemical works, none of which has come down to us.[47] Vandenhoff concludes that Ahob's treatise is no more than the work of Nathniel with a few additions.[48] This is probably slightly too harsh, but Ahob's text can indeed be seen as a further development of that of Nathniel. Even if Ahob should be equated with Ayyub of Seleucia, which would make the two authors contemporaries, it is indeed not impossible that Ahob made use of his colleague's work. Fragments of Ahob's *Aims of the Psalms*, in their turn, were used in Ishoʿdad's introduction to the Psalter, and one is found in Theodore bar Koni.[49]

3. Further Sources

As we have seen, fragments of Ahob were also quoted by Ibn at-Tayyib in his biblical commentaries in Arabic. From there they found their way to Ethiopia, where they were first translated into Gəʿəz and later received a place in the Amharic *andəmta* commentary tradition. Further references to Ahob can be found in Bar Bahlul's *Lexicon* and in Isaac Eshbadnaya's own prose commentary on his *Poem on the Divine Government of the World from the Creation to the Consummation* (15th century).

EXEGETICAL TRADITION AND GLOSSES IN THE LANGUAGE OF QATAR

In terms of the exegetical tradition in which Ahob stands, two points should be made. First, it is abundantly clear that Ahob

---

[46] Jean Maurice Fiey, *Assyrie chrétienne* 3 (Beirut: Dar el-Machreq, 1968), p. 69.

[47] Assemani, 'Carmen Ebedjesu', p. 224.

[48] Vandenhoff, *Exegesis Psalmorum*, pp. 5–6.

[49] Van den Eynde, *Psaumes* [version], p. xxxiv.

stands in the East Syrian tradition. He is following Theodore of Mopsuestia and on a number of occasions, both in the material studied by Cowley and in the comments on Genesis and Psalms which we have referred to above, he can be shown actually to summarize or paraphrase Theodore's opinions. He therefore formed part of the movement to make Theodore's work easily accessible. The possible quotation of Ephrem in one of the fragments given by Cowley does not contradict this: both the East Syrian and West Syrian tradition kept referring to this great fourth-century exegete and poet. Ahob's use of earlier material, possibly including that of his contemporary Nathniel of Shirzor, was standard practice. The goal was not to be original, but to hand down the opinions of Theodore and the tradition of the East Syrian church—a tradition which on the one hand went back to Ephrem and the School of Edessa, but on the other hand was taking pains to explain Theodore and deal with objections to his exegesis.

The second point which should be mentioned is Ahob's appeal to other languages. The *Diyarbakır Commentary* offers four references to the language of Bet Qatraye, and the *Anonymous Commentary* adds some eight in the same section of the Pentateuch. We have suggested above that these additional readings could very well come from Ahob, to whose work the editor of the *Anonymous Commentary* had direct access. It is even possible that *Diyarbakır*'s original four readings come from Ahob, as there is already some anonymous Ahob material there. Alternatively it could be suggested that Rabban Gabriel Qatraya was their source, but the references do not form part of explanations ascribed to him. As we have seen, Ahob also explains Aṭar in Gen. 50:10 on the basis of Egyptian. In the *Denha-Gregory Commentary* a number of references to the language of Bet Qatraye are found as well.

What exactly the language of Bet Qatraye was, remains somewhat enigmatic.[50] Linguists have studied some of the glosses found

[50] For this, see Riccardo Contini, 'La lingua del Bēt Qaṭrāyē', in J. Lentin and A. Lonnet (eds.), *Mélanges David Cohen: Études sur le langage, les langues, les dialectes, les littératures, offertes par ses élèves, ses collègues, ses amis; présentés à l'occasion de son quatre-vingtième anniversaire* (Paris: Maisonneuve & Larose, 2003), pp. 173–81, with further references.

in our texts. They appear to contain some words that cannot be explained, some Persian material, and some words of Semitic stock. Some of the possibly Semitic words seem closer to Arabic than to Aramaic, and it is conspicuous that there is no trace of the emphatic state which is so characteristic of Aramaic and especially Syriac. On the other hand, Riccardo Contini did find one feature that reflects an Aramaic morphology and phonology. He therefore does not object to Anton Schall's categorization of the language of Qatar as 'Southeastern Aramaic'.[51] He also expresses the hope that further studies into the Aramaic substrate of the neo-Arabic dialects of Eastern Arabia will provide new clues. An alternative might perhaps be to see it as a form of Arabic written down by someone used to writing Aramaic.

In addition to the explanations of difficult words in the Peshitta on the basis of the language of Qatar, Ahob also appealed to the Hebrew text as an alternative to the Peshitta. We have seen that in this respect he was actually an important source to Ishoʿdad. Interestingly, Theodore of Mopsuestia would probably not have approved of these references. Since Eusebius of Emesa, it was an established fact within the Antiochene School of exegesis that the Greek Septuagint was a translation of the Hebrew text, and that translations could confuse those who only knew the receiving language, for instance, when an idiom was translated literally. Theodore knew all this, and in his earlier works, he did refer to the three Jewish revisions of the Septuagint. However, later he changed his opinion: he came to believe that the Septuagint, precisely because of its literalness and the fact that it was translated by seventy excellent Jewish scholars, was the best way to access the original text. He criticized Jerome for making his own rendering of the Hebrew, whereas he had learned Hebrew only at a later age, and he was especially critical of the Syriac Peshitta, as it was not known who had

[51] Anton Schall, 'Der nestorianische Bibelexeget Īšōʿdāḏ von Merw (9. Jh. n. Chr.) in seiner Bedeutung für die orientalische Philologie', in Maria Macuch *et al.* (eds.), חכמות בנתה ביתה: Studia semitica necnon iranica Rudolpho Macuch septuagenario ab amicis et discipulis dedicata (Wiesbaden: Otto Harrassowitz, 1989), pp. 271–82, esp. p. 281.

produced it.[52] Ahob obtained his references to the Hebrew probably by consulting an informant, who must have interpreted the Hebrew or one of the Targumim for him: procedures Theodore would certainly condemn. We can therefore say that by giving these references, Ahob stood in the Antiochene tradition, but did not follow Theodore.

CONCLUSION

Through the study of the later East Syrian collections, even in their Arabic or Gəʿəz renderings, we can get access to fragments of the work of Ahob of Qatar. He must have been an exegete from the Bet Qatraye region, living in the sixth or seventh century, rather than the tenth, as Assemani thought. Given the fact that we have few sources for the East Syrian exegesis of the sixth and seventh centuries, these data are precious. In general, Ahob shows himself a disciple of Theodore of Mopsuestia, but in his use of the spoken language of Qatar he is an innovator. His references to the Hebrew, finally, may have been in line with earlier Antiochene practice, but it does not agree with the practices of the one who was considered the Interpreter par excellence. However, this did not stop later East Syrian exegetes from adopting these readings and some of his other comments from Ahob's works.

---

[52] See my *A Syrian in Greek Dress. The Use of Greek, Hebrew, and Syriac Biblical Texts in Eusebius of Emesa's Commentary on Genesis* (Traditio Exegetica Graeca 6; Leuven: Peeters), pp. 135–39.

GABRIEL OF BETH QATRAYE AS A WITNESS TO SYRIAC INTELLECTUAL LIFE C. 600 CE

SEBASTIAN BROCK
UNIVERSITY OF OXFORD

ABSTRACT

Gabriel Qatraya's extensive Commentary on the East Syriac liturgical services is preserved in a single manuscript of the thirteenth century. On internal evidence Gabriel must have been writing c. 600 (and not the late seventh century, as previously thought). His work happens to be an important witness to intellectual developments in the Church of the East at this significant time in its history, during the lifetime of the Prophet Muhammad, and these developments are discussed in this paper.

According to the evidence of Syriac literary sources, the Church of the East had a presence in Beth Qatraye for roughly half a millennium, from the fourth to the ninth century CE, but it is only from the seventh century that we have surviving texts by authors from Beth Qatraye who wrote in Syriac. In the case of three authors, Gabriel Qatraya, Isaac of Nineveh and Dadishoʿ Qatraya, the extent of their surviving writings is considerable. While the main focus of the present paper will be on Gabriel's extensive Commentary on the Liturgical Offices, attention will also be given to the witness of the monastic writings of Isaac and Dadishoʿ to the intellectual background that these three writers shared.

It so happens that we have references to no less than eight Gabriels who had some sort of connection with Beth Qatraye in the seventh century.[1] Three, or perhaps four, of these can probably be identified as a single writer, who is also curiously known as 'Gabriel Arya', ('Gabriel the Lion');[2] he was the author of a lost biblical commentary which, however, was cited as an authoritative source by several later commentators.[3] This particular Gabriel, who probably belongs to the latter part of the seventh century, was certainly a different person from Gabriel Qatraya bar Lipeh, who definitely belonged to the beginning of the seventh century, thanks to his mention of a contemporary bishop, Shubhalmaran, the metropolitan bishop of Karka d-Beth Slokh (modern Kirkuk), who was active in the first decade and a half of the seventh century.[4] This dating of Gabriel bar Lipeh to the early seventh century led the Chaldean liturgical scholar Serhad Jammo to identify him with a Gabriel Qatraya who was the collator and owner of a manuscript of the Syriac New Testament that was copied in Nisibis in the 25th year of Khusrau II, i.e. 614/615 CE, and is preserved today in the British Library, London.[5] Though attractive, this identification seems unlikely, since the Gabriel of the manuscript from Nisibis was evidently a young man, probably just a student at the time.

---

[1] For some further details and discussion, see my 'Syriac writers from Beth Qatraye', *Aram* 11–12 (1999–2000), pp.85–96.

[2] The *arya* can also mean 'leprosy', but the term for 'leper' would be *aryana*.

[3] This Gabriel Qatraya was evidently their source for several references to the language of Beth Qatraye; for this, see R. Contini, 'La lingua del Bet Qatraye', in J. Lentin and A. Lonnet (eds), *Mélanges David Cohen* (Paris, 2003), pp.173–181.

[4] British Library, Or. 3336, f.109r. Shubhalmaran's 'Book of Gifts' has now been edited, with English translation, by D.J. Lane, *Shubhalmaran, The Book of Gifts* (Corpus Scriptorum Christianorum Orientalium 612–613, Scriptores Syri 236–7; Louvain, 2004).

[5] Add. 14,471.

Apart from his being described as 'bar Lipeh' and 'Qatraya' in the single manuscript containing his Commentary on the Liturgical Offices, we thus have no more information about this Gabriel, and so it is to his Commentary that we need to turn.[6] The manuscript in question was copied in the thirteenth century in a monastery on the slopes of Mount Qardu, where (according to Syriac tradition) Noah's Ark landed after the Flood;[7] the exact date of the manuscript is unfortunately not clear, since one of the digits has been damaged, leaving three different possibilities, 1228, 1268 and 1288. The Commentary consists of five discourses (*memre*), the first four containing questions and answers on the liturgical offices of Ramsha (Evening Service) and Sapra (Morning Service) on weekdays and on Sundays, while the fifth concerns the 'Office of the (Eucharistic) Mysteries', of which the second section, in the form of a commentary on the rite, is the only one so far to have been published and translated.[8]

The significance of the work, from the point of view of the history and development of the East Syriac liturgy, lies in the fact that Gabriel was writing not long before the influential liturgical reforms of the Catholicos Ishoʿyahb III (649–659). From our present point of view, however, our interest will be focused primarily on a number of passages where Gabriel cites from earlier authors, for it is these which will provide us with some sort of indication of his intellectual background and of what sort of texts were available to him.

---

[6] His interest there in monastic usage strongly suggests he was a monk.

[7] Or. 3336; a very brief description is given by G. Margoliouth, *Descriptive List of Syriac and Karshuni MSS. in the British Museum acquired since 1873* (London, 1899; repr. Piscataway NJ, 2002), p.15; the details concerning the place of copying are given in a misleading form by S. Jammo, in his 'Gabriel Qatraya et son commentaire sur la liturgie chaldéenne', *Orientalia Christiana Periodica* 32 (1966), pp.39–52; see further my Gabriel of Qatar's Commentary on the Liturgy', *Hugoye* 6:2 (2003), pp.197–248 (reprinted, but without the Syriac text, in *Fire From Heaven: Studies in Syriac Theology and Liturgy* [Variorum Reprints, 2006], chapter 17).

[8] See the references in the previous note.

First, however, it is worth noting the geographical horizons of his knowledge; this comes out especially in a passage where he is discussing the variety of liturgical usages. 'In this region of Beth Parsaye', that is, within the Sasanian Empire, he observes that 'the Great Monastery of Izla and the holy Monastery of Rabban Shabur' have preserved the older liturgical usage in a certain matter, and 'have not been persuaded to make changes in the ordering of the earlier Fathers', that is, by introducing certain innovations.[9] These references might possibly indicate that Gabriel had at some time visited these two famous monasteries. The 'Great Monastery of Izla' was none other than the Monastery of Abraham of Kashkar, the great sixth-century reformer who revitalised the East Syriac monastic tradition;[10] at the time when Gabriel was writing, its superior will very probably have been one of the most important figures of the Church of the East, Babai the Great (d. 628). The mention of the other monastery, that of Rabban Shabur (in the region of Shuster, W. Iran),[11] is intriguing, for it was with this monastery that both Isaac and Dadishoʿ were later to be connected; this perhaps suggests that there was some longer lasting link between monks of Beth Qatraye and this monastery. Varying liturgical practices in different unnamed monasteries are also mentioned by Gabriel on a number of other occasions, and at one point he describes what 'I have seen with my own eyes a few years ago'.[12] All this suggests that he had travelled fairly extensively. Much earlier in his Commentary Gabriel shows an awareness of liturgical usage in churches of the Rhomaye (or, Byzantines) and of Antioch;[13] and elsewhere he refers to the distinctive tonsures of monks and bishops in the

---

[9] Or. 3336, f.76r.

[10] See especially S. Chialà, *Abramo di Kashkar e la sua comunità* (Magnano, 2005), and F. Jullien, *Le monachisme en Perse. La réforme d'Abraham le Grand* (CSCO 622, Subsidia 121; Louvain, 2008).

[11] F. Jullien, 'Rabban Shapor. Un monastère au rayonnement exceptionel. La réforme d'Abraham de Kashkar dans le Beth Huzaye', *Orientalia Christiana Periodica* 72 (2006), 333–348.

[12] Or. 3336, f.75r.

[13] Or. 3336, f. 2v.

Byzantine Empire.[14] This information should probably be attributed to hearsay rather than to any direct knowledge; in any case it should be remembered that Gabriel was writing at a time when many provinces of the Eastern Roman Empire were under Sasanian occupation. A further indication of his wide geographical horizon comes in his discussion of the etymology of *basiliqe* in the liturgical term *ʿonitha d-basiliqe*, a feature of the Office of Ramsha (Vespers).[15] He takes the term to be derived from Greek *basilika*, denoting the place (*beth*) of the emperor (*basileus*), that is, the place before the altar accorded to the emperor Constantine, according to the Council of Nicaea (325). Anticipating that someone might object that the word for 'king' in Greek was *qesar*, that person, he says, 'should realize that *qesar* is Latin'. Although this is obvious enough for a modern academic reader, it would not have been so for someone in the Sasanian Empire, for whom the Grecised form *kaisar* (whence Syriac *qesar*) would have been the standard term of reference for the Byzantine emperor; Gabriel's knowledge of the Latin origin of the word was, in fact, exceptional, in that Latin impinged on the Syriac-speaking world only through the intermediary of Greek, and so the Latin origin of a word would by no means be always obvious to a Syriac reader.

A good indication of the intellectual background of a particular author is often provided by the range of authors whom he mentions or directly quotes from. Gabriel was in fact fairly sparing in the number of writers to whom he refers, or whom he quotes.[16] The only previous Syriac author whom he cites is the poet Narsai, who was closely associated with the famous School of Edessa and then that of Nisibis, of which he was the Director, as we learn from the Statutes of 496. Greek authors, known to him in Syriac translations, receive more attention: the choice of Christian writers is of well-known figures of authority, Basil of Caesarea, Gregory of Nazianzus, Evagrius, Theodore of Mopsuestia, and 'Dionysius the

---

[14] Or. 3336, f.224v.

[15] Or. 3336, f.27v–28r.

[16] Gabriel's quotations are discussed in more detail in my 'Patristic quotations in Gabriel Qatraya's Commentary on the Liturgical Offices', forthcoming in the Festschrift for P. Géhin.

Areopagite'; but also included among the authorities to whom he refers are Aristotle and Pythagoras. Each of these provides us with some illuminating information.

Gabriel has three quotations in succession from Basil,[17] with an indication of the specific work given for the first and third, while the second is simply described as 'another teaching'. The first quotation is introduced as being from Basil's Letter to Gregory, that is, Letter 2 in the modern numbering. This letter was clearly widely read in monastic circles and a considerable number of manuscripts of the Syriac translation survive, but what is intriguing is the fact that the passage which is quoted by Gabriel comes from a supplement that features solely in a small number of manuscripts, all of a later date than Gabriel, who thus turns out to be the earliest witness to the supplementary text.[18] The third quotation, introduced as being from 'the Questions to the Brothers', comes from another popular monastic text.[19] The middle passage, described as being from 'another teaching of his', turns out to be from a work by the intellectual par excellence among monastic authors, Evagrius of Pontus, namely his *Gnostikos*, where Evagrius gives a citation from Basil.[20] Gabriel has two further quotations from Evagrius, this time attributed to him by name; the second comes from

[17] Or. 3336, f.95r–v.

[18] The quotation corresponds to Sections 52, 53–55 of my edition of Letter 2, in preparation.

[19] The so-called 'Small Asceticon', whose Greek original is lost (a Latin translation, however, also survives); Babai the Great also cites from this work in his Commentary on Evagrius' *Kephalaia Gnostica.*

[20] Chapter 45, in A. and C. Guillaumont, *Evagre le Pontique, Le Gnostique* (Sources chrétiennes 356, 1989). There are two Syriac translations of this work; Gabriel cites the one published by Frankenberg from British Library, Add. 14,578 (p.552, his no. 147). Babai the Great's Commentary on Evagrius' *Kephalaia Gnostica* (ed. Frankenberg, from Vatican Syr. 178, f.9r) also quotes this passage, as does Dadishoʿ in his Commentary on Abba Isaiah's *Asceticon* (p.155).

Evagrius' *Kephalaia Gnostica* (IV.25),[21] the work to which Babai the Great devoted a whole commentary.

Two different works by Gregory of Nazianzus are quoted,[22] his homily against the Emperor Julian (Discourses 4–5), and his Apologia (Discourse 3). Gabriel evidently knows the early Syriac translation of Gregory's Discourses, made c.500; this must have been circulating quite widely in East Syriac circles, for it was also known to Babai the Great, who quotes from a number of Gregory's Discourses (all different from the two cited by Gabriel).

Gabriel provides an extended quotation from the man he calls 'the blessed Dionysius, bishop of the city of Athens, disciple of the blessed Paul', that is, the mysterious author of the famous Pseudo-Dionysian corpus. His quotation, from the treatise on the Divine Names (I.4), comes from the first Syriac translation of the Pseudo-Dionysian corpus, made by Sergius of Reshʿaina, who died in 536. Gabriel, together with his contemporary Babai the Great,[23] is the earliest East Syriac writer to show knowledge of, and to quote from, this influential work. Most remarkably, Gabriel also quotes at length, though without acknowledgement, from Sergius of Reshʿaina's own Discourse on the Spiritual Life,[24] which in now known for certain to have prefaced his translation of the Dionysius corpus as preserved in the unique manuscript, Sinai Syriac 52.[25] In this connection it is worth recalling that Sergius's Introduction to Aristotle's Categories was addressed to a bishop within the Persian

---

[21] Or. 3336, f. 218rv; the wording indicates the Gabriel was using the widespread Syriac recension, S1, edited by A. Guillaumont, Patrologia Orientalis 28:1 (1958).

[22] Or. 3336, f.96r.

[23] Commentary on Evagrius (ed. Frankenberg), pp.38/40 (f.18r–v) and 142 (f.66v).

[24] Or. 3336, f.107v–108v; the passage can be identified as sections 35–39 of Sergius' Discourse, ed. P. Sherwood in *L'Orient Syrien* 5 (1960), pp.458 (for sections 35–38), and 6 (1961), p.96 (for section 39).

[25] For the scattered constituent parts of this manuscript, see P. Géhin, 'Manuscrits sinaïtiques dispersés, I. Les fragments syriaques et arabes de Paris', *Oriens Christianus* 90 (2006), pp.23–43, here 37–38.

Empire, Theodore of Karkh Juddan, on the Tigris (in the vicinity of Samarra).

That Gabriel should quote from 'the Interpreter', that is, Theodore of Mopsuestia, is no surprise, given the great authority this Greek writer enjoyed in the Church of the East. Works by him were already being translated into Syriac in Edessa in the first half of the fifth century, thus ensuring their survival despite the condemnation of Theodore and his writings at the Council of Constantinople in 553. The brief quotations that Gabriel makes, however, seem to be from works that are now lost in Syriac as well; they are of interest in that they speak of the torment of Gehenna as having an end, an idea taken up at greater length by Isaac of Nineveh (who likewise quotes Theodore, though not the same passages).

It is particularly interesting that Gabriel provides quotations from the two famous pagan authors, Pythagoras and Aristotle, both in connection with number symbolism. He introduces Pythagoras as 'a lover of silence', and then goes on:

> He defines everything by number, and by means of certain numerical symbols he used to transmit the mystery/secret of his teaching to his disciples … He handed down that the number one is the equivalent of the Maker, whom he in truth confesses as being one. The number two (symbolizes) matter, and three species, and four the elements, providing four equivalents. And just as the numbers 1, 2, 3 and 4 make up the number 10, so, by the power of the Creator, who is one in the simplicity of his nature,[26] this whole world came into being, with the number of its elements and the full (number) of its natural constituents (lit. natures), bearing the equivalence of the perfect number of ten.

The reference is to Pythagoras' famous *Tetraktys*, which forms the subject of Book 1 of Augustine's *De Musica*. A Discourse by Pythagoras and a collection of his sayings in Syriac translations are known from other sources, but Gabriel must have derived this information from somewhere different.

---

[26] 'Simplicity of his nature' reflects Neoplatonic terminology.

Gabriel then introduces Aristotle, whom he describes as 'the skilled philosopher and exact investigator of natural phenomena', and continues:[27]

> Accordingly, imitating this ordering, the skilled philosopher and exact investigator of natural phenomena, Aristotle, himself counted up and defined with ten genera (*gense*) all the simple appellations (*kunnaye pshite*) of the world's phenomena; within these (ten *gense*) all the natures, and all that are within the natures, are contained. First of all he had skilfully constructed that fourfold higher level of substance (*ousia*), accidents, the common and the individual; and then from it he generated those ten *gense*, which are the ten categories (*qategoris*); and for this writing he made the *Eisagoge*, and the foundation of all the rational knowledge of philosophy.

It would appear that Gabriel has taken Aristotle himself to be the author of Porphyry's famous *Eisagoge*, or Introduction to Aristotle's logical works. The first Syriac translations of both Aristotle's *Categories* and Porphyry's *Eisagoge* were made in the early sixth century by an unknown person (not Sergius of Reshʿaina, as has sometimes been suggested), and Gabriel's reference to them usefully indicates that these translations were already available in the Persian Empire by the early seventh century.

Turning now to the two authors from Beth Qatraye who flourished in the late seventh century, Isaac and Dadishoʿ, it is of interest to compare their knowledge of earlier literature in Syriac with that of Gabriel. Both quote from the same Greek authors as Gabriel, and occasionally from the same passage. Evagrius is especially popular, which is hardly surprising in specifically monastic authors. The range of authors quoted by Isaac and Dadishoʿ is, however, considerably greater, with Macarius, Mark the Monk and the *Apophthegmata,* or Sayings, of the Egyptian Fathers featuring prominently, all writings of monastic, rather than liturgical interest, and in any case, the sixth-century translations of the Sayings of the Desert Fathers had only achieved prominence in the Church of the East thanks to the edition, entitled 'The Paradise of the Fathers',

[27] Or. 3336, f.144v–145r.

compiled by ʿEnanishoʿ at the request of the Catholicos Gewargis (660–680/1).

In the case of Syriac authors, a passage of Narsai probably features in the background of a christological interpretation by Isaac of a passage in Exodus 25,[28] though he is not mentioned by name. The two other Syriac authors quoted are Ephrem and the early fifth-century monastic author, John the Solitary, or John of Apameia. The latter was given a number of different appellations, one being 'the prophet, the Seer of Thebes',[29] a rare case of the designation 'prophet' for a Christian author.[30]

Like Gabriel, both Isaac and Dadishoʿ were not averse to quoting from, or making use of pagan Greek writings. Aristotle's *Categories* receive mention, along with the *Peri Hermeneias* and *Apodeiktikos* (or *Posterior Analytics*), in Dadishoʿ's Commentary on Abba Isaiah's *Asceticon*, but, unlike Gabriel, his reference is very negative, these being books which in his (and Evagrius') opinion are used by the demons to distract monks and make them proud. Quoted in a much more favourable light, both by Dadishoʿ and by Isaac, are the words of certain pagan philosophers in praise of virtues that were highly valued also by monks. Dadishoʿ, in his Discourse on Stillness (*shelya*), gives examples of the advice of several unnamed pre-Christian philosophers.[31] Isaac, too, in the course of a discussion on patience and endurance, adduces examples of pagan philosophers; although he does not name the protagonists, the narratives can be identified: one is from the Life of Secundus 'the Silent Philosopher', a widely known work of the second century CE,[32]

---

[28] Part II, xi.14.

[29] Dadishoʿ, *On Stillness* (ed. A. Mingana, *Early Christian Mystics*, Woodbrooke Studies VII, pp.207–8 (text), 86 (translation)). Dadishoʿ in fact distinguishes between several different Johns.

[30] In the *Historia Monachorum* (I.1), the ultimate source, it is just stated that he had 'the charism of prophecy'.

[31] Woodbrooke Studies VII, p.226 (text), 111–112 (translation).

[32] In Isaac's Discourse 57 (ed. Bedjan, pp.403–404; see my 'Secundus the Silent philosopher. Some notes on the Syriac tradition', *Rheinisches Museum* 121 (1978), pp.94–100 (reprinted in *Studies in Syriac Christianity*

while a little further on Isaac very probably has an allusion to the story of Alexander the Great's encounter with the Brahmin philosopher Dindamis, found in Greek in Palladius' *On the peoples of India and on the Brahmins*. The Syriac translations of both narratives are known from other sources, and intriguingly they are found together in a Melkite monastic anthology preserved in a manuscript in St Catherine's Monastery, Mount Sinai.[33] It thus seems quite likely that Isaac came across them in a manuscript of similar content. It so happens that there is a certain amount of evidence for contacts between monks of the Church of the East and St Catherine's Monastery from the late sixth to the ninth century,[34] either in the form of visits in the course of pilgrimages to Jerusalem and/or the Egyptian monasteries, or in the migration of manuscripts; a good example of this is one of the Syriac manuscripts among 'New Finds', for M20N contains a work by the seventh-century East Syriac monastic author Babai of Nisibis.[35]

SUMMARY

Although it is impossible to say with certainty whether or not it was at a School of higher education in Beth Qatraye itself that these various Syriac authors from Beth Qatraye first acquired their wide knowledge of earlier writings in Syriac, it is nevertheless the case that Gabriel, Dadisho^{c} and Isaac can be described as being

[Variorum Reprints, 1992], chapter 9), where a translation of the Syriac translation of the Life is also given.

[33] Sinai Syr. 14; the excerpt with Alexander's meeting with Dandamis is edited and translated in my 'Stomathalassa, Dandamis and Secundus in a Syriac monastic anthology', in G.J. Reinink and A.C. Klugkist (eds), *After Bardaisan. Studies on Continuity and Change in Syriac Christianity in Honour of H.J.W. Drijvers* (Orientalia Lovanensia Analecta 89, Leuven, 1999), pp.35–50, esp. 40–46.

[34] The evidence can be found in my 'Syriac on Sinai: the main connections', in V. Ruggieri and L. Pieralli (eds), *Eukosmia. Studi miscelanei per il 75o di Vicenzo Poggi SJ* (Soveria Manelli, 2003), pp.103–117.

[35] For the identification, see P. Géhin, 'Fragments patristiques syriaques des Nouvelles découvertes du Sinaï', *Collectanea Christiana Orientalia* 6 (2009), p.76.

amongst the most highly educated and widely read of all the many known East Syriac writers of the seventh century, being surpassed only by Babai the Great. It is particularly significant that our authors from Beth Qatraye were clearly cognisant of the sixth-century translations of the early books of Aristotle's collection of books on logic, known as the Organon, or 'Tool': this represented the cutting-edge of higher education in the Syriac-speaking world: it rapidly became the basis for all higher studies among the Syrian Orthodox communities within the Late Roman Empire, and was soon to do so within the Church of the East as well.[36] It is pleasing to think that the various monastic ruins that have been discovered in various locations in the Gulf[37] were once home to these learned writers.

It is clear that these seventh-century Syriac authors from Beth Qatraye were very much a part of the intellectual world of the Church of the East which had been stimulated by the translations of books of Aristotle's Organon made in the previous century by Syriac scholars living within the Byzantine Empire. Looking at matters from a wider perspective, one can observe how both the Syriac Orient and the Latin West were co-heirs of the Alexandrian Greek intellectual tradition for which Aristotle, as read by the Neoplatonists, was the great authority. The role played by Sergius of Resh'aina and others in the Syriac-speaking world, by way of translating and commenting on Aristotle, had its counterpart in the Latin West in the works of Boethius. It was thanks to these parallel developments in the Latin West and the Syriac Orient, with the

---

[36] As witnessed, for example, by the bizarre account, using technical Aristotelian terms, by Hnanishoʿ II concerning the dispute over his election at a synod of 775/6; cf. J-B. Chabot, *Synodicon Orientale* (Paris, 1902), p.246 (text), 517 (French translation).

[37] For these, see especially, R.A. Carter, 'Christianity in the Gulf during the first centuries of Islam'. *Arabian Archaeology and Epigraphy* 19 (2008), 71–108; J-F. Salles, 'Chronologies du monachisme dans le Golfe Arabo-Persique', in F. Jullien and M-J. Pierre (eds.), *Monachismes d'Orient* (Paris, 2012), pp.291–312; J-F. Salles and O. Callot, 'Les églises de Koweit et du Golfe persique', in F. Briquel-Chatonnet (ed.), *Les églises en monde syriaque* (Études syriaques 10, 2013), 237–268.

subsequent translations of the same works of Aristotle into Arabic, often at first by way of Syriac, that it came about that the medieval Latin West and its contemporary Arabic East shared the same philosophical heritage, with the result that the works of Ibn Sina/Avicenna and others proved to be so highly appreciated in Latin translations made in twelfth-century Spain, thus providing a new stimulus to the western European philosophical tradition.

THE FUTURE OF THE PAST: THE RECEPTION OF SYRIAC QAṬRAYE AUTHORS IN LATE MEDIEVAL IRAQ

THOMAS A. CARLSON
OKLAHOMA STATE UNIVERSITY, USA

ABSTRACT

Several authors from Beth Qaṭraye are cited by Isḥaq Shbadnaya, a priest from northern Iraq in the fifteenth century. Shbadnaya's 'Poem on God's Government from "In the Beginning" until Eternity' is a long didactic poem, with a prose commentary consisting primarily of quotations from earlier authors. Ten citations attribute ideas and opinions to Isaac of Nineveh, to Aḥobh Qaṭraya, to Gabriel Qaṭraya, to Rabban Gabriel Qaṭraya, or to an author identified simply as 'Qaṭraya'. A poem quoted anonymously by Shbadnaya also cites Isaac of Nineveh, raising the question how his reception of these authors was mediated. This paper presents a first edition and English translation of these quotations from Shbadnaya's larger work, and explores the character and genre of these quotations, most of which seem to be exegetical or chronological. This is a first step toward charting the reception of the Qaṭraya corpus in later East Syriac literature and thought.

INTRODUCTION

The fame of an author depends not only on the works which he produced for his own period, but much more on how those works continued to be read long after the author's death. Almost all ancient authors are known only because some medieval scribes decided their works were worth copying out, or at least some portion of their works. These scribes preserved what they did because it served a purpose in their own time and place, and they formed images of the ancient authors which continue to inform our own ideas about these authors today. Therefore it is important to look not just at what we can know about the Syriac authors of Beth Qaṭraye, but also at how they formed a part of later Syriac tradition, which has preserved their works and passed them down to us.

The study of how all subsequent Syriac authors and scribes used the writings of the Syriac authors of Beth Qaṭraye exceeds what I am able to accomplish in my limited lifetime. Rather, it is a research agenda which will require the collaboration of many scholars over a long period. But as a start, in this paper I will analyze the use of the Qaṭraye authors in one particular work, the long 'Poem on God's Governance from "In the Beginning" until Eternity' by an Iraqi priest of the fifteenth century named Isaac Shbadnaya. This choice is not haphazard. In this work, Shbadnaya selected the highlights of the Eastern Syriac tradition available to him in order to create a digest of the most essential components of Christian teaching, as he saw them. In eleven passages, Shbadnaya referred to one or another author from Beth Qaṭraye. This paper presents an edition of those passages and an analysis of how they fit within Shbadnaya's project in his major work.

SHBADNAYA AND HIS POEM

Little is known about the life of this priest from northern Iraq.[1] The only reliable date is the composition of three liturgical poems in the year 1751 A.G. / 1440, and some manuscripts specify that he is from the Sendi region near Zakho. He is known primarily as a poet, whose works included these three liturgical poems, incorpo-

[1] For a summary of what is known regarding this author, see Carlson, 'Shbadnaya's Life and Works'. Additional details, such as his birthdate and parentage, are found in a note on CUA Hyvernat Syr. Ms. 7, f. 132b, but it is unclear whether these details have any historical value. The use of Anno Domini dates rather than the Seleucid calendar in that note suggests it is of late composition.

rated into the Khamis collection of liturgical poetry for the Church of the East, and his masterpiece, the very long 'Poem on God's Governance from "In the Beginning" until Eternity'.

This long poem runs to around 1500 lines, and is divided into thirty sections (Syriac *sedre*). Each section has a separate title which specifies the theme, and they address the Trinity, the individual days of Creation, the fall of humanity, the Incarnation of the Word of God and various aspects of the life of Christ, the Passion, the Resurrection, the descent of the Spirit at Pentecost, and the expectations for the last days. In addition to the poetry, the author supplemented most sections with a prose commentary adding detail to his poetic narrative. In this commentary, Shbadnaya's own remarks are interspersed with citations of earlier authors to give a range of opinions drawn from the tradition on a variety of subjects. The authors he cites range from Ephrem to John of Zoʿbi in Syriac and from Josephus to John Chrysostom in Greek, and it is among those earlier authorities that he cites the authors from Beth Qaṭraye.

The citations take a variety of forms. Sometimes merely the name of the earlier author is invoked in order to lend his authority to the point at hand. Other times Shbadnaya will paraphrase the earlier material in order to rephrase it in his own words. In some cases the citation is presented as a quotation of the written work of the earlier author in question. Even here, however, the notion of 'quotation' must be used with caution, as it is clear from various examples that Shbadnaya frequently rearranged and sometimes partly rephrased the passages he quotes.[2] Nor is it always clear whether Shbadnaya is the person responsible for the adjustments, since he may well have received any particular passage through the mediation of an intervening source which he does not name.[3] This

[2] This is the conclusion of ten Napel, 'Some Remarks on the Quotations from Emmanuel Bar Shahhare's Hexaemeron in Isḥaq Šbadnaya's Prose-Commentary on the Divine Providence'. It is confirmed by Shbadnaya's quotations of Theodore bar Konay which I have compared with the critical editions.

[3] This is clear in the case of passage 8 below, but may apply to other passages as well.

is less plausible for longer passages, which are more likely to have been taken directly from the work indicated, but in any case, these citations of earlier authors must be understood primarily in the context of their use by Shbadnaya in the fifteenth century, before they can be considered as textual witnesses to earlier works.

EDITORIAL METHODOLOGY

It is worth saying a few words about the challenges specific to editing a late medieval Syriac text. Unlike the late antique texts which are the bulk of all edited Syriac works, by the time Shbadnaya sat down to compose his masterpiece, there were a variety of additional writing tools at his authorial disposal. Some vowel marks were probably in the original text he composed, as well as a more elaborate system of punctuation than was available to Narsai a millennium earlier. It is likely that he used red ink alternately with black to call attention to certain portions of his text. To present a bare consonantal text of Shbadnaya's masterpiece, especially in an Estrangelo unfamiliar to him, would be to create an artificially archaic text different from what he himself composed in fifteenth-century Iraq.

But each of these presents the editor with a challenge, as scribes could and did change these features without necessarily creating a 'textual corruption'. Vowel marks are optional in Syriac, and later scribes might add or omit vowels without changing the meaning of the text. Individual scribes seem to have used punctuation differently, and changed which mark was used in order to fit their own scheme. Which portions were highlighted in red could be a stylistic choice. Consequently, these aspects of the text are less stable than the consonantal text of the work, and most variations, such as the presence or absence of a particular vowel sign, are not meaningful. For the edition of the passages presented here, I have adopted a maximal approach to vowel signs, including any vowel sign included in any of the various manuscripts of the text. But the manuscript tradition also reveals considerable confusion as to which vowel to use between the two different *a* vowels and between the two *e* vowels. Where such meaningless variation occurs, I have followed the majority of manuscripts and only indicated a variation when it implies a different interpretation.

Punctuation is even trickier, and I have arbitrarily adopted the punctuation of the earliest extant manuscript, even when it is clearly problematic. Red ink poses an additional economic challenge in the world of modern computer typesetting and printing, so I have omitted any indication of red ink in the manuscripts, except in two cases. When the beginning of a citation is indicated exclusively by the earlier author's name in red ink, I have imitated some later scribes by adding a ❖ character to set off the name from the following quotation. In passage 9 below, Syriac letters are used as numbers in two places, and this usage is indicated in the original manuscripts by red ink; I have indicated it here with an overline. As with punctuation, I have only indicated a variation in the use of red ink where it reveals a difference of interpretation.

Certain other scribal features were also excluded from this edition as not meaningful. These excluded phenomena include variation in the consonantal spelling of words where either alternate is correct (for example, ܥܕܥܕܐ or ܥܕܥܐܕܐ), and differences in word division which are not meaningful (for example, ܚܡܫܡܐܐ or ܚܡܫ ܡܐܐ). The edition also does not note the frequent erroneous original readings of a manuscript which the first scribe evidently caught and corrected. Thus original and corrected readings of a manuscript are only noted in the apparatus where the original reading agrees with another witness, in which case a manuscript's original reading is indicated by an asterisk (such as B*) while the corrected reading is shown by a superscript *c* (such as B^c).

LIST OF WITNESSES

A	**Cambridge Add. Ms. 1998** Dated to the sixteenth century on palaeographical grounds, this is the earliest surviving manuscript. It is marked with the signet ring of Metropolitan Ishoʿyahb of Ṣoba (Nisibis) and Armenia, the same ring which marked the colophon of Cambridge Add. Ms. 1988, which is dated 7 October 1558.
B	**Harvard Syr. Ms. 152** This manuscript is dated to the seventeenth century on palaeographical grounds. It is challenging to read, in part due to the scribe not having followed any discernible ruling.
C	**Berlin orient. fol. Ms. 1201 [Syriac 85]** According to the colophon on f. 107b, this manuscript was finished on 22 July 1725 in the village of Darband in the Tergawar district of the Hakkari mountains.

D	**Oxford Bodleian Syr. Ms. c. 9** According to the colophon on f. 129b, this manuscript was finished on 29 April 1726. If the colophon once recorded the location of the copying, that leaf has been lost.
E	**Catholic University of America Hyvernat Syr. Ms. 7** According to the colophon on f. 130a, this manuscript was finished on 29 July 1889 in the village of Alqosh north of Mosul.
F	**London British Library Or. Ms. 9358** According to the colophon on f. 111b, this manuscript was finished on 4 July 1895 in Alqosh. It bears a very strong resemblance to manuscript G, so strong that they almost always share page breaks and often even line breaks. Since these two manuscripts were finished just over a month apart, it seems likely they were copied from the same exemplar and mostly reproduced the page divisions of that manuscript.
G	**Birmingham Mingana Syr. Ms. 57** The date this manuscript was completed is slightly illegible. According to the colophon on f. 111b, the manuscript was completed on a Monday, the twelfth day of the month, in the year 1895. The month name looks like it was originally written Tammuz (July), but 12 July 1895 was a Friday. The original name has been crossed out, and it is not clear what the correction reads, but Ab (August) seems most likely, as the only month of that year whose twelfth day was a Monday. The manuscript was copied in Telkepe north of Mosul.
H	**Oxford Bodleian Syr. Ms. c. 13** This manuscript was completed on 24 May 1904 according to a colophon on f. 88a, and it was copied from a manuscript from the year 2106 AG / 1795. It was copied in the village of Qudshanis in the Hakkari mountains.
I	**Vatican ms. sir. 592, ff. 41a–92b** This manuscript was finished on 'the middle day' of Adar (16 March), 1918, in Mosul, copied for the Chaldean priest Marutha bar Petros Ḥakim of Amid. It is unusual in that the scribe copied only the commentary sections, neglecting the poetic sections which structure the work. It is also copied in Serto script, unlike the East Syriac script of all the other manuscripts, although the vocalization is almost exclusively Eastern.

STEMMA CODICUM

While a complete stemma must await the complete collation of all the available witnesses for the work as a whole, at the present time the following stemma may be proposed as most probable. It is based on a complete collation of four witnesses (ACFG) and a partial collation of the remaining manuscripts. The two main points of uncertainty are whether A shares an ancestor with BD or whether it is independently derived from α, and whether D is in fact a direct descendant of B rather than a descendant of a sibling of B. Regarding the latter question, the places I have so far found where B is in error but D is not could be argued to be correctable errors, so at present the relationship of B to D is uncertain. In the stemma below, the Greek letters represent hypothetical texts which are not extant. Their place chronologically is not significant, but represents only the textual relationship between their descendants. The sole exception to the rule that hypothetical manuscripts are not anchored in time is the immediate ancestor of H, whose date is given in the colophon of H.[4]

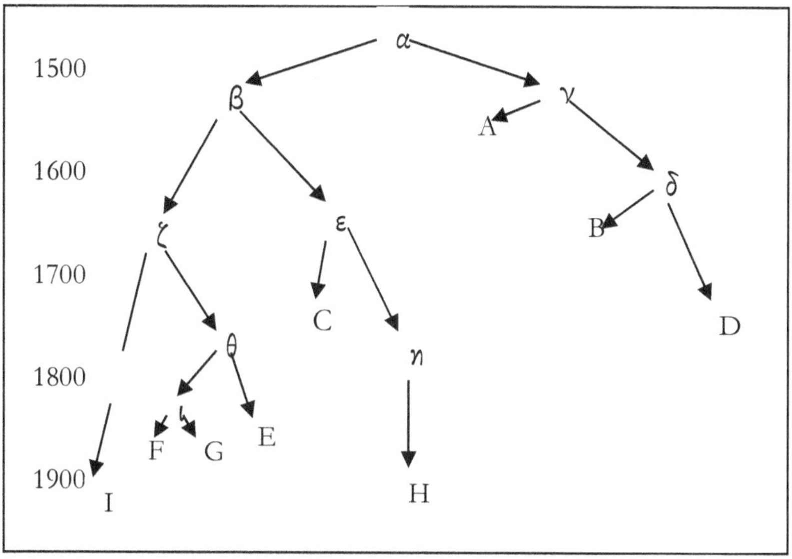

[4] H, f. 88a.

Passage 1:

Witnesses:

This is a marginal note contained in only four of the manuscripts: A, f. 53b; B, f. 52a, D, f. 31a; and E, f. 32a.

Text:

ܘܣܗܕ ܥܠ ܗܠܝܢ ܡܪܝ ܐܝܣܚܩ ܕܢܝܢܘܐ:

Translation:

And Mar Isaac of Nineveh testifies concerning these things.

Commentary:

In the context of a discussion of varieties of afflictions which people experience, Shbadnaya discusses causes of unexpected death and the tendency to attribute such events to Satan. Shbadnaya contends that Satan does not have the power to overrule the Creator's care for humans, and at that point inserts this marginal note. It is unclear which particular passage by the earlier Isaac of Nineveh may be in the mind of Isaac Shbadnaya.

Passage 2:

Witnesses:

A, f. 83b; B, ff. 80b–81a; C, f. 41b; D, f. 46b; E, f. 51a; F, f. 41b; G, f. 41b ; H, f. 35b; I, f. 53a

Text:

ܩܛܪܝܐ܀ ܒܫܬܐ ܒܟܢܘܢ ܐܚܪܝ ܐܥܡܕ ܦܪܘܩܢ. ܒܝܘܡ ܫܒܬܐ.

Translation:

Qaṭraya: On the sixth of latter Kanun (January) our Savior was baptized, on a Saturday.

Commentary:

This passage does not specify which author from Beth Qaṭraye is cited. This is of course the normal date for Epiphany, and the date may be derived from the liturgical commentary of Gabriel Qaṭraya rather than an exegetical context. On the other hand, a commentary of Gabriel Qaṭraya on Epiphany does not seem to be known, so the passage may be taken from an exegetical work by either Aḥobh or the exegete Gabriel.[5] In Shbadnaya's masterpiece, this brief remark follows a discussion of details regarding John the Baptist (how he was transported to the wilderness, what he ate there, and what he wore) and precedes a discussion of the meaning of the baptism of Christ. The additional detail that Jesus was baptized 'on Saturday' likely ties the baptism of Christ more closely to the baptism of Christians, as earlier in his commentary Shbadnaya had quoted Ishoʿdad of Merv to indicate that Christians were baptized after fasting 'on the Saturday which is the type of the burial' of Christ.[6]

Passage 3:

Witnesses:

A, f. 91b; B, ff. 88a; C, f. 45b; D, f. 50b; E, f. 55b; F, f. 45a; G, f. 45a ; H, f. 38b; I, f. 55b

Text:

ܩܛܪܝܐ܀ ܐܬܚܒܫ ܝܘܚܢܢ ܒܝܬ ܐܣܝܪ̈ܐ ܫܢܬܐ ܚܕܐ. ܘܐܬܩܛܠ ܩܕܡ ܚܫܘܗܝ ܕܡܪܢ ܒܫܢܬܐ ܚܕܐ.

Translation:

Qaṭraya: John was locked in prison one year, and he was killed one year before the suffering of our Lord.

Commentary:

Again, it is unclear which author of Beth Qaṭraye is intended, and this passage is again chronological. But since this concerns the passage of years rather than of months, there is no clear liturgical significance to this statement, and we may expect this to be derived from an exegetical work of either Aḥobh Qaṭraya or the exegete Gabriel Qaṭraya. This passage and the preceding one are short enough that they may easily have been transmitted through an intermediate source, which may explain the absence of the author's

---

[5] For a list of the various known authors named Gabriel Qaṭraya, see Brock, 'Beth Qaṭraye', pp. 89–92.

[6] A, f. 80b.

first name, although if so the intermediate source is unknown.[7] This passage occurs at the end of a section of commentary on Christ's baptism, immediately following a citation of John Penkaya which lists the durations of different components of Christ's life. Perhaps it serves to fit the end of the life of John the Baptist into the chronology provided by Penkaya, with the result of dividing the three years of Christ's ministry between the baptism and the crucifixion into thirds, one year before John was imprisoned, one year while John was in prison, and one year after John was executed.

Passage 4:

Witnesses:

A, f. 108b; B, f. 105a; C, f. 57a; D, f. 61a; E, f. 67a; F, f. 54a; G, f. 54a; H, ff. 45b–46a; I, ff. 58a–b

Text:

ܐܡܪ ܘܡܬܚܙܝܐ ܡܫܠܡܢܐ܀ ܠܘ [8] ܡܣܬܒܪܐ ܕܐܣܝܪܗ ܠܝܘܚܢܢ ܥܠ ܡܠܝ
ܠܗܘܪܕܝܣ. ܐܠܐ ܐܝܟ ܕܐܡܪ ܡܦܫܩܢܐ ܕܐܘܢܓܠܝܘܢ. ܟܕ ܐܣܪܗ [9] ܠܝܘܚܢܢ.
ܗܘܐ ܫ̈ܢܝܢ ܡܢ ܒܬܪ ܕܥܡܕ ܡܪܢ: ܘܐܚܕܗ ܠܟܪܘܙܘܬܐ ܘܠܡܠܦܢܘܬܐ. ܘܐܬܬܚܒܫ
ܘܒܬܪܗ ܡܠܟܐ ܐܝܟ ܕܡܘܕܥܢܘܬܗ. ܘܐܡܪ ܡܦܫܩܢܐ ܕܐܘܢܓܠܝܘܢ. ܕܗܘܐ ܟܠܗ ܫܢܬܐ ܟܠ
ܡܫܬܠܛ ܗܘܐ ܒܟܠܗܘܢ. ܒܗܝ ܫܢܬܐ. ܐܠܐ [10] ܠܫܢܬܐ ܕܬܠܬܝܢ ܘܚܕܐ ܐܣܝܪ.
ܘܗܘܐ ܬܠܬ ܫܢܝܢ ܒܬܪ [11] ܕܐܬܩܛܠ. ܐܠܐ ܟܕ [12] ܒܬܪ ܗܢܐ [13] ܐܬܩܛܠ
ܗܘܐ ܠܬܠܬ ܫܢܝܢ. ܘܐܬܩܛܠ ܒܗ ܗܢܐ ܫܢܬܐ ܘܝܘܚܢܢ ܚܕ ܡܢ [14] ܫܢܝܐ
ܗܘܐ. ܘܠܘܬ ܚܕܐ ܗܘܬ. ܟܕ ܐܝܬ ܕܐܡܪܝܢ ܕܫܢܬܐ. ܢܦܩ [15] ܗܘ [16]

[7] A quick check of the commentaries of Ishoʿdad of Merv yielded no match in the obvious locations.

[8] ACEFGHI] BD insert ܚܕܐ

[9] ABCEFGHI] D ܐܣܝܪ

[10] ACFGHI] BDE insert ܕܝܢ

[11] ABCDEFGI] H ܫܢܝܢ

[12] ACEFGHI] BD omit word

[13] ACEFGHI] BD insert ܗܘܬܐ

[14] ABCDEFGI] H omits word

[15] AᶜBDEFGI] A*CH ܢܦܩܗ

[16] ABCDEFGI] H ܗܘܐ

ܘܬܠܡܝܕܘܗܝ ܘܒܬܘ[17] ܒܛܘܪܐ[18] ܕܙܝܬܐ. ܘܩܕܡ[19] ܒܨܦܪܐ ܘܥܒܪ[20] ܥܒܪܐ ܠܟ
ܐܝܪܝܚܘ. ܘܐܣܝ ܠܒܪ ܛܝܡܝ.

Translation:

Aḥobh and Gabriel Qaṭraya: When he raised Lazarus, our Lord did not enter Jerusalem at once, but as John the Evangelist said, 'When he raised Lazarus, some of those who saw these things went and spoke to the priests and the Pharisees, and they gathered together and took counsel in order to destroy him'.[21] And the Evangelist says, 'Jesus was not walking around openly among the Jews, but to the city which is named Ephrem'.[22] And many were seeking for these days to be fulfilled, but when he had remained there a little while he came to Bethany, and they prepared a feast for him there, and Lazarus was one of those at the feast.[23] And it was the Sabbath. But when the sun had set, he and his disciples went out and spent the night on the Mount of Olives,[24] and he got up early and went across to Jericho, and he healed Bar Timaeus.[25]

Commentary:

This passage is exegetical in character, and opens the section of commentary on the famous entrance of Jesus into Jerusalem. It is chronological in import, indicating the temporal relationship between two known events in the life of Christ. The citation of both Aḥobh and Gabriel by name is problematic, since no work is known to have such a dual authorship. This passage is perhaps not a quotation at all but is Shbadnaya's summary of what he thought to be a position shared between these two earlier authorities,[26] or it

[17] ABCDEFGI] H ܘܒܬܘ
[18] ABCDEFGI] H ܠܛܘܪܐ
[19] CDEFGHI] AB ܘܩܕܡܘ
[20] ABCEFGHI] D omits word
[21] Jn 11:46–53.
[22] Jn 11:54.
[23] Cf. Jn 12:1–2.
[24] Cf. Lk 21:37.
[25] Mk 11:46–52.
[26] For a clear example of Shbadnaya doing this with other authors in another context, see A, ff. 206b–207a.

may reflect Shbadnaya's knowledge that the biblical exegete Gabriel Qaṭraya quoted the earlier work of Aḥobh Qaṭraya on this subject.[27]

Passage 5:

Witnesses:

A, ff. 118a–b; B, ff. 115b–116a; C, f. 62a; D, ff. 66b–67a; E, f. 72b; F, f. 59a; G, f. 59a; H, f. 50a; I, ff. 60b–61a

Text:

ܫܒܕܢܝܐ܀ ܟܕ ܠܟܡ ܐܡܠܟ[28] ܐܠܐ ܚܘܒܐ ܕܒܪܘܝܐ ܘܐܬܟܠܝܬܘܢ ܒܗ܆ ܒܬܪܗ
ܡܫܘܕܥܐ ܡܢ ܫܡܝܐ[29] ܆ ܕܡܣܟܢܘܬܗܘܢ ܢܣܬܟܠ ܒܚܝܘܬܗܘܢ܂ ܘܒܝܬ ܦܐܫܢܐ
ܢܬܡܠܘܢ[30] ܒܟܘܬܗܘܢ[31]܂ ܘܟܕ ܐܣܬܪܗ ܠܦܬܓܡܐ ܕܒܪܢܫܐ ܡܢܗ ܡܠܝܠܘܬܐ.
ܗܘ ܕܝܢ ܡܠܟܐ ܗܘܐ ܒܪܚܡܬܗܘܢ ܕܐܠܗܐ[32] ܐܡܝܪܐ ܐܟܚܕ ܗܘܐ. ܘܠܡܪܐ ܘܡܫܝܚ
ܗܘܐ[33] ܘܠܡܪܐ ܥܠܡܐ. ܘܟܕ ܗܘܐ ܕܠܐܢܫܐ ܣܓܝܐܐ[34] ܢܡܪܐ[35]܆ ܢܚܙܘܢ ܕܠܟܠ
ܒܢܝ. ܠܟܠܗܘܢ ܕܝܢ[36] ܕܝܘܕܝܐ[37]. ܘܟܕ ܝܠܝܕܐ ܠܐ ܢܫܬܟܚ ܕܢܗܘܐ ܠܟܠܗܘܢ
ܐܒܗܐ ܕܠܐ ܢܣܬܒܪ ܐܝܟ ܠܡ. ܘܐܝܟ ܕܒܟܬܒܐ[38] ܫܢܝܐ ܗܘܐ[39] .. ܗܢܘ[40]
ܕܝܢ. ܒܢܝܐ ܗܢܘ[41] ܕܒܢܝܢܫܐ[42] ܗܢܘܢ ܐܝܟ ܕܡܫܝܚܐ ܢܬܝܠܕ. ܘܟܕ ܐܬܝܠܕ ܕܝܢ[43]
ܘܚܢܢ. ܐܬܚܙܝ ܘܐܬܓܠܝܬ ܠܟܠܗܘܢ ܠܓܢܣܗܘܢ..

---

[27] The biblical exegete is number 3 in Brock's typology of Gabriels: Brock, 'Beth Qaṭraye', pp. 89–92.

[28] ACEFGH] BD ܐܡܠܟܗ

[29] ABCDFGHI] E ܡܫܡܝܐ

[30] ABDEFGI] CH ܢܬܡܛܘܢ

[31] ABCDEI] FG ܒܟܘܬܗܘܢ | H ܒܟܘܬܗܘܢ [*sic* no seyame]

[32] ABCDEFGI] H ܠܐܠܗܐ

[33] ABCDEFGI] H omits word

[34] ACEFGHI] BD ܡܢ ܣܓܝܐܐ

[35] ABCEFGHI] D ܢܡܪܐ

[36] ABCDEFGI] H omits word

[37] ABCDEFGI] H ܕܝܘܕܝܐ

[38] ACEFGHI ܘܐܝܟ ܕܒܟܬܒܐ] B ܘܒܟܬܒܐ | D ܘܕܒܟܬܒܐ [*sic*]

[39] ABCDEFGI] H ܠܟܠܗܘܢ

[40] CEFGHI] A ..܀ ܗ | BD ܀ ܗ

[41] ABCDEFGI] H omits word

Translation:

Qaṭraya:[44] When Herod and his son Archelaus ruled over Judah, the Jews requested from Caesar that he would leave their laws in their hands, and on the day of Passover they were completing their order. And when they arrested our Lord, they brought him before Pilate. He was familiar with their custom, that they would choose two prisoners, and one they would crucify and the other they would release. And when he was asking, 'Which of them shall I release?' they said, 'Barabbas, but Jesus should be crucified'. And when he found no reason that he deserved death, they shouted, 'We have a law, and according to what is in our Law he is condemned to death'. That is, 'This is our custom, that on this day we can do as we please'. And when they took the blood of the innocent one, he scourged him and delivered Jesus over to their will.

Commentary:

This passage is also exegetical, and so we might suspect it derives from a gospel commentary by Aḥobh or Gabriel Qaṭraya, although the full name is not given. Shbadnaya includes it between two sections of his own prose exegetical discussion of some of the details of the Passion narrative, such as the number of times Jesus was stripped, and the source of the purple cloth which the Roman soldiers put on Jesus to mock him. It could be that for other details, Shbadnaya was content to assert his interpretation on his own, with appropriate indications of humility, but for this aspect of the interpretation, he thought it important to borrow the authority of the earlier author.

Passage 6:

Witnesses:

A, ff. 122a–123a; B, ff. 119b–121a; C, ff. 64a–b; D, ff. 69a–b; E, ff. 74b–75a; F, ff. 61a–b; G, ff. 61a–b; H, ff. 51a–b; I, f. 62b

---

42 ABCDEFGI] H ܕܝܘܡܢܐ

43 ACEFGHI] BD ܕܡܢܐ

44 The first vowel on the name is a problem, and in many of the passages several of the manuscripts read 'Qeṭraya' instead of 'Qaṭraya'. The source of this variation is not clear, but I do not think it is meaningful.

Text:

ܡܛܠ ܐܣܘܢ ܡܠܟܐ܀ ܟܕ ܗܘܐ ܒܫܢ̈ܬܐ ܠܝܘܢܝܐ. ܕܐܝܬܝܗ ܕܫܢ̈ܝ ܗܘܬ
ܐܪ̈ܡܢܝܘܬܐ ܒܡܠܟܘܬܐ. ܗܘܝܢ ܗܘܘ ܗܠܝܢ ܐܬܩ̈ܦܘ. ܕܡܠܟܝܢ ܗܘܘ ܚܕ ܠܚܕ ܒܚܕ
ܬܘܡܐ.. ܗܢܘܢ ܕܝܢ[45] ܐܪ̈ܡܢܝܘܬܐ. ܘܡܠܟܘܬܐ[46] . ܒܡܠܟܘܬܐ ܕܐܬܩܒܠܘ ܕܠܐ ܢܚܬܘܢ
ܒܗ ܟܠ ܚܕ. ܘܠܐ ܐܘܣܦܘ ܬܘܒ ܒܟܠܗ ܒܝܬ ܡܡܠܟܘܬܗܘܢ.
ܘܐܪ̈ܡܢܝܘܬܐ[47] . ܕܩܕܝܡ[48] ܕܐܝܬ ܠܗ ܒܗܘ ܙܒܢ ܦܝܫܐ ܘܟܠܗ ܒܚܘܪܐ
ܘܐܦܠܓܗ. ܟܕ ܕܝܢ ܗܘܐ ܒܡܠܟܘܬܐ ܕܫܒܥ ܡܠܟܐ ܟܘܪܟܝ. ܐܬܚܙܝ ܠܗܘܢ
ܠܝܘܢܝܐ. ܕܢܬܚܒܪܘܢ ܠܬܘܡܐ ܕܥܕܬܐ: ܘܢܫܬܘܬܦܘܢ ܡܥܡܘܕܝܬܐ ܒܟܪܣܛܝܢܘܬܐ. ܒܫܢܬ
ܚܕܘܬܐ.. ܗ̈:[49] ܘܡܠܟ ܘܐܫܠܡ[50] ܥܡ ܟܝܢܐ. ܟܕ ܕܚܝܢ ܙܒܢ ܦܝܫܐ
ܒܬܘܡܐ ܕܥܕܬܐ. ܘܡܫܬܟܚܝܢ ܦܝܫܐ ܡܠܟܘܬܐ: ܠܗ ܕܝܢ[51] ܠܗܘܢ ܦܝܫܐ. ܗ̈: ܡܠܟܘܬܐ..
ܡܬܝܚܕܝܢ ܗܘܘ ܥܡ ܝܘܢ[53] ܚܕܘܬܐ[52]. ܡܬܒܛܠܢܝܬܐ ܡܠܟܘܬܗܘܢ. ܐܝܟ ܩܠܝܠܬܐ
ܘܡܬܠܟܢ ܘܡܬܡܨܝܢ ܡܢܗܘܢ ܕܝܠܗܘܢ[54] ܘܡܠܟܐ ܗܢܐ ܕܗܟ ܐܝܟ ܕܐܚܝܕܝܢ ܗܘܘ.
ܘܠܐ ܡܬܡܠܟܝܢ ܗܘܬ ܠܗܘܢ ܢܘܟܪܝܐ[55] . ܒܚܐܪܘܬܐ ܕܐܪ̈ܡܢܝܘܬܐ[56] . ܒܗܕܐ ܒܠܚܘܕ: ܗܠܝܢ
ܡܫܠܡܝܢ ܗܘܘ[57] ܠܡܠܟܐ: ܟܕ ܗܫܐ ܐܢܛܘܢܝܢܘܣ ܥܡ ܐܢܛܘܢܝܢܘܣ. ܠܗܢܘܢ
ܕܒܝܘܡܝ ܐܢܛܘܢܝܢܘܣ ܡܠܟܐ. ܘܠܡܠܟܘܬܐ[58] ܐܢܛܘܢܝܢܘܣ[59] ܕܘܡܢܐ ܡܠܟܘܬܐ. ܘܗܟ[60]
ܒܝܘܢܝܐ[61] ܕܗܕܐ ܐܪܡܢܝܐ ܡܬܬܢܝܐ[62] ܠܗܢܐ[63] ..

---

45 CEFGHI ܗܢܘܢ ܕܝܢ] A ..ܗ̈: | B ܗ. ܡ̈: | D ܗ̇
46 ABCDEFGI] H ܘܡܠܟܘܬܐ
47 ABCEFGI] D ܘܒܪܡܢܝܘܬܐ | H ܘܐܪܡܢܝܘܬܐ [sic]
48 ABCEFGDI] H ܕܩܕܝܡ
49 CDEFGHI] AB add in margin: ܚܕܘܬܐ ܕܗܘܐ ܒܫܢܬ ܬܡܢܐ ܡܫܬܠܛܢܐ
50 ABDEFGHI] C ܘܐܫܠܡ
51 ABCEFGHI] D ܒܗ ܠܗ
52 AB^c^CDEFHI] B*G omits word
53 ABCEFGHI] D ܝܘܢ̈ܝܐ
54 ABCEFGHI] D ܕܝܠܗܘܢ
55 ABCEFGHI] D ܢܘܟܪܝܐ
56 ABCEFGH] DI ܕܐܪܡܢܝܘܬܐ
57 ACEFGHI] BD insert ܠܗܘܢ
58 ACEFGHI] BD ܘܠܐܢܛܘܢܝܢܘܣ
59 ACDEFGHI] B ܐܢܛܘܢܝܢܘܣ
60 ACEFGHI] BD ܕܗܟ
61 ABCEFGHI] D ܒܝܘܢܝܐ
62 ACEFGHI] BD insert ܡܠܟܐ

Translation:

Mar Aḥobh Qaṭraya: The Jews had a custom that when the fourteenth falls on a Saturday, there were two laws which break each other on the same day, namely the fourteenth and the Sabbath. Regarding the Sabbath they were commanded, 'You shall not do any work on it',[64] and 'you shall not light a fire in the whole area of your habitation'.[65] And regarding the fourteenth, 'Between the evenings you shall kill the Passover lamb and roast it with fire and eat it'.[66] When this happened in the year our Lord suffered, it appeared to the Jews that they should have the feast on the sixth day, and call it a 'participant' in the feast, that is Friday, i.e. mingled and mixed with the feast. While they were slaughtering the Passover lamb on the sixth day, and reckoning the Passover a Sabbath, for the same day of Passover was a Sabbath, they were preparing on Friday cold foods like beets and salt and some wild vegetables, etc. This is also what was handed down to eat for those who were far off and were not going to visit in the time of the fourteenth in Jerusalem. When they compared obligation with obligation, the obligation of the Sabbath was for those who were in Judea, and the obligation of the holy place was for those nearby. And Jews everywhere still do the same thing until now.

Commentary:

Like the preceding passage, this text concerns an ancient Jewish custom in the time of Jesus, although this one is asserted to continue to the present. Also, while the former passage discussed the relationship of Jewish and Roman law, this addresses the relationship between two apparently conflicting laws in the Torah, which are alleged to have come into conflict in the year that Jesus was crucified. The calendrical implications of this conflict are brought out more fully by Shbadnaya in his comments immediately following, where he discusses the date on which the Passover fell in

---

63 ABCDEFGI] H ܗܨ̈ܪ̈

64 Ex 20:10; Deut 5:14; 16:8.

65 Ex 35:3.

66 Cf. Ex 12:6, 8.

that year, in both the solar and the lunar calendar, and the reasons why the Jewish Passover lines up with the Christian Holy Week some years but not others.

Passage 7:

Witnesses:

A, ff. 129b–130a; B, ff. 127b–128a; C, f. 67b; D, f. 73b; E, f. 78b; F, f. 64b; G, f. 64b; H, f., 53b; I, ff. 65a–b

Text:

ܪܒܐ ܡܪܝ ܐܝܣܚܩ ܐܦܝܣܩܘܦܐ[67] ܕܢܝܢܘܐ: ܬܐܘܪܝܐ ܕܚܫܗ ܕܒܪܐ ܕܡܛܠ ܟܠܐ:
ܠܐ ܡܒܛܠܢܝܬܐ ܗܝ[68] ܕܕܝܢܐ ܕܠܥܠ. ܐܠܐ ܡܓܠܝܢܝܬܐ ܗܝ. ܕܬܐܘܪܝܐ ܕܐܪܙܗ[69]
ܕܕܝܢܐ. ܒܗܿ ܕܚܫܗ ܕܒܪܐ ܕܚܠܦ ܟܠܐ: ܚܘܒܐ ܕܐܒܐ ܗܘܐ ܒܗܕܐ ܝܕܝܥܐ[70]. ܕܝܢ
ܐܢ ܥܠ ܒܪܗ ܠܐ ܚܣ: ܡܛܠ ܚܘܒܗ ܕܠܘܬܢ. ܐܠܐ ܐܫܠܡܗ ܚܠܦ ܟܠܢ.
ܐܝܟ ܠܐ ܒܠܡܝܬܝܢ ܢܦܫܗ ܝܗܒ ܠܢ. ܒܝܕ ܗܘ ܡܟܝܠ ܚܝܠܗ ܕܚܘܒܐ[71].
ܕܥܒܕ ܒܪܗ ܐܬܝܗܒ ܒܒܢܝܬܗ. ܒܝܕ ܥܘܕܪܢܐ ܕܐܢܫܝܢ ܕܡܝܬ. ܘܗܘܐ ܡܘܬܐ: ܕܠܐ
ܠܐܢܫܝܢ ܕܡܣܝܒܝܢ ܠܗ ܡܝܬ: ܐܠܐ[72] ܠܐܢܫܝܢ ܕܡܝܬ[73] ܠܗܘܢ ܩܢܐ ܠܗ.
ܘܚܠܦ ܡܘܬܐ ܡܘܬܢܐ ܕܡܬܚܣܝܢ: ܒܗܝ ܕܚܝܐ ܒܡܫܠܡ ܡܢܬܗܘܢ
ܡܬܚܘܝܢ ܒܚܕܒܫܒܐ. ܘܐܢܫ ܦܘܠܘܣ ܕܒܗ[74] ܐܢܫ ܒܡܠܟܘܬܐ ܢܬܚܕܬ
ܒܥܠ ܐܠܗܐ[75] ܡܚܕܐ. ܕܚܠܝܢܝܢ ܕܬܠܝܢ.

Translation:

The great Mar Isaac, the bishop of Nineveh: The *theoria* of the suffering of the Son on behalf of all is not the abolisher of the future judgment, but it is the revealer of the *theoria* of the mystery of judgment, in that the suffering of the Son was for all, the love of

[67] ABCDEFGI] H omits word
[68] ABCEFGHI] D omits word
[69] ACEFGHI] BD ܕܐܪܙܗ
[70] ABCDEHI] FG ܡܠܟܐ
[71] ABCDEFGI] H ܕܚܘܒܗ
[72] ABCDEFHI] G ܐܢܫܝܢ
[73] ACEFGHI] BD ܕܒܬܪ ܡܝܬ
[74] ABCDEFGI] H ܒܗ
[75] CEFGHI] ABD omit word

the Father makes the Son the cause. 'If he did not spare his Son because of his love toward us, but gave him up for all of us, how will he not give us everything with him?'[76] Thus is known the power of love, that not even his Son was honored in his eyes in comparison with those whom he loves. And this is a marvel, that it is not those who love him that he loves, but that those whom he loves hate him. And instead of the loved person having amazement and glory, how many times are they fiercely moved to blasphemies with their voices! And according to Paul, 'While we were enemies God was reconciled with us',[77] etc., that are about these things.

Commentary:

This passage, the only substantial citation of Isaac of Nineveh, is theological or perhaps devotional in nature. Shbadnaya incorporates it into his commentary on the crucifixion, not to clarify historical details as with the preceding passages, but to state the purpose of the death of Christ: namely to reveal the depth and power of God's love even for people who hate God.

Passage 8:

Witnesses:

A, ff. 130b–131a; B, f. 129a; C, f. 68a; D, f. 74a; E, f. 79a; F, f. 65a; G, f. 65a; H, f. 54a; I, f. 65b

Text:

ܗܳܟܰܢܳܐ ܟܬ݂ܰܒ ܡܳܪܝ ܐܝܣܚܩ. ܒܦܶܠܓܽܘܬܶܗ ܗܳܝ ܚܰܡܫܰܝܬܳܐ.
ܚܰܫܳܐ ܕܡܶܬܩܰܒܠܺܝܢ ܚܰܛܳܝܶܐ. ܡܶܢ ܢܶܓ݂ܕܶܐ ܕܓܶܗܰܢܳܐ[78] ..
ܦܣܩܐ ܡܢ ܠܒܢܝܗ[79] ܕܪܒܬܐ. ܗܘ ܕܡܫܬܒܚ ܗܘܐ ܠܥܠܡܝܢ:

Translation:

Thus wrote Mar Isaac, in that fifth chapter of his, 'The suffering which sinners undergo from the torments in Gehenna has a

---

[76] Rom 8:32.

[77] Rom 5:10.

[78] ABCDEFGH] I ܘܕܓܗܢܐ

[79] ABCDEFGI] H ܒܢܝܗ

likeness to the suffering of the Son, that which he endured for our sakes.'

Commentary:

These three lines are taken from a poem which Shbadnaya quotes immediately following the preceding passage, which he attributes solely to 'one clothed with the Spirit' (ܓܒܪܐ ܠܒܝܫ ܪܘܚܐ). Shbadnaya quotes a number of authorities anonymously in this fashion (the citation following this one is also anonymous), and until we have a searchable text corpus covering medieval Syriac literature, the identification of these passages is dependent upon a scholar happening to have read the source recently. This anonymous poem is in a 7+7 meter, and is a metrical meditation on Christ suffering on the Cross, which freed humanity from the curse of sin, from suffering, and from death. At the end of the portion which Shbadnaya quotes, just before these three lines, the anonymous poem turns its attention to those who reject Christ's suffering for them, and in this context it appeals to Isaac of Nineveh.

Passage 9:

Witnesses:

A, f. 171a; B, f. 171a; C, f. 87a; D, f. 98a; E, f. 100b; F, f. 85b; G, f. 85b; H, f. 69a; I, f. 78a

Text:

ܓܒܪܝܐܝܠ ܩܛܪܝܐ܀ ܗܘܬ ܠܗ ܩܝܡܬܗ ܕܡܚܝܢܢ ܝܗ ܒܢܝܣܢ ܒܣܗܪܐ: ܘܟܚ ܒܐܕܪ ܒܫܡܫܝܐ. ܕܬܡܝܗ ܕܬܡܝܗܬܐ ܘܡܫܒܚܐ[80] ܒܚܕܬܬܐ[81] ܀܀܀܀܀

Translation:

Gabriel Qaṭraya: The resurrection of our life-giver was 15 Nisan (April) in the lunar calendar and 28 Adar (March) in the solar, the wonder of wonders and glorified in new things.

Commentary:

This citation closes Shbadnaya's commentary in his section on the Resurrection of Christ, and like passage 2 above, it provides the month and day for events in the life of Christ. Unlike that earlier passage, it is not clear what liturgical significance these dates would have, since the date of Easter moves around in the solar calendar, and according to passage 6, the Passover was observed a day earlier than its typical 14 Nisan in that year. We may suspect, therefore, that this passage is taken from a biblical commentary by the exegete Gabriel Qaṭraya, rather than the author of the liturgical commentary.

Passage 10:

Witnesses:

A, ff. 182a–183a; B, ff. 182b–183b; C, ff. 92b–93a; D, ff. 105a–b; E, ff. 106b–107a; F, ff. 91b–92a; G, ff. 91b–92a; H, ff. 73b–74a; I, ff. 80b–81a

Text:

ܬܘܒ ܡܛܠ ܥܕܢ[82]. ܒܝܘܠܦܢܐ[83] ܡܠܟܝܐ[84]. ܕܝܠܗ ܕܓܒܪܝܐܝܠ ܩܛܪܝܐ. ܟܕ ܡܦܪܫ ܘܡܚܘܐ ܒܦܘܫܩܐ[85] ܡܫܬܡܠܝܢ[86]. ܘܡܢܝܢ ܠܗ[87] ܠܦܘܪܩܢܗ ܕܥܠܡܐ.

---

[80] ABCDEFGI] H ܘܡܫܒܚܘܗ

[81] ABCDEFGI] H ܒܚܕܬܬܐ [*sic* no seyame]

[82] ACEFGHI] BD omit word

[83] ABDEFG[c]I] CG*H ܒܝܘܠܦܢܐ

[84] ABDI] CEFGH make word red and omit following punctuation, which links it with the following title

[85] ABCDEFGI] H ܒܦܘܫܩܐ

ܕܡܠܦܢܐ ܠܦܝܫܬܗ ܗܘܕܢܢܐ ܠܠܫܢܐ ܢܘܪܢܐ ܠܫܢܐ ܡܢ ܕܢܦܩ ܐܝܟܢܐ ܘܕܡܘܬܐ
ܕܒܗ ܕܗܠܝܢ ܕܦܘܫܩܘܗܝ ܘܗܢܐ . ܬܐܘܠܘܓܝܐ ܕܟܠ ܕܩܕܝܫܝܐ ܗܢܐ ܟܕ ܡܦܫܩܢܐ
ܕܐܬܘܪܐ ܕܡܢܐ ܡܛܠ . ܗܕܐ ܕܡܢܬܐ ܠܕܘܟܬܐ ܠܗ . ܗܢܘܢ ܕܡܫܒܚܬܐ ܣܘܟܠܐ
ܒܢܝܢܐ ܗܟܢ : ܡܫܬܠܡ ܕܡܫܒܚܢܐ ܫܘܒܚܗ ܕܒܟܠ ܕܡܢܐ ܒܗ . ܐܬܒܘܪܟܘ ܗܠܝܢ
ܕܡܬܕܢܚܐ ܠܡܬܡܨܝܘ ܡܣܬܟܠ ܕܝܢ ܗܟܢܐ . ܦܪܨܘܦܐ ܐܝܟ ܙܗܝܐ ܡܣܘܪܐ [88] ܘܦܪܝܢ
[90] ܡܦܫܩܢܐ ܕܡܠܦܢܐ ܗܘܘ ܡܬܒܥܐ ܕܟܠ ܐܝܟ ܗܢ ܐܠܗܝܐ . [89] ܡܣܘܪܐ ܐܝܟ ܘܡܬܘ
ܕܒܫܘܒܚܗ . ܢܛܘܪܘܗܝ ܕܫܡܗ ܘܐܘܪܝܬܐ ܬܐܘܠܘܓܝܐ ܝܗܒܘ . ܕܐܚܝܕ ܐܣܝܪܐ [91]
ܕܚܢܢܐ . ܡܣܘܪܐ ܐܝܟ :ܗ . [92] ܠܥܠܡܗ ܕܗܘܠܐ ܡܢܗ ܘܐܡܪܐ . ܘܡܣܘܪܐ ܚܢܢܐ
ܣܘܟܠܐ ܐܝܟ ܗܟܢ . [93] [94] ܘܡܬܒܪܟ ܗܘ ܐܝܟ ܘܕܬܘܪܓܡܗ [95] . ܕܒܠܗܘܢ ܐܝܟ
[96] ܠܫܢܐ ܡܢ ܦܘܪܫܢܐ ܕܡܦܩܝܢ ܐܝܠܝܢ ܘܡܬܒܪܟܝܢ : ܕܡܫܒܚܢܐ ܒܫܘܒܚܐ ܐܚܪܢܝܢ
ܡܬܚܠܦܝܢ ܒܙܒܢ ܒܙܘܢܐ ܒܟܠܗ . ܗܘܘ ܡܫܠܡܝܢ ܠܐ ܐܠܗܐ ܡܢ ܕܝܠܗ . ܠܠܫܢܐ
ܘܐܠܝܢ ܠܗܘܢ ܡܢ ܘܡܬܚܙܐ . ܕܝܕܥܝܢܗܘܢ ܐܝܟ [97] ܠܗ ܗܘܘ ܘܡܢܨܚܝܢ . ܗܘܘ
. ܐܢܫܐ ܕܚܢܢܐ ܠܗܘܢ ܠܐ . ܦܝܫܘ ܕܠܗܘܢ ܕܫܡܝܐ ܣܘܟܠܐ ܒܫܡܗ . ܗܟܢ
. ܕܒܠܗܘܢ ܡܬܚܙܐ ܠܕܝܢܝܢܐ ܐܠܐ

Translation:

[At the end of a list of authorities who seem to disagree with (Pseudo-)Dionysius the Areopagite regarding the place of seraphim in the angelic hierarchy] … with the one wise in all the exalted theology,[98] Rabban Gabriel Qaṭraya, while confirming and demonstrating with strong proofs. And he reveals the cunning of [the

[86] ABCDEFGI] H omits word
[87] BCDEFGI] A ܠܗ | H omits word
[88] ABCDEFGI] H omits word
[89] ABCDFGHI ܐܝܟ ܡܣܘܪܐ] E ܡܣܘܪܐ ܐܝܟ
[90] ACEFGHI] BD make word red
[91] ABCEFGHI] D ܘܫܘܒܚܘܗܝ
[92] ABCEFGHI] D ܠܥܠܡܐ
[93] ABCDEFGI] H ܕܒܠܗ
[94] ACDEFGHI] B inserts ܐ
[95] BCcD] C*H ܘܡܬܒܪܟ [AEFGI unclear]
[96] ABDEFGHI] C ܠܠܫܢܐ
[97] ACEFGH] I ܠܗ | BD omits word
[98] Or 'in all theology, the exalted'

translator of Pseudo-Dionysius], and of his fellow Kumai who translated from the Greek language into the Syriac language the works of the blessed Interpeter. When in the treatise on faith, and in the one on the incarnation of our Lord, one *qnoma* is placed in Christ, it was Kumai who said it this way, because the great man of God, Mar Theodore, whenever he was speaking about the unity of Christ, was saying 'two natures and two *qnome*, one person'. But Kumai changed the expression of the saint and put 'one *qnoma*'. For it is clear that it was impossible for the blessed Interpreter, the light of the world, to refute the faith and the confession which was established by him, of the duality of natures and *qnome*, and to say something foreign to his truth, i.e. one *qnoma*. For their own opinion and that of Origen are the same and corrupted, for scribes do a lot of damage in the books, and especially those who translate books from one language to another, if it is the case that they do not fear God. They were transforming the entire shape of a book, and they were composing it according to their opinion, and these two more than any others made a corruption in the books which they translated, not according to true opinion, but according to their own corrupt opinion.

Commentary:

The occasion for this outburst against translators is that Shbadnaya is disagreeing with certain people who assert that the seraphim are the highest rank of angels, and his opponents cite (Pseudo-)Dionysius the Areopagite in their favor. Shbadnaya contends that what the saint actually wrote does not support their position, but was changed by its translator, and he lists other authorities who agree with his view. At the end of this list he includes 'Rabban Gabriel Qaṭraya', who, according to Shbadnaya, demonstrated the 'falseness' of the translation of Pseudo-Dionysius and also the error of Kumai, whose translations of Theodore of Mopsuestia include the phrase 'one *qnoma*' despite the fact that the standard Christology of the East Syrian tradition since long before Shbadnaya's time was two *qnome*. Shbadnaya of course takes it for granted that the actual theology of the revered Interpreter agrees with that of his tradition. Whatever work of Rabban Gabriel Qaṭraya contained these arguments is now lost, and it is unknown how much of this passage is influenced by Rabban Gabriel's words, and how much is Shbadnaya's paraphrase.[99]

Passage 11:

Witnesses:

A, f. 214a; B, f. 214b; C, ff. 49a–b; D, f. 123a; E, ff. 124a–b; F, f. 107b; G, f. 107b; H, ff. 84b–85a; I, ff. 90b–91a

Text:

ܐܚܘܒ ܩܛܪܝܐ܀ ܡܫܠܡܝܢ ܐܝܬ[100] ܐܢܫܝܢ ܕܩܘܪܒܢܐ ܘܬܘܕܝܬܐ ܕܐܫܠܡ ܡܪܢ. ܐܝܟ ܘܢܩܘܡ ܐܠܦ ܘܚܡܫܡܐܐ ܘܬܫܥܝܢ ܘܫܬ[101] ܫܢܝܢ[102]. ܟܡܝܘܬܐ ܕܩܡܘ ܩܘܪܒܢܐ ܕܐܘܪܫܠܡ ܘܢܡܘܣܐ.

ܗܘ ܗܘ ܛܘܒܢܐ܀ ܡܫܠܡܢܐ ܗܘܐ ܕܢܗܘܐ ܥܠܡܐ ܬܠܬܥܣܪܐ ܐܢܕܩܛܝܘܢ ܗܘܐ[103] ܡܢ ܫܘܪܝܗ[104] ܥܕܡܐ ܠܫܘܠܡܗ. ܥܣܪܐ ܐܝܬ ܩܕܡܝܐ ܩܕܡ ܡܐܬܝܬܗ ܕܡܫܝܚܐ[105]. ܘܬܠܬܐ ܡܢ ܡܐܬܝܬܗ ܥܕܡܐ ܠܫܘܠܡܐ.

Translation:

Aḥobh Qaṭraya: Some pass down that the offerings and thanksgiving which our Lord delivered will endure 1596 years, the quantity that the offerings of Jerusalem and the Law continued.

The same blessed one: It is also passed down that the world will be thirteen indictions from its beginning until its end, ten former ones before the coming of Christ, and three from his coming until the end.

---

[99] This 'Rabban Gabriel Qaṭraya' is plausibly the author of a Christological treatise mentioned as number 7 by Brock, 'Beth Qaṭraye', pp. 90–92.

[100] ABCDEFGI] H omits word

[101] ABCD^{c}EFGI] D*H omits word

[102] ABCDEFGI] H ܘܫܢܝܢ

[103] ABCDHI] EFG omit word

[104] ABCDEFGI] H ܫܘܪܢܐ [*sic*]

[105] ABCDFGHI] E omits the four following words

Commentary:

These are two passages attributed to Aḥobh Qaṭraya predicting the time of the end, one based on symmetry with the sacrificial system of the Old Testament, and the other by numerology. 'Indiction' in this context means the 532-year cycle of Easter dates in the Julian calendar, so that both of these passages agree on a period of 1596 years following the coming of Christ. The duration of 1596 years from the Exodus to the coming of Christ is shorter than the figure of 1629 probably implied by the thirteenth-century Solomon of Baṣra's *Book of the Bee*,[106] and the *Book of the Bee* gives a slightly longer period from creation to Moses than the 7 indictions or 3724 years implied by the calculation here ascribed to Aḥobh Qaṭraya.[107] It is also not clear whether the periods of 1596 years were thought to transition at the birth of Christ or at his resurrection. In any event, Shbadnaya includes these two calculations following a quotation of Emmanuel bar Shahhare describing the final judgment, evidently to allow a more concrete expectation of when these will occur. The fact that 1596 years after the resurrection of Christ is almost exactly the year 1000 in the Hijri calendar suggests that this calculation was influenced by the expectations of the apocalypse of Pseudo-Methodius.

CONCLUSIONS AND GENERAL REMARKS

These eleven passages represent a diverse body of material which Isaac Shbadnaya had received from the Syriac authors of Beth Qaṭraye. Calendrical considerations figure prominently in passages 2–4, 9, and 11, while passages 4–6 have a more exegetical character. Some of these passages are attributed to Aḥobh,[108] some to Gabri-

[106] Solomon of Baṣra ascribes 655 for all the Judges (apparently including Moses and Joshua), followed by 455 for the kings, after which he lists the rulers from Darius Hystaspes until the birth of Christ (and afterward): Solomon of Akhlat, *Book of the Bee*, pp. 67–68, 120–121. He does not mention the exile, but I have included it in calculating the total.

[107] The duration was 3868 according to Solomon of Baṣra: Ibid., p. 65.

[108] The name 'Jacob Qaṭraya' is reported to be in the work of Shbadnaya according to Brock, 'Beth Qaṭraye', p. 94 on the authority of

el, one to both of them together, and three are attributed to 'Qaṭraya' without specifying the author further. There is no apparent distinction in Shbadnaya's citations between Gabriel the liturgical commentator and Gabriel the biblical exegete, and the joint citation of Aḥobh and Gabriel in passage 4 suggests that the late medieval East Syrian tradition knew both names but did not sharply distinguish between these authors. By contrast, passages 1, 7, and 8 reveal that Isaac of Nineveh was the person to cite regarding divine love and the sufferings in Gehenna, the same subjects for which he was cited by the thirteenth-century author Solomon of Baṣra.[109] Finally, the extended rant regarding translators given in passage 10 seems to indicate a separate Rabban Gabriel Qaṭraya with Christological interests.

Until these passages may be identified in manuscripts containing them in the context of the work as a whole, it is hard to know how Shbadnaya may have modified or paraphrased the words he ascribes to the earlier authors he cites. Nor is it clear which of these passages he was reading for himself from the original works, or which of these he collected from intermediate sources which included the same citation, as is clearly the case with passage 8. The calendrical passages are typically very short, and might easily have been found by Shbadnaya in the work of an unidentified intermediary author. A quick check of the plausible passages in the gospel commentaries of Ishoʿdad of Merv did not indicate that he was an intermediary for Shbadnaya, as he seems to have been for the quotations of Aḥobh Qaṭraya which surface in the Ethiopic commentary tradition.[110] But the exegetical passages are longer and thus more likely to have been taken by Shbadnaya directly from the original work, as is passage 7 from Isaac of Nineveh. On the other hand, these longer passages may not reflect the exact words of the sources either, but simply the later author's paraphrase. So further work on the reception of the Syriac authors of Beth Qaṭraye is nec-

---

Reinink, *Gannat Bussame*, p. 50, n. 15. It appears that Reinink's 'Jakob' has accidentally replaced 'Aḥob', which does not occur in the list given there.

[109] Solomon of Akhlat, *Book of the Bee*, pp. 139–140.

[110] Cowley, 'Ahob of Qatar', p. 340. Of course Shbadnaya extensively cites Ishoʿdad of Merv as well.

essary to clarify not only how typical Shbadnaya's reading of these authors' texts were, but also the form in which he encountered these quotations.

DADISHOᶜ QAṬRAYA'S COMPENDIOUS COMMENTARY ON THE PARADISE OF THE EGYPTIAN FATHERS IN GARSHUNI—A CASE OF MANUSCRIPT MISTAKEN IDENTITY

MARIO KOZAH
AMERICAN UNIVERSITY OF BEIRUT

ABSTRACT

The seventh century monastic writer Dadishoᶜ Qaṭraya was a member of the Church of the East and an author of ascetic and monastic literature in Syriac. Dadishoᶜ Qaṭraya was a native of the Qaṭar region, as his demonym "Qaṭraya" suggests. This paper gives an overview of his life and works before considering his as yet unpublished Commentary on the Paradise of the Egyptian Fathers originally written in Syriac then subsequently translated into Garshuni. An account is given of the rediscovery and identification of the Garshuni translation.

The Monastery of Rabban Shabūr[1] in Beth Huzaye / Khuzistan, in the heart of the former Sassanian Empire, was the final resting

[1] The location of this monastery is identified by A. Scher as being in the environs of the town of "Šouštar" (or Tustar). See A. Scher, "Notice sur la vie et les oeuvres de Dadishoᶜ Qaṭraya", *Journal Asiatique*, 10:7 (1906), p. 109, n. 1. J-M. Fiey, suggests that if the monastery was founded to the south of the town of "Tuster" in the direction of the village of

place of Isaac of Nineveh or Isaac Qaṭraya, who alongside Ephrem of Nisibis and Jacob of Serugh, is one of the most well-known and influential authors in Syriac literature, and it is where he spent his last days in prayer, study and composition.[2] It is with this same monastery that the late seventh century monastic writer Dadishoʿ Qaṭraya was associated and which he himself mentions on a number of occasions in his writings.[3] This Syriac author of monastic and ascetic literature, a Church of the East monk, was a native of the Qatar region, as his demonym "Qaṭraya" indicates. Dadishoʿ seems to have become a monk at the otherwise unknown monastery of Rab-kennārē before dwelling for a time at the monastery of Rabban Šābūr and at that of the "Blessed Apostles".[4]

Dadishoʿ's name and works are to be found recorded at the beginning of the fourteenth century in the catalogue of ʿAbdishoʿ bar Brikā who states:[5]

Dūlāb, the birthplace of Rabban Shabūr himself, then it might be identified with "Dayr Ḥamīm" mentioned in the Muslim sources. See J-M. Fiey, "L'Elam, première des metropoles ecclésiastiques syriennes orientales", *Melto* 5 (1969), p. 247, n. 126. For a more recent article on the Monastery of Rabban Shabūr but which does not make any advance on Fiey's conclusions concerning its location see F. Jullien, "Le couvent de Rabban Shapour et le renouveau monastique en Perse", in M. Vannier, *Connaissance des Pères de l'Eglise, N° 119, septembre 20 : Isaac de Ninive.* Nouvelle Cité, 2010.

[2] "Afterwards he grew old and advanced in years (ܣܓܝ ܒܫܢ̈ܝܐ) and departed to our Lord. He was buried in the Monastery of Mar Shabūr (ܐܬܬܣܝܡ ܒܕܝܪܐ ܕܡܪܝ ܫܒܘܪ)", see I.E. Rahmani, *Studia Syriaca*, I. Charfet, 1904, p. ܟܠ. "When he became very advanced in age, he departed from temporal life (ܚ̈ܝܐ ܙܒܢ̈ܝܐ) and his body was buried in the Monastery of Shabūr (ܐܬܬܣܝܡ ܦܓܪܗ ܒܕܝܪܐ ܕܫܒܘܪ)", see J.B. Chabot, "Le livre de la chasteté composé par Jésusdenah, évéque de Baçrah", p. 64.

[3] ܘܗܘܐ ܡܢ ܟܠܗ ܒܗܘ ܙܒܢܐ ܕܗܘܝܬ ܒܕܝܪܐ ܕܡܪܝ ܫܒܘܪ See A. Scher, "Notice sur la vie et les oeuvres de Dadishoʿ Qaṭraya", *Journal Asiatique*, 10:7 (1906), p. 111.

[4] Ibid., pp. 103–111.

[5] As was first established by A. Scher in the above-cited article on Dadishoʿ Qaṭraya.

> The renowned Dadishoʿ (ܕܕܝܫܘܥ ܩܛܪܝܐ), wrote a commentary (lit. commented) on the Paradise of the Occidentals [monks] (ܦܪܕܝܣܐ ܕܡܥܪ̈ܒܝܐ); he elucidated [the book of] Abbā Isaiah; he wrote a book on the [monastic] way of life (ܥܠ ܕܘܒܪܐ); treatises on the sanctification of the cell; consolatory dirges (ܡܐܡܪ̈ܐ ܡܒܝܐܢܐ ܕܒܘܝܐܐ); he also wrote letters and inquiries (ܐܓܪ̈ܬܐ ܘܫܘܐ̈ܠܐ) on quietude in the body and the soul (ܥܠ ܫܠܝܐ ܕܦܓܪ ܘܢܦܫܐ).[6]

The commentary on the twenty-six discourses of Abbā Isaiah has been edited and translated by René Draguet.[7] However, all the extant manuscripts of this work only reach the end of the commentary on the fifteenth discourse. Interestingly, a later anonymous commentary[8] in Syriac which is in fragmentary form incorporates sections from the subsequent discourses by Dadishoʿ proving that he did in fact complete this work. A more complete Garshuni translation exists of this anonymous commentary.[9] This anonymous commentary consists of a thematically arranged selection of excerpts and, according to R. Draguet's hypothesis,[10] was compiled in the first half of the eighth century by a disciple of Isaac of Nineveh. Could this disciple have undertaken this work at the Monastery of Rabban Shabūr with which both Isaac and Dadishoʿ were associated? It is certainly the case that disciples of Isaac were to be found in this very same monastery as is attested by a Syrian Orthodox notice in which a pupil of a certain Mar Dāzedeq (ܡܪܝ ܕܐܙܕܩ) named Būshīr (ܒܘܫܝܪ) appears to be a monk in Rabban Shabūr who is not only familiar with the teachings of Isaac but is able to

---

[6] J.S. Assemanus, *Bibliotheca Orientalis Clementino-Vaticana*, III/1. Rome, 1725, pp. 98–99.

[7] R. Draguet, *Commentaire du Livre d'abba Isaïe* (*logoi I–XV*) *par Dadišo Qaṭraya*, in *CSCO*, 326–327, Scr. Syr. 144–5. Louvain, 1972.

[8] R. Draguet, *Commentaire anonyme du Livre d'abba Isaïe* (*fragments*), in *CSCO*, 336–337, Scr. Syr. 150–151. Louvain, 1973.

[9] Ibid., tr., p.xviii. Draguet refers to two manuscripts which contain this Garshuni translation: Paris syr. 239, ff. 226ʳ–280ᵛ and Cambridge D.d. 15.2 ff. 227ᵛ–269ʳ.

[10] Ibid., tr., pp. xxv–xxvi.

send these teachings to Mar Dāzedeq. This suggests that these teachings were to be found in written form at the monastery and that Būshīr considered them worthy enough of being disseminated resulting in many others also becoming disciples of Isaac. Mar Dāzedeq writes in his letter to Būshīr:

> I know that the keys of the Kingdom have been gained by you in life, because you have filled our monastery with teaching that is filled with life. For we confess that we are pupils of Mar Isaac (ܘܬܠܡܝܕ̈ܐ ܚܢܢ ܕܡܪܝ ܐܝܣܚܩ) the bishop of Niniveh.[11]

In addition to this commentary, the other writings by Dadisho' to survive are a letter to Abqosh[12] and a number of discourses or treatises on stillness.[13] One more very important work of his survives that is catalogued by 'Abdisho' bar Brikā but which remains unedited and with no translation. This is, of course, Dadisho''s commentary on 'Nānisho''s *Paradise of the Fathers*,[14] which is the Syriac version of the *Paradise of the Egyptian Fathers* translated and compiled in the seventh century. Until recently this commentary was also only to be found surviving in an incomplete form in manuscripts at the British Library, Cambridge University Library and the Paris Bibliothèque Nationale.[15] However, the discovery of the complete text in the Metropolitan Library of the Church of the East in Baghdad has attracted the interest of a number of distinguished

---

[11] I.E. Rahmani, *Studia Syriaca*, I. Charfet, 1904, p. ܠܗ.

[12] An edition and French translation exists. See A. Guillaumont and M. Albert, "Lettre de Dadisho' Qaṭraya à Abkosh sur L'Hesychia", in E. Lucchesi and H.D. Saffrey, *Mémorial A-J. Festugière.* Geneva, 1984, pp. 235–245.

[13] Edited and translated by A. Mingana, *Woodbrooke Studies*, vol. 7, 1934, pp. 70–143/201–47.

[14] Some excerpts were published and translated by N. Sims-Williams, "Dādišo' Qaṭrāyā's Commentary on the *Paradise of the Fathers*", in *Analecta Bollandiana*, 112, 1994, pp. 33–64.

[15] Ibid., p. 33.

scholars and a critical edition and translation of this important text are now underway.[16]

What is, perhaps, less well known is that a Garshuni translation of Dadisho^c's commentary features in a number of manuscripts, one of which was first identified in Berlin by Eduard Sachau in 1899. On the very first folio the text itself attributes the work at the outset to Philoxenos of Mabbug, referred to as *Fīloksīnūs al-Siryānī*:

> I begin with the compendium (ܒܡܟܬܨܪ) of the book of the stories (ܐܟܒܐܪ) of the Egyptian monks and its explanation (ܘܬܦܣܝܪܗ) by Fīloksīnūs (ܠܦܝܠܘܟܣܝܢܘܣ) the Syrian.[17]

Sachau was apparently the first to establish the relationship between this Garshuni abridged version or compendium of Dadisho^c's commentary and a Syriac abridged version to be found in the British Library (Add. 17175)[18] in 1899. He did not, however, identify the author of both texts as Dadisho^c leaving this important conclusion for Anton Baumstark to point out 23 years later in a brief and mostly unnoticed sentence to be found in his *History of Syriac Literature* published in German in 1922,[19] identifying both as being authored by Dadisho^c not Philoxenos of Mabbug.[20] The same Garshuni compendium was consequently identified in a number of other manuscripts to be found in the Vatican, St. Pe-

---

[16] A critical edition of Dadisho^c's "Commentary on the Paradise of the Fathers" is being prepared by D. Phillips. See R. Kitchen, "Dadisho Qatraya's *Commentary on 'Abba Isaiah'*. The *Apophthegmata Patrum* Connection", in *StPatr* 41, 2006, pp. 35–50.

[17] Berlin Syr. 244, f. 1^{v}: ܐܒܬܕܝ ܒܡܟܬܨܪ ܟܬܐܒ ܐܟܒܐܪ ܐܠܪܗܒܐܢ ܐܠܡܨܪܝܝܢ ܘܬܦܣܝܪܗ ܠܦܝܠܘܟܣܝܢܘܣ

[18] Add. 17175.

[19] A. Baumstark, *Geschichte der syrischen Literatur mit Ausschluß der christlich-palästinensischen Texte*. Bonn, 1922, p. 226, footnote 7.

[20] The manuscript is Berlin Syr. 244, ff. 1^{v}–112^{v}. See E. Sachau, *Verzeichniss der syrischen Handschriften der Königlichen Bibliothek zu Berlin*. Vol. II. Berlin, 1899, p. 742; A. Baumstark, *Geschichte der syrischen Literatur mit Ausschluß der christlich-palästinensischen Texte*. Bonn, 1922, p. 226, footnotes 7, 8.

tersburg, Jerusalem and Birmingham.[21] Although Alphonse Mingana published his *Catalogue of the Mingana Collection of Manuscripts* in 1933, it seems that Baumstark's conclusions had eluded him as can be seen from his catalogue entries for the four manuscripts that include the Garshuni compendium. In fact, it is only in the 1990s that this erroneous ascription is finally cleared up completely with an article by Prof. Nicholas Sims-Williams entitled: "Dādišoʿ Qaṭrāyā's Commentary on the *Paradise of the Fathers*", in *Analecta Bollandiana*, 112, 1994, p. 38. Interestingly, Sims-Williams points out[22] that the first scholar to argue that Dadishoʿ was the author of the Garshuni compendium was in fact Baron Victor Rosen in his catalogue of Arabic manuscripts entitled *Notices sommaires des manuscrits arabes du Musée Asiatique* published in 1881,[23] forty-one years before Baumstark and unnoticed by Sachau and Mingana. Rosen's argument is based on internal evidence from the Garshuni compendium manuscript he was describing to be found in the Asiatic Museum in St Petersburg. His argument is partly based on the identification of two books referred to and cited from in the Garshuni compendium as having been composed by Dadishoʿ using the catalogue of ʿAbdishoʿ bar Brikā in order to corroborate this identification. The two works are the *Commentary on the Book of Abbā Isaiah* (كتاب تفسير انبا اشعيا), and *The Book of Perfection of Disciplines*, (كتاب التدبير الكامل). The identification of the *Commentary on the Book of Abbā Isaiah* as having been composed by Dadishoʿ is, of course, correct. On the other hand, *The Book of the Perfection of Disciplines* was in fact a monastic work, extant today in only three other known fragments,[24] written by Theodore of

[21] For details see N. Sims-Williams, "Dādišoʿ Qaṭrāyā's Commentary on the *Paradise of the Fathers*", in *Analecta Bollandiana*, 112, 1994, pp. 38.

[22] Ibid., p. 34, footnote 5 and p. 38, footnote 25.

[23] V. Rosen, *Notices sommaires des manuscrits arabes du Musée Asiatique, I.* St. Petersburg, 1881, pp. 6–12.

[24] F. Graffin, "Une page retrouvée de Théodore de Mopsueste", pp. 29–34 in *A Tribute to Arthur Vööbus: Studies in Early Christian Literature and Its Environment, Primarily in the Syrian East.* Edited by Fischer, Robert H. Chicago, Illinois: The Lutheran School of Theology at Chicago, 1977.

Mopsuestia whose works were translated from Greek into Syriac in Edessa in the first half of the fifth century and who enjoyed a great deal of authority in the Church of the East being quoted extensively by authors such as Dadishoʿ. The confusion lies in the fact that all the names and titles of the doctrinal and monastic authorities specifically venerated by the Church of the East, such as Theodore of Mopsuestia, have been omitted or changed in the West Syriac manuscript witnesses and their Garshuni translations. Thus "Theodore the Blessed Interpreter" is often reduced to "the blessed interpreter" or "the interpreter saint" or even changed to "Abba Evagrius", who is Evagrius of Pontus, the universally revered monastic intellectual and author. The same is the case with Dadishoʿ himself who is transformed, as we have seen, into "Philoxenos the Syrian" at the outset of the Garshuni compendium.

Clearly, the conscious attribution of this text in its opening rubric to Philoxenos of Mabbug, one of the most important Syriac Orthodox theologians from the sixth century, at the outset of many of these manuscripts, is an indication of the West Syriac Orthodox tradition to which they belong. Furthermore, a Syriac manuscript at the British Library (Add. 17264) reveals that a Syriac Orthodox copyist has omitted the name of Dadishoʿ who, as mentioned earlier, was a member of the Church of the East, and also omitted the name of his monastery but left his demonym "Qaṭraya", a very useful clue! In fact, an older Church of the East manuscript tradition also survives with Dadishoʿ Qaṭraya's name fully intact.

Unlike ʿNānishoʿ's *Paradise*, the Garshuni compendium is divided into four parts (ܐܓܙܐ / ܓܙܘ). In the copy to be found in the Vatican library[25] the first part is attributed to Philoxenos, the second to Barsanuphius, the third to Hieronimus and the fourth to Palladius.[26] The Berlin copy, however, as well as the oldest copy to be found in the Mingana collection[27] (1480 C.E.) both clearly attribute the whole commentary to Philoxenos the Syrian (ܦܠܟܣܝܢܘܣ ܐܠܣܪܝܐܢܝ) at the very outset whereas the division of

---

[25] Vat. ar. 85.

[26] See E. Tisserant, "Philoxène de Mabboug", in *DThC* 12, 1935, pp. 1521–1522.

[27] Mingana Syr. 403.

the parts and their attribution to Hieronimus (ܚܝܪܘܢܐܡܝܣ) for the third part[28] and Palladius (ܒܠܐܕܝܣ) for the fourth part[29] relates to Philoxenos's (Dadishoʿs) reading of ʿNānishoʿ's *Paradise.* The first two parts do not seem to be attributed to anyone based on the rubric with which the second part begins[30] although it may be argued, given the opening attribution, that they may be understood as both being attributed to Philoxenos. What must also be taken into consideration is that both the Berlin, Mingana and Vatican Library copies are acephalous and refer to themselves as such. It remains to be verified whether the copy in St Petersburg is different in this regard as well as in the attribution of the parts, and consequently representing perhaps a different manuscript tradition. A preliminary investigation based on Rosen's catalogue entry, however, suggests that this is not the case.

It is not at all the case that the selected content which is commented upon in each of these parts can be located in the equivalent part of ʿNānishoʿ's *Paradise.* For example, the story of the vision of two great boats in one of which Abba Arsenius was travelling in silence with the spirit of God while in the second was Abba Moses and the angels of God who were feeding him honey from the comb which is found in part III of the *Paradise*[31] is in fact to be found on folios 3^{v}–4^{r}[32] of the Garshuni compendium in Ber-

---

28 Berlin Syr. 244, f. 29^{v}: "The compendium of the third part is complete, the part which belongs to ʿĪrūnāmīs who wrote the inquiries". ܟܡܠ ܡܟܬܨܪ ܐܠܓܙܘ ܐܠܬܐܠܬ. ܓܙܘ ܚܝܪܘܢܐܡܝܣ ܐܠܕܝ ܘܟܬܒ ܐܠܡܣܐܝܠ.

29 Berlin Syr. 244, ff. 29^{v}–30^{r}: "The fourth part which is the last of the stories of the solitaries written in the book *The Paradise.* From the last part which Balādīs wrote". ܐܠܓܙܘ ܐܠܪܐܒܥ ܘܗܘ ܐܠܐܟܝܪ ܡܢ ܐܟܒܐܪ ܐܠܡܬܘܚܕܝܢ ܐܠܡܟܬܘܒܗ ܦܝ ܟܬܐܒ ܐܠܦܪܕܘܣ. ܡܢ ܐܠܓܙܘ ܐܠܐܟܝܪ ܐܠܕܝ (sic) ܟܬܒܗ ܒܠܐܕܝܣ.

30 Berlin Syr. 244, f. 25^{r}: "That [which] was abridged from the second part is complete and God is my strength". ܬܡ [ܡܐ] ܐܟܬܨܪ ܒܥܘܢ ܡܢ ܐܠܓܙܘ ܐܠܬܐܢܝ ܘܐܠܠܗ ܐܠܡܥܝܢ ܒܥܢ܀

31 E.A.W. Budge, *The Book of Paradise*…, 2 vols. London, 1904, vol. 1, pp. 597–8.

32 Berlin Syr. 244, ff. 3^{v}–4^{r}: "He saw two boats in a river and Arsānīyūs was in one of them in silence and the spirit of God was with

lin and therefore in the first part of the commentary. This four part division is not to be found in the full version of Dadisho^c's commentary in Syriac as is apparent in the second most complete extant manuscript at the British Library (Add. 17264), the first part of which is damaged, and which is organized into two books, the first of which covers Books I–III of the *Paradise* while the second book corresponds to Book IV. It remains to be seen through comparative textual analysis whether the abridged version of the commentary in Syriac or *Epitome*, also to be found in the British library (Add. 17175), is, like the Garshuni compendium, divided into four parts or follows the same ordering.[33] What might be concluded at this stage is that both the full version and the *Epitome* in Syriac as well as the Garshuni compendium all seem to be acephalous for different reasons. The full Syriac version (Add. 17264) is acephalous due to the fact that the first two quires are lost, while the first 19 folios of the *Epitome* in Syriac (Add. 17175) which is partially mutilated at the beginning appears to contain lost material from the beginning of Dadisho^c's full commentary.[34] This hypothesis, first proposed by N. Sims-Williams was recently confirmed in an article by David Phillips[35] who relying upon the recent discovery of the most complete text to date found in the Metropolitan Library of the Church of the East in Baghdad and comprising the full Syriac

him and Anbā Mūsā was in the other and the angels and saints were with him and were feeding him honey from a comb". ܦܪܐܝ ܡܪܟܒܝܢ ܦܝ ܢܗܪ : ܘܐܪܣܢܝܘܣ ܦܝ ܐܚܕܗܡܐ (sic) ܦܝ ܐܠܟܘܪܗ ܘܪܘܚ ܐܠܐܠܗ ܡܥܗ : ܘܐܢܒܐ ܡܘܣܐ ܦܝ ܐܠܐܟܪ ܘܐܠܡܠܐܝܟܗ ܘܐܠܩܕܝܣܝܢ ܡܥܗ ܘܗܡ ܝܛܥܡܘܢܗ ܥܣܠ ܡܢ ܫܗܕ.

33 D. Phillips, "The Syriac Commentary of Dadisho' Qatraya on the *Paradise of the Fathers*. Towards a Critical Edition", in *BABELAO* 1, 2012, pp. 1–23, states on p.16: "The beginning and end are missing and there are no subdivisions into books. No numbering system has been applied to questions and answers, but each question-and-answer group has been supplied with a title written vertically in the margin".

34 See N. Sims-Williams, "Dādišoʿ Qaṭrāyā's Commentary on the *Paradise of the Fathers*", in *Analecta Bollandiana*, 112, 1994, p. 38.

35 D. Phillips, "The Syriac Commentary of Dadisho' Qatraya on the *Paradise of the Fathers*. Towards a Critical Edition", in *BABELAO* 1, 2012, pp. 1–23.

version of the commentary that includes most of the missing section at the beginning[36] states:

> Until the discovery of G [=the Baghdad MS] the initial logia (ff° 1r°–19v°) were not immediately identifiable in DQC [=Dadisho'’s full commentary] and Sims-Williams suggested, that they were “based on lost material” from DQC I. His hypothesis has been vindicated by the material now made available by G: the initial logia in g [=Add. 17175] do indeed find parallels in DQC as attested by the Baghdad manuscript.[37]

In contrast, the Garshuni compendium actually begins towards the end of the answer to question I/14 and includes the six concluding topics[38] which makes it most likely the case that the Garshuni compendium is a translation either of an acephalous *Epitome* or the product of direct contact with an acephalous full Syriac version. This is further verified by the fact that the end of the first part of the compendium refers to what it calls “the first copy” (ܢܣܟܗ ܐܠܐܘܠܗ) which states that first “forty inquiries” (ܐܪܒܥܝܢ ܡܣܐܠܗ) are missing:

> The first part is complete with God’s aid and it is mentioned in the first copy that forty inquiries are missing at its beginning.[39]

Given that the material at the beginning of the full Syriac version and of the *Epitome* has been established[40] as coming at the end of the answer to question I/14 (ܐܪܒܥܬܥܫܪ) and not forty (ܐܪܒܥܝܢ) could this error, which originates in II/14 of the full Syriac version, have

---

36 Ibid., p. 12: “…there are some missing folios at the beginning and the end”.

37 Ibid., p. 16.

38 These six topics are listed simply as numbers in the Garshuni. Berlin Syr. 244, f. 4r : ܐܠܪܐܒܥ ; f. 4v : ܐܠܬܐܠܬ ; f. 8r : ܐܠܬܐܢܝ ; f. 11r : ܐܠܚܐܡܣ ; f. 12r: ܘ̄.

39 Berlin Syr. 244, f. 18v: ܟܡܠ ܐܠܓܙܘ ܐܠܐܘܠ ܒܡܥܘܢܗ ܐܠܠܗ ܘܕܟܪ ܦܝ ܢܣܟܗ ܐܠܐܘܠܗ ܐܢܗ ܢܩܨ ܡܢ ܐܘܠܗ ܐܪܒܥܝܢ ܡܣܐܠܗ

40 See N. Sims-Williams, “Dādišoʿ Qaṭrāyā’s Commentary on the *Paradise of the Fathers*”, in *Analecta Bollandiana*, 112, 1994, p. 37.

been inherited by the Garshuni compendium indirectly through the *Epitome*? There is also, however, the possibility that the error may have come directly from the full Syriac version if the Garshuni compendium in fact reveals itself to be different from the *Epitome*. Given that the *Epitome* is not completely preserved in the British Library manuscript (Add. 17175) which is damaged at the beginning and end, the publication and translation of the Garshuni compendium[41] will help reconstruct this *Epitome* as well as reveal any material that has been preserved in the Garshuni but has been lost in both the *Epitome* and the full Syriac version of Dadishoʿ's commentary.

A concluding point is that the Garshuni compendium does not mark the end of the literary journey of Dadishoʿ's commentary for, in fact, an Ethiopic (Ge'ez) translation of the compendium survives in numerous copies and which is yet to be fully edited or translated.[42] The importance of investigating the history of the translation process of Dadishoʿ's commentary from Syriac into Arabic then consequently into Ethiopic is that it will provide a very rare opportunity to acquire certain important insights into the transmission of knowledge and cultural material from an originally Syriac work into other languages and cultures over the course of over one thousand years, from the seventh century to the most recent Garshuni and Ethiopic manuscripts from the eighteenth and nineteenth centuries. The academic questions raised at each stage might include: what material was omitted or altered and who first undertook this in both the Garshuni and Ethiopic translations? When was the attribution to Philoxenos introduced? Was the Garshuni version undertaken during the Abbasid translation movement or later? Are certain Syriac references retained in the Garshuni manuscripts? Finally, how independent were the Garshuni and Ge'ez translators at each stage: did they simply copy and

[41] This is currently underway. Edition based on all available manuscripts. Translation: Mario Kozah, Abdulrahim Abu-Husayn, and Suleiman Mourad.

[42] See W. Witakowski, "Filekseyus, the Ethiopic version of the Syriac Dadisho Qatraya's Commentary on the Paradise of the Fathers", in *Rocznik Orientalistyczny*, 59, 2006, pp. 281–296.

translate what they were given or did a process of adaptation take place based on careful discerning decisions for their contemporary readerships? Only complete editions of the Syriac, Garshuni, and Ge'ez versions of Dadisho''s commentary on the *Paradise*, itself structured in a question and answer format, will reveal the precious answers to the many tantalizing questions related to the work of this great literary survivor from Beth Qaṭraye.

LOST AND FOUND: DADISHOᶜ QATRAYA'S COMMENTARY ON THE PARADISE OF THE FATHERS AS A WITNESS TO THE WORKS OF THEODORE OF MOPSUESTIA

DAVID PHILLIPS
CATHOLIC UNIVERSITY OF LOUVAIN

ABSTRACT

The works of Dadishoᶜ Qatraya, and in particular his Commentary on the Paradise of the Fathers *are important documents for understanding seventh century East Syriac ascetic and mystical thinking. Dadishoᶜ regularly makes abundant references to several authors, including Evagrius, Mark the Hermit and Theodore of Mopsuestia. In doing so, Dadishoᶜ becomes a secondary witness to writings which, in some cases, are otherwise lost or badly attested. This paper deals with the case of Theodore. Many of his extremely influential works have been lost, but the* Commentary on the Paradise *contains no less than thirty quotations from his works, including a long and so far unique quotation of* The Book of Perfection. *These quotations provide a new store of information on Theodore's writings.*

INTRODUCTION

The works of Dadishoᶜ Qatraya, and in particular his *Commentary on the Paradise of the Fathers* are important documents for understanding seventh century East Syriac ascetic and mystical thinking. From a literary point of view, his *Commentary* is unique as being the only full-length running commentary on the Sayings of the Desert Fathers in Christian Antiquity. Although an original thinker, he draws largely on his predecessors among monastic writers in order to explain questions at issue and obscurities in the Apophthegmata as well as expanding on themes of importance to his readers. His approach is a scholarly one, comparing what a given text says to other similar or divergent ones taken from the corpus he is commentating on, but he also refers to authors whom he and his community considered to be authoritative personalities. Dadishoʿ regularly makes abundant references to several writers of whom we can single out Evagrius, Mark the Hermit, abba Isaiah and Theodore of Mopsuestia, to mention only those who are the most often quoted. By so doing, Dadishoʿ becomes a secondary witness to writings which, in some cases, are otherwise lost or badly attested. This paper will deal with the case of Theodore who, in East Syriac sources, is the second-to-none authority and referred to as the 'Blessed Interpreter' ܛܘܒܢܐ ܡܦܫܩܢܐ. Condemned over a hundred years after his death, which took place in 428 CE, many of his extremely influential works have been lost; however his continued veneration in the East Syriac Church has ensured the transmission of fragmentary quotations of his writings. The *Commentary on the Paradise* contains almost thirty such references, some of which are to works the existence of which is attested elsewhere, while others appear to be totally new, and some of them have been brought to light thanks to the work undertaken for our critical edition of the *Commentary* currently in preparation.[1]

In this hit-parade of patristic authors to whom Dadishoʿ habitually refers, the winner—hardly surprisingly—is Evagrius who is mentioned no less than 86 times, followed by Mark the Hermit (or Solitary) who is quoted in 42 places and then comes Theodore with 28, more or less at equals with abba Isaiah. This corroborates the same literary centre of gravity which is attested in Dadishoʿ's other

[1] Phillips, *Towards a Critical Edition*. We shall refer to our forthcoming edition as DQC.

full-length commentary on abba Isaiah's *Ascetikon* where we find the same kind of distribution.[2]

We can group these references to Theodore's writings according to the works from which they are drawn:

a) Theological and ascetical works	
The Book of Perfection of Disciplines	5 references[3]
The Book of Pearls	1 reference[4]
The Book on Priesthood	2 references[5]
Against Original Sin	1 reference[6]
b) Exegetical Works	
On Luke	6 references[7]
On Romans	1 reference[8]
On the Lord's Prayer	1 reference[9]
New Testament explanations without a work being specified	5 references[10]

c) General allusions with no work specified: 7 references[11]

The limits of this paper prevent the analysis of all these references and so we shall concentrate on the most singular elements.

By far the most important finds are the substantial quotations from the *Book of Perfection of Disciplines*, a monastic work of which

---

[2] Draguet, *Commentaire du livre d'abba Isaïe*, vol. 2, pp. 255–257.

[3] DQC I:6, 24, 33; II: 100, 200.

[4] DQC I:18.

[5] DQC I: 32; II:155.

[6] DQC II:290.

[7] DQC I:18, 21; II:94, 183, 213, 251.

[8] DQC II:116.

[9] DQC II:191. A specific work with this title does not seem to have been attributed to Theodore (Geerard, *Clavis patrum Graecorum*, pp. 344–361; Geerard and Noret, *Clavis patrum Graecorum: Supplementum*, pp. 220–226) so this may, in fact be a reference to another exegetical writing.

[10] DQC I:43, 89, 98; II:135, 212

[11] DQC I:34, 97 (2 references); II:188, 194, 272, 275.

only three other fragments are known,[12] two of which come from other works composed by Dadishoʿ. Compared however with his other writings, it is his *Commentary on the Paradise* which contains the largest amount of material drawn bodily from Theodore's *Book of Perfection*, elsewhere we have to make do with allusions or résumés, while here we have, at last, clear textual citations. It is to the five quotations made by Dadishoʿ in his *Commentary* that we shall turn our attention.

First of all, the title of Theodore's work requires some brief comments. In Dadishoʿ, as well as in ʿAbdishoʿs famous 14th century catalogue[13] the name appears as (ܟܬܒܐ) ܕܡܫܡܠܝܘܬܐ ܕܕܘܒܪ̈ܐ which has been, as Graffin pointed out,[14] variously translated by modern authors. Rendering the Greek πολιτεία in this context, the Syriac ܕܘܒܪ̈ܐ takes on a highly polysemic field of meaning, ranging from 'dispensation' to 'way of life'. Among monastic and spiritual authors the word refers, in a technical sense, to the different general kinds of monastic life, for example coenobitic, anchoretic, solitary, wandering, as well as to specific ascetic practices performed by individual monks, or groups of them, following a particular 'rule'. In the translations here, we have opted for 'conduct' for the secular ܕܘܒܪ̈ܐ and 'discipline' when it concerns monks. The sense of ܡܫܡܠܝܘܬܐ is made clear by the start of the first quotation we shall analyze: it is the monk who professes to lead the 'perfect' way of life or conduct and so the 'perfection of disciplines (or conduct)' means undertaking the monastic life as being the best, or most perfect, way of life. Theodore's *Book of Perfection of Disciplines* thus appears to be a manual for monastic life and this will be borne out by the information we can glean from Dadishoʿ's quotations of it.

---

[12] Graffin, 'Une page retrouvée de Théodore de Mopsueste', pp. 29–34.

[13] Assemani, *Bibliotheca Orientalis*, vol. 3.1, p. 34.

[14] Graffin, 'Une page retrouvée de Théodore de Mopsueste', pp. 29–30.

DQC I:6

Let us then start with DQC I:6 which contains the single most extensive quotation of this work so far brought to light. The context is that of a long series of questions and answers concerning the superiority of the monastic ways of life compared with the secular ones (DQC I:4–14), and almost constitutes a literary sub-unit on this theme within the *Commentary*. Dadishoᶜ is at pains to explain to the brothers with whom he is in conversation that even virtuous seculars who perform all kinds of good and exemplary deeds are inferior even to dissolute and lax monastics. Since the topic ranges over ten questions and is placed almost at the beginning of the *Commentary*, it is quite clear that the issue was of the first importance to the author and his readers. Basically, it boils down to proving that monastic life is, in almost every case, better than a secular life-style, be it an exemplary one. Although the scene is thoroughly set at the outset of the first part of his work, Dadishoᶜ will come back to it yet again in the second part (DQC II:15).

Faced with the, albeit rhetorical, surprise shown by the brothers, our author marshals up his arguments in order to demonstrate his point of view. He does this by lining up three groups of proof-texts taken respectively from the Gospels, the Blessed Interpreter and the divine revelations granted to some of the Desert Fathers, saying that any debate concerning the 'fear of God' should be confirmed by 'the testimony of the Holy Scriptures, the Doctors [of the Church] and the monastic fathers'. This is probably an implicit reference to the idea that two or three witnesses are required to establish a case at Law, according to Deut 19:15 and echoed in several places in the New Testament.[15]

Up to DQC I:15, we only possess two manuscripts to which I have attributed the *sigla* G and g.[16] G is an East Syriac witness pre-

[15] Mt 18:16, 2Cor 13:1, 1Tim 5:19, Heb 10:28.

[16] For a complete description of the codicological material, see Phillips, *Towards a Critical Edition*, pp. 10–18. The *sigla* used in this paper to designate the manuscripts are as follows: A = British Library Add 17264; B = British Library Add 17263; C = British Library Or 2311; G = Bagh-

served at the Archbishopric of the Church of the East at Baghdad and probably to be dated to the first half of the 9th century, according to a recent study made by Kaplan.[17] Because it is the only East Syriac manuscript of DQC of any length, it is of invaluable importance, notably, in so far as it contains intact all the names and titles of the doctrinal and monastic authorities specifically venerated in the Church of the East, whereas in all the other manuscript witnesses, being West Syriac, the names have been omitted or changed. This is the case in manuscript g for the section being examined here which has, rather clumsily, changed 'Theodore the Blessed Interpreter' into 'one of the blessed interpreters'.

The three-fold witness structure of Dadisho^c's reply to the brothers is clearly emphasized in G by the presence of three rubricated sub-titles:

- Testimony from the Holy Gospel on the matter
- Testimony from the Blessed Interpreter
- Testimony from the divine revelations granted to the saints concerning this matter

While the sub-titles may well be editorial, they do highlight the author's own intention. This structure has been completely lost in g which has an abbreviated form of the text, leaving out the sub-titles and the introductory phrase to the second section. This may either have been for concision, since g represents the shorter or 'epitome' version of the text[18] or in order to leave out the reference to Theodore entailing in its wake the omission of the other two sub-titles as well.

The issue of the pre-eminence of monastic over secular life is, of course, a corner-stone for Dadisho^c's whole edifice which, in the guise of a commentary on the first corpus of monastic writings, is a defence and justification of the whole monastic system. That he should lay this corner-stone with Theodore as one of his main

dad Archbishopric of the Church of the East Manuscripts Library 210; g = British Library Add 17175.

[17] Kaplan, *Expertise paléographique*, p. 119.

[18] Sims-Williams, 'Dādišoᶜ Qatrāyā's Commentary', pp. 35–36; Phillips, *Towards a Critical Edition*, pp. 16–20.

props shows, if it were necessary to do so, to what extent the Interpreter constituted a supreme authority, not only for doctrinal and exegetical questions, but also for monasticism.

Here is the text, followed by a translation of the relevant portion of DQC I:6 (G ff° 4v°–5v°; g ff° 10v°–11v°; the variants in our edition are indicated in the notes for the sake of completeness)

ܘܠܐ ܢܐܙܠ ܡܕܒܪܐ. ܡܛܠ ܕܐܦ ܠܐܒ ܦܐܡܝܢ ܐܢܐ ܡܢ ܡܬܟܫܦܢܐ ܕܛܘܒܢܐ ܠܐܪܣܢܝܘܣ ܩܕܝܫܐ. ܐܝܟ ܕܒܬܫܥܝܬܐ ܕܝܠܗ ܕܡܕܒܪܐ

<u>ܫܘܕܥܬܐ ܡܢ ܛܘܒܢܐ ܩܕܝܫܐ</u>

ܐܡܪ ܓܝܪ ܒܟܬܒܐ ܕܫܘܥܪܢܐ ܕܐܒܗܬܐ[19] ܗܟܢܐ. ܡܫܝܚܐ[20] ܗܘ ܠܡܣܟܝܢܐ ܘܡܬܟܪܝܐ ܕܫܘܥܪܢܐ ܕܐܒܗܬܐ ܘܕܒܪܐ ܗܘ ܡܥܠܐ: ܐܝܟ ܕܡܬܚܙܐ[21] ܕܦܩܕ ܘܒܪܗ ܠܐܝܠܐ ܕܫܩܝܠ ܡܫܟܚ ܘܫܒܩ ܢܦܫ ܕܕܝܠܗ ܠܐܠܗܐ ܡܢ ܐܠܘܗܝ ܒܪܘܚܐ: ܘܠܐ ܡܢ ܗܘܐ ܕܡܬܒܥܐ ܡܢ ܟܠܗܘܢ ܗܠܝܢ ܐܝܟܢܐ ܘܡܢܐ[22] ܟܠܗ ܠܐܠܗܐ ܡܢ ܒܪܐ ܟܘܢܐ ܕܟܠܝܐ: ܢܛܝܪ ܘܡܬܢܛܪ ܒܗ. ܠܗܘ ܐܡܪ. ܕܗܘ ܡܢܟܝ ܘܡܬܛܪ ܘܟܘܢܐ ܘܒܪܐ ܘܡܬܝܒܐ ܡܢ ܕܟܠܝܬܐ ܡܬܛܪܐ. ܐܝܟ ܕܡܬܛܪ ܗܘܐ ܘܟܘܢܐ ܘܒܪܐ ܘܡܬܢܝܚ ܠܗ ܕܠܘܬܗ. ܡܢ ܘܒܪܐ ܘܡܬܐܬܐ ܢܠܗ. ܡܬܐܬܐ ܠܡ ܡܢ ܛܒ ܟܠ ܐܦ ܠܡܫܡܫܬܐ ܕܝܠܗ ܕܡܪܢ ܘܡܬܚܫܒܢܘܬܗ ܡܪܬܐ[23] ܗܘܬ ܘܡܬܚܦܛܐ. ܐܠܐ ܐܦܢܝܗ ܡܢ ܐܡܪ. ܡܬܐܬܐ ܡܬܐܬܐ. ܡܪܬܝ[24] ܘܡܬܪܥܝܢܬܝ ܥܠ ܣܓܝܐܬܐ. ܠܡܬܚܡ ܕܐܦ ܡܚܣܢ. ܡܛܠ ܕܡܬܚܡܠ ܟܠܗܘܢ ܗܠܝܢ. ܘܟܠܗܝܢ ܒܠܚܘܕ ܐܡܝܢܐ ܗܘܬ ܒܢܝܫܬܐ ܕܡܚܝܢܘܬܐ ܡܢ ܘܠܐ ܫܒܩܐ ܙܡܢܐ ܗܘܬ ܠܗ ܘܢܬܚܐ ܥܠ ܓܒ ܩܪܝܒܘܬܗ ܘܠܐ ܫܒܩܐ ܚܙܝܐ ܗܘܬ ܒܗ. ܡܢ ܢܦܫܐ ܒܠܝ ܡܬܩܢܝܢ ܘܒܗܘܢ ܡܬܬܪܥܝܢܐ ܠܗ ܠܬܘܩܢܐ ܗܘ ܕܠܗܝܢ. ܘܡܢ ܡܬܦܪܢܣܐ ܗܘܬ ܒܫܘܒܐ ܕܟܠܐ ܡܬܬܪܬܐ. ܡܬܡܛܠ ܗܘܐ ܙܒܢܐ ܘܪܚܝܩ ܡܢ ܛܘܦܣܗ ܕܟܠܗ ܗܘܐ. ܘܒܟܠܗ ܕܟܠܝ ܐܝܟ ܕܡܥܪܩܪܩܢܘܬܐ[25] ܢܝܫܐ ܗܘܬ. ܕܐܝܟ ܗܘܝܐ

[19] ܐܡܪ ܓܝܪ ܚܕ ܡܢ] ܡܛܠ ܕܐܦ ܠܐܒ ܦܐܡܝܢ ܐܢܐ ... ܒܟܬܒܐ ܕܫܘܥܪܢܐ ܕܐܒܗܬܐ g ܛܘܒܢܐ ܩܕܝܫ[ܘ]ܬܐ

[20] ܡܫܝܚܐ] ܘܡܫܝܚܐ g

[21] ܕܡܬܚܙܐ] ܕܡܬܚܙܐ g

[22] ܘܡܢܐ] ܘܡܢܐ g

[23] ܡܪܬܐ] ܡܪܬܐ *cfr* Psh Lk 10, 41

[24] ܡܪܬܝ] ܡܪܬܝ G = Psh Lk 10, 41

[25] ܕܡܥܪܩܪܩܢܘܬܐ] *cum seyame* [g]

ܐܝܬܘܗܝ ܕܒܪܐ ܕܝܗܘܕܝܐ ܒܗܘܝܐ ܕܟܝܢܐ. ܘܠܕܘܒܪܗ ܕܬܘܡܟܝܟܘܬܐ ܡܢܝܢ ܕܟܝܢܐ.
ܘܐܝܟ ܕܠܐ ܢܒܠ ܗܘܐ ܡܢܬܐ ܠܒܘܟܪܐ ܟܝܢܐ ܘܓܡܝܪܐ ܕܪܘܚܢܐ ܕܡܢܝܢ ܥܡܗ ܗܘ
ܕܡܫܡܠܝܐ ܗܘܐ ܠܟܠ ܡܕܡ. ܗܟܢܐ ܠܐ ܙܓܝܡ[26] ܠܥܡܡ̈ܐ ܦܠܚ̈ܝ[27] ܡܫܬܘ̈ܬܐ
ܓܠܚܢ̈ܬܐ ܒܦܓܪܗܘܢ ܘܒܪܘܩ̈ܬܐ: ܕܒܘܟܪܐ ܟܝܢܐ ܘܓܡܝܪܐ ܕܡܢ ܝܗܘܕܝܐ
ܟܡܠܐ ܡܫܡܠܝܐ. ܟܕ ܙܒܢ ܗܘܐ ܠܗܘܢ ܠܥܒܕܗ. ܘܐܡܝܢܐ ܕܡܫܬܡܪܐ ܢܩܡܐ
ܒܟܝܢܐ ܡܢ ܦܓܪܐ. ܗܟܢܐ ܡܫܡܠܝ ܕܒܪܐ ܟܝܢܐ ܕܟܡܠܐ ܡܢ ܝܗܘܕܝܐ
ܡܬܦܠܚ ܡܢ ܕܒܪܐ ܓܠܝܐ ܘܡܫܡܠܝܐ ܕܥܡܡ̈ܐ: ܕܒܦܓܪܗܘܢ ܘܒܢܦܫܗܘܢ
ܒܟܠܗܘܢ ܡܫܡܠܝܢ. ܘܐܝܟ ܕܡܬܚܫܒ ܕܒܪܐ[28] ܘܡܠܐܟܐ ܡܢ ܕܒܫܡܝܐ. ܗܟܢܐ
ܡܬܚܫܒ ܦܘܠܚܢܐ ܕܝܗܘܕܝܐ ܡܢ ܕܥܡܡ̈ܐ ܡܫܡܠܝܐ. ܘܐܝܟ ܕܡܬܚܫܒ ܘܡܫܡܠܝ ܗܘܟܐ
ܘܐܠܗܐ ܡܢ ܗܘܟܐ ܕܒܫܡܝܐ. ܗܟܢܐ ܡܬܚܫܒ ܘܡܫܡܠܝ ܦܘܠܚܢܐ ܕܝܗܘܕܝܐ ܡܢ
ܦܘܠܚܢܐ ܕܥܡܡ̈ܐ. ܡܛܠ ܕܥܡܡ̈ܐ ܠܒܪܝܬܐ ܚܠܦ ܦܠܚܝܢ[29] ܠܐܠܗܐ.
ܝܗܘܕܝܐ ܕܝܢ ܠܒܪܘܝܐ ܐܠܗܐ ܦܠܚܝܢ ܠܗ. ܗܘ ܕܝܢ ܠܥܒܕܝܢ ܠܐ ܢܣܓܕܘܢ ܘܡܕܡ
ܠܐ ܙܓܝܢ: ܡܢ ܟܠ ܕܒܫܡܝܐ ܘܟܕܐ ܐܘ ܒܐܪܥܐ ܐܘ ܒܥܡܩܐ: ܐܘ ܒܬܗܘܡܐ ܗܘܐ ܐܘ
ܒܟܠܗ ܕܠܥܠ. ܐܠܐ ܐܘ ܠܡܘܬܗ ܕܐܠܗܐ ܕܥܡܗ ܡܫܘܐ ܡܫܝܚܐ ܘܠܒܪܗ.
ܠܥܡܡ̈ܐ[30] ܕܝܢ ܐܦ ܙܘܩ̈ܐ ܦܠܚܝܢ ܘܠܡܫܪ̈ܝܬܐ ܡܣܝܡܝܢ ܘܠܟܘܟܒ̈ܐ
ܡܕܒܪ̈ܝܢ:[31] ܘܒܦܓܪܗܘܢ ܠܘܬ ܢܦܫܗܝ. ܐܠܐ ܙܒܢܘܗܝ ܠܒܪܝܬܐ ܦܓܪ̈ܢܝܬܐ
ܡܫܡܠܝ. ܠܒܪܝܬܐ ܕܐܪܥܐ. ܠܒܪܝܬܐ ܕܫܡܝܐ ܠܒܪܝܬܐ ܕܐܬܪ̈ܐ. ܠܒܪܝܬܐ
ܘܐܝܠܢ̈ܐ. ܠܒܪܝܬܐ ܕܒܝܡ ܝܒܫܐ. ܠܒܪܝܬܐ ܕܡܝܐ.[32] ܘܫܡܫ ܗܘ ܙܘܓܐ
ܘܡܫܬܘܕܥܝܢ ܐܝܟ ܡܫܠܡܢܘܬܗ ܕܡܢ ܡܢ ܩܕܡ ܘܙܘܙ̈ܐ. ܘܐܝܬܝܗܝܢ ܡܬܕܒܪܢ
ܕܟܠܗ ܘܪܦܝܗ: ܘܢܘܗܪܐ ܘܫܘܚܠܦܝܗ ܪܗܛܘܗ ܘܡܬܚܒܪܢܗ. ܝܗܘܕܝܐ ܕܝܢ
ܒܪܚܡܬܗܘܢ ܠܟܠܗܘܢ ܗܠܝܢ ܕܒܪܝܬܐ ܥܠܝܗ ܣܒܪܘ[33] ܡܫܝܚܝܢ. ܘܚܕܐ ܙܡܝܢ
ܒܪܘܡܗܘܢ ܕܒܥܡܩܐ ܦܪܨܘܦܗܘܢ: ܠܟܠ[34] ܘܐܬܓܠܝ[35] ܘܚܙܝܘܗܝ. ܟܕ ܓܠܝ

26 ܙܓܝܡ] *cum seyame* g
27 ܦܠܚ̈ܝ] ܦܠܚܝ g
28 ܕܒܪܐ] ܦܘܠܚܢܐ G
29 ܦܠܚܝܢ] ܦܠ̈ܚܝܢ g
30 ܠܥܡܡ̈ܐ] *sine seyame* g
31 ܡܕܒܪ̈ܝܢ] ܡܕܒܪܝܢ G
32 ܕܡܝܐ] *cum seyame* g
33 ܣܒܪܘ] *add waw* G
34 ܠܟܠ] ܠܟܠܗ g
35 ܘܐܬܓܠܝ] ܘܐܬܓܠܝܘ g

ܠܡܗܘܪܐ ܗܘܐ ܘܕܘܒܪܗܘܢ. ܘܠܡܫܪܪܐ ܗܘܐ ܦܘܪܫܢܗܘܢ. ܘܡܛܠ ܠܗ ܩܫܝܐ
ܘܕܘܡܝܐ ܒܟܬܒܗܘܢ ܕܒܪܝܫܝܬ ܕܟܬܒܐ܀ ܗܢܐ ܕܝܢ ܕܡܬܐܡܪܐ ܡܢ ܗܘܢܝܬܐ:
ܕܟܬܒܐ ܢܒܝܐ ܘܡܫܬܪܐ: ܕܦܫܝܛ ܙܘܥܐ ܘܡܫܬܪܪܐ ܠܡܬܩܢܐ ܘܡܟܝܪ ܠܠܚܡܪܐ
ܘܡܢܝܢ ܠܡܫܬܪܪܐ: ܡܛܠ ܗܘ ܡܢ ܡܣܒܪܐ: ܡܛܠ ܕܗܘ ܠܡܦܫܩܢܐ ܛܘܒܢܐ
ܡܦܫܩܢܐ: ܗܟܢ ܕܝܢ ܠܟܬܒܐ: ܕܒܓܘܗܝ ܐܘ ܡܫܡܥ ܦܘܪܫܢܗ ܡܢܗ. ܠܐ ܟܪܐ ܐܢܐ
ܘܐܡܬܝ ܡܫܬܒܚܢܘܬܐ ܥܠ ܦܘܪܫܢܗܘܢ:[36] ܐܝܟ ܡܬܚܫܒܢܘܬܗܘܢ ܓܒܪ ܕܗܘܠܝܢ
ܩܛܠܐ. ܡܬܚܙܝܢ[37] ܐܝܟ ܒܠܚܘܕܝܐ ܐܘ ܡܢ ܢܘܟܪܝܘܬܐ:[38] ܘܠܓܒܪܐ ܠܐܝܬ ܠܐ ܡܟܝܢ
ܘܡܢ ܐܝܟ ܠܐ ܡܬܡܠܠܝܢ ܘܠܐܝܬ ܠܐ ܡܬܚܫܒ. ܡܬܚܙܝܢ[39] ܕܝܢ ܐܦ ܡܢ ܡܠܐܟܐ.
ܡܛܠ[40] ܡܢ ܐܝܟܢܐ ܒܟܠܗ ܘܡܬܬܢܝܐ: ܘܠܐܠܗܐ ܒܟܠܗ ܡܫܡܫܝܢ
ܘܡܫܡܫܝܢ: ܐܡܪ ܐܢܐ ܕܝܢ ܒܬܘܒ ܘܒܪܚܡܐ ܘܡܬܢܒܝܐ. ܐܠܐ ܗܠܝܢ ܡܛܠ ܩܫܝܢ
ܡܢ ܢܟܦܘ ܕܡܫܡܫܢܐ.

Translation—for the sake of the clarity in the analysis latter on I shall indicate the different blocks of text with letters:

A ‘I shall now bring together some [testimonies] from the teaching of the blessed Theodore the Interpreter in order to confirm the matter.

Testimony from the Blessed Interpreter

B Now he says thus in the *Book of Perfection of Disciplines*, "It is shameful for a monk who professes the perfection of discipline and a dire disgrace if it appears that his discipline is comparable to that of one who, although in marriage, is very zealous in the fear of God and mindful about it and if [the monk] is not recognized as being better than [the married man] by being above human con-

36 ܦܘܪܫܢܗܘܢ] ܦܘܪܫܢܗ G
37 ܡܬܚܙܝܢ] *cum seyame* g
38 ܢܘܟܪܝܘܬܐ] ܡܣܟܢܐ g
39 ܡܬܚܙܝܢ] *cum seyame* g
40 ܡܛܠ] *add waw* g

> siderations with his gaze turned towards God in the perfect discipline of quietude".[41]

[Theodore] also says,

C The discipline of monks is much higher, better and perfect than that of virtuous seculars, just as the conduct of Mary, Lazarus's sister[42] was better than that of her sister Martha's. Martha was indeed very mindful about serving our Lord and his disciples and laboured for this, however he reprimanded her saying, "Martha, Martha you are mindful and anxious about many things" (Lk 10:41). Mary he praised because she had left all this and remained with him alone in perfect love, listening to him insatiably, sitting at his feet and gazing ceaselessly at him. Drawn by his words, she imagined through them the image[43] to come and flew by love towards virtue; her mind bore her away far from the image of this world and she gazed upon the world to come as though in a hallucination. The discipline of monks is like this when they are in quietude which resembles that of the blessed Mary.[44] Just as Martha did not know the hidden and perfect discipline of her sister Mary's mind which she showed to our Lord, so seculars who perform visible virtuous deeds through their bodies and through alms are not conscious of the hidden and perfect discipline performed by monks in quietude. It is meet that they should know that just as, in

---

[41] I have opted for this voluntarily awkward translation of ܫܠܝܐ in order to bring out its specifically technical nature in Syriac spiritual literature with a semantic field ranging from tranquillity, quietness or stillness of the mind (partially corresponding to the Greek ἡσυχία in Byzantine literature) to physical solitude.

[42] The Martha mentioned in Lk 10:41 is assimilated to the one in Jn 11:1. The assimilation made by Theodore is recurrent in Dadisho's *Commentary*.

[43] τύπος.

[44] Lazarus's sister, of course, not Christ's mother.

> nature, the soul is more excellent than the body, so the hidden and perfect discipline carried out by monks in quietude is more excellent than the visible and virtuous discipline of seculars which is performed through their bodies and their possessions in the world. Just as the conduct of angels is more exalted than that of men, so the labour of monks is more exalted than that of virtuous seculars. Just as the love of God is more exalted and excellent than the love of men, so the labour of monks is more exalted and excellent than the labour of seculars. Seculars please God through the love of men, while monks please him through the love of God. In other words, they love and desire nothing whatsoever among all that has been made and created in earth or in heaven, in this world or in the world to come except the love of God through our Lord Jesus Christ and the vision of him. Even though seculars give alms, bring relief to the harassed, and give help to the oppressed and can also be chaste in their bodies, yet in their minds they are divided between many loves: love for a wife, love for children, love for parents, love for brothers, love for people of a family or love for possessions. The seed of their virtue is choked, as our Lord says, by thorns and thistles,[45] which are the cares and worries of the world, the enticement and downwards attraction of its many affairs and dealings. Monks however have voluntarily stripped themselves of these things and cast them off, their mind being vested and clothed solely with the love of their Creator manifested through Christ our Saviour. Hence their discipline is worthy of marvel and their reward deserving of wonder and there is nothing comparable or similar among any of the disciplines of the world.'

We now come to an important methodological point concerning quotations in Dadishoᶜ's writings. In general we know exactly when

---

[45] Mt 13: 7 = Mk 4:7 = Lk 8:7. In fact both the Peshitta and the two Old Syriac versions only use the term 'thorns' in these passages.

the quotation starts, because of the introductory formula, but it is often much less easier to know when it stops to let Dadishoʿ take up the pen again himself, since his argument runs on from the text he is using almost seamlessly.

In the passage here, the text continues immediately as follows:

D 'As for what is said by the uneducated,[46] that a chaste and virtuous secular who gives alms, feeds orphans, helps the afflicted and gives relief to the harassed is more excellent than a monk, because the latter is only profitable to himself while the former is profitable to many, which would mean that the former's reward would be better than the latter's! I am quite incapable of telling at greater length all their foolishness. According to the idea of these idiots, seculars are even more excellent than anchorites who never see anybody, never speak with anyone and never give relief to a soul. In which case they would also be more excellent than the angels, and even more so than the upper and higher ranks[47] [of angels] who serve and glorify God alone!—by which I mean the cherubim, seraphim and thrones.

E Now these few considerations taken from the teaching of the Interpreter will have to suffice.'

On the one hand, the last phrase of this passage (E) would lead us to conclude that this paragraph (D) is also part of the quotation, but on the other the fact that Dadishoʿ is using the first person when introducing the quotation right at the beginning (A) and the text switches back to the first person at the beginning of this last paragraph (D) would bring us to the conclusion that in fact the quotation stops at the end of block C.

There is perhaps a piece of external evidence which can help us to decide. The angelology of block D quite manifestly betrays

---

[46] ἰδιώτης.

[47] τάγμα.

the influence of Pseudo-Dionysius's *Celestial Hierarchy* (6:2)[48] since it considers the triad cherubim-seraphim-thrones to be a superior class of angels unlike the New Testament where the texts which enumerate the angelic hosts (Col 1:16, Rom 8:28, Eph 1:21) do not introduce such a hierarchy. Although the dating of the Pseudo-Dionysian corpus is the subject of much controversy, we are dealing, at the earliest, with a late fifth or sixth century source.[49] In other words, unless the angelic hierarchy presupposed in the text goes back to a hypothetical common source, block D is more likely to have come from Dadishoʿ's seventh century hand rather than Theodore's fourth or early fifth century one.[50] We shall thus consider the quotation from Theodore's *Book of Perfection* to end with block C—block D is a parenthetical aside made by Dadishoʿ in order to prolong and emphasize Theodore's point of view with what he considers to be a scathing *reductio ab absurdum* against an opposing standpoint. The separation of the concluding formula (E) from the text to which it really refers (C) by D is thus not really significant.

DQC I:24

The context is that of a question concerning the duty of taking in sick and old monks in a monastery. Dadishoʿ criticizes certain ab-

---

[48] Luibheid, Rorem and Roques, *Pseudo-Dionysius. The Complete Works*, pp. 160–161. For the Greek text, see Heil and Ritter, *Pseudo-Dionysius Areopagita*, p. 26.

[49] Luibheid, Rorem and Roques, *Pseudo-Dionysius. The Complete Works*, pp. 12–21; Roques, Heil and de Gaudillac, *Denys l'Aréopagite: La Hiérarchie céleste*, p. xviii.

[50] Pseaudo-Dionysius was transmitted to the 7th century Syriac authors via the sixth century translation made by Sergius of Reshaina and the specific Dionysian angelology is attested among several of them (Beulay, *La lumière sans forme*, pp. 158, 174–179). We might mention, in passing, that although the same angelic hierarchy is to be found in the *Book of the Holy Hierotheos*, (Marsh, *The Book of the Holy Hierotheos*, pp. 15*–21*; 18–22), Dionysius's eponymous initiator to whom he explicitly attributes the triad, it seems unlikely that *Hierotheos* served as a transmitter of Dionysian thought in the East Syriac churches (Beulay, *La lumière sans forme*, pp. 181–183).

bots who prefer receiving healthy and vigorous men, despite their bad character, probably because they are more apt for handling the monastery's worldly affairs! To make his point he brings into play the weight of Theodore's authority and gives a long quotation from the *Book of Perfection*.

Now it so happens that another treasure-hunter who was in search of quotations from the Interpreter unearthed the same prize, without however noticing the interest of the treasure chest which contains it. In 1977, Graffin published a find which had been made by Paramelle in Migne's *Patrologia Graeca*.[51] In a series of texts purportedly attributed to Anthony the Great, Paramelle had noticed the quotation from Theodore which we about to discuss and asked Graffin to publish it. Ultimately the source for Migne goes back to an Arabic manuscript used by Abraham Ecchellensis in editing Anthony's works. What Graffin failed however to realize was that the whole text attributed in Migne to Anthony is in fact a citation of Dadisho'''s *Commentary on the Paradise* but which itself contains a citation from Theodore—that is to say a quote within a quote. Our Syriac text thus not only provides the ultimate source for Graffin's fragment of Theodore but also the larger text containing it and which had been left unidentified by Graffin and Paramelle.

Given this fact, it will be worthwhile to provide here the whole text of the *Commentary*'s question and reply because it provides not only a complete parallel both to Graffin's fragment from Theodore, but also to what, apparently unbeknown to him, is an extract from DQC (A ff° 4v°–5r°, G ff° 12r°–12v°, g ff° 20r°–20v°):

ܐܝܢܐ ܚܝܠܐ ܢܠܒܫ ܡܢ ܗܢ ܕܐܡܪ ܐܢܘܢ[52] ܒܦܘܪܫܐ ܠܟܘܠܐ ܦܫܝܩܐ ܠܡܥܒܕܘ
ܡܢ ܢܦܩ ܡܢ ܥܠܡܐ. ܕܐܢ ܙܟܐ ܐܝܬ ܠܥܡܘܕܐ ܕܢܦܫܐ ܐܠܐ ܠܗ ܠܥܘܡܪܐ ܕܐܝܢܐ
ܡܫܬܐܠ. ܐܝܟ ܕܡܫܡܫܝܢ ܕܐܦ ܒܪܘܚܢܐܝܬ ܢܫܬܪܪܘܢ܀

---

[51] Graffin, 'Une page retrouvée de Théodore de Mopsueste', p. 32 concerning Migne, *Patrologia Graeca*, vol. 40, col. 1085B.

[52] ܐܢܘܢ] *add* ܐܚܐ Gg

ܕܟܠ ܓܒܪܐ ܕܒ̈ܢܝܐ[64] ܟܕ[65] ܐܡܪ.[66] ܦܩܕܝܢ[67] ܠܗܘܢ ܕܢܣܒܠܘܢ
53 ܘܪܡܥܘܗܝ] ܗܕܐ Ag
54 ܘܢܣܒ] *add* ܚܣܝܪܘܬܐ Gg
55 ܠܐܢܢ̈ܩܐ] *sine seyame* G
56 ܚܣܝܪܘܬܐ] *om* Gg
57 ܕܪ̈ܚܡܐ] ܕܪܚܡܐ A
58 ܡܦܩܕܝܢ] ܡܫܠܡܝܢ AG
59 ܠܟܠܢܝ̈ܫܐ] ܠܟܠܢܫܐ g
60 ܘܡܫܡܠܝܘܬܐ] ܘܫܦܝܪܘܬܐ G ■ ܘܡܫܬܪܝܘܬܐ g
61 ܘܦܩܕ] *om* A
62 ܒܗܠܝܢ] ܗܢܐ g
63 ܛܘܒܐ ܡܫܡܠܝܐ] ܡܫܡܠܝܐ A ■ ܐܝܟ ܡܢ ܗܕ̈ܐ ܛܘܒܐ g
64 ܒܟܠܟܠ ܕܟܠ ܓܒܪܐ ܕܒ̈ܢܝܐ] *om* g
65 ܟܕ] *om* g
66 ܐܡܪ] *add waw* g
67 ܦܩܕܝܢ] ܡܦܩܕܝܢ G
68 ܗܘ] *om* G
69 ܘܦܘܪܣܐ] ܘܦܘܠܚܢܐ Gg
70 ܒܥܕܬܐ] ܒܥܕܐ A
71 ܟܕ] *om* A
72 ܡܢܗܝܪ] ܡܢܗܝܪ Gg

ܦܘܩܕܢܐ[74] ܕܐܬܡܠܠ ܠܗ. ܐܝ ܡܢ ܡܫܡܥܘܬܐ ܐܘ ܡܢ ܡܗܝܡܢܘܬܐ ܢܐܡܪ
ܕܐܡܪ ܗܘܐ. ܐܦ ܩ̈ܕܡ[75] ܕܒܢ̈ܝ ܗܘܐ ܢܦܩ ܕܡܫܠܡܘܬܐ. ܡܡܟܝܢ ܘܡܦܠܚܝܢ[76]
ܠܐܢܫܐ ܕܢܦܩ ܕܦܘܠܚܢܐ ܘܕܘܒܪ̈ܐ[77] ܕܒܥܠܡܐ. ܐܦ ܗܘܐ ܕܡܕܡ: ܥܠ
ܡܫܠܡܘܬܐ. ܘܟܠܗ ܡܢ ܚܒܪ̈ܐ ܕܡܫܠܡܘܬܐ. ܐܠܐ ܡܢ ܦܘܠܚܢܐ ܦܓܪܢܝܐ[78] ܕܒܗܘܐ
ܚܒܪ̈ܐ. ܢܬܝܕܥܘܢ ܒܫܠܡܗܘܢ ܐܝܟ ܕܫܡܠܝܢ ܘܐܝܟ ܕܚܙܝܢ. ܘܐܦܠ ܦܘܡ
ܐܡܪ. ܕܐܢ ܗܘܘ[79] ܐ̈ܚܐ[80] ܐܚܝ̈ܐ. ܘܟܕ ܗܘܐ ܒܥܠܡܐ ܗܟܢ. ܘܐܚܪܢܐ[81]
ܡܫܠܐ ܟܕ ܡܕܘܐ. ܘܐܚܪܢܐ ܡܫܡܫ ܒܫܘܡܠܐ ܗܟܢܐ. ܠܐܚ̈ܝܗܘܢ[82] ܟܕ
ܦܘܠܚܢܐ ܐܡܝܢܗܘܢ. ܘܡܘܫ ܗܘܐ ܡܕܝܠ. ܕܒܘܚܪܢܐ ܕܦܓܥ̈ܐ ܪܘܚ[83]
ܘܗܘܘ.[84] ܠܗ ܒܠܒܗܘܢ ܣܓܝ̈ܐܬܐ[85] ܘܡܫܡܫܝܢ. ܐܠܐ ܐܦ ܐܢ̈ܫܐ[86] ܩܪ̈ܝܒܐ ܘܫܒ̈ܒܐ
ܡܫܬܠܐ ܕܡܫܬܠܡܝܢ[87] ܘܐܢ̈ܫܐ ܠܘܬ[88] ܕܢܦܩܝܢ ܘܡܫܝܢ ܒܥܠܡܐ

A — 'The brothers: What can we learn from the word that Anthony addressed to his disciple Paul the Simple at the outset when he left the world, "If you want to be a monk, go to a monastery with many brothers who are able to support your sickness"?

---

73 ܘܪܗܛ] ܘܪܗܛ A
74 ܦܘܩܕܢܐ] ܦܘܠܚܢܐ Gg
75 ܩ̈ܕܡ] *sine seyame* G
76 ܘܡܦܠܚܝܢ] ܘܡܫܡܠܝܢ AG
77 ܘܕܘܒܪ̈ܐ] *om waw* A
78 ܦܓܪܢܝܐ] ܒܥܢܝܐ g
79 ܗܘܘ] ܗܘܐ
80 ܐ̈ܚܐ] *sine seyame* Gg
81 ܘܐܚܪܢܐ] *om waw* A
82 ܠܐܚ̈ܝܗܘܢ] *sine seyame* Gg
83 ܪܘܚ] ܪܘܚ A ■ *om* g
84 ܘܗܘܘ] *om* g
85 ܣܓܝ̈ܐܬܐ] ܣܓܝܐܬܐ g
86 ܐܢ̈ܫܐ] *sine seyame* G
87 ܕܡܫܬܠܡܝܢ] ܕܡܫܡܫܝܢ g
88 ܠܘܬ] *om* Gg

B Dadishoʿ: We learn from this story that it is fitting to receive with joy and love those who are old, ill, weak, blind or lame; those who have acquired a favourable will towards virtue through that which they are capable of, even if they are hindered from other things because of their weakness. Here it is the leaders and heads of monasteries who are admonished because they do not receive the weak even though they are very loyal and virtuous, but who eagerly take in vigorous youths, doubtless with a view to the administration of business and external affairs,[89] despite the fact that they are rabid, harsh and insolent.

C In his *Book on the Perfection of Disciplines*, the blessed Interpreter reprimands them by saying, "They leave off inciting their disciples to virtue and do as though they supervised worldly business and bodily pleasure for those who are gathered together in the name of virtue without giving them respite from worldly labour. They give orders to all and sundry, scorning and reprimanding whoever does not carry out what was entrusted to him with great diligence and finding fault with him—whether this becomes apparent on account of his weakness or on account of his negligence. Even if he showed concern about virtue thousands of times, [these leaders prefer to] praise and extol whoever is mindful of worldly labour and affairs, even if he despises virtue. It is not because of the works of virtue, but because of bodily labour in the guise of works that the zealous and the lazy are recognized as such among these people.

D Now abba Poemen says, "If three [monks] are together: one in good quietude, another is sick but gives thanks and the last serves with an upright mind, all

[89] Literally: 'going out onto the roads'.

> three accomplish the same labour". The holy man showed by this that in a monastery with many brothers, it is good that there be not only brothers in good health who serve, but also sick brothers and infirm elderly brothers who have to be served as well as brothers who keep quietude and remain in it.'

The entire text A, B, C and D appear as such in Graffin's text in the same order.[90] He considers D not to be part of the Theodore quotation but does not explain its presence or purpose. The question thus arises as to what it is doing here. Now that we know that we are in fact dealing with Dadishoʿ's *Commentary on the Paradise* as the larger context for the quote from *The Book of Perfection* we can perhaps shed some more light on the question, which is germane since we want to try and delimit the Theodore quote with greater accuracy. Is it Dadishoʿ who is adding on a rider by bringing in the words of abba Poemen, taken of course from the Apophthegmata themselves,[91] or were they already part of Theodore's text? It would seem that it is the former. The *logion* in question is another of Dadishoʿ's cornerstones for building up the edifice of monastic life—right at the beginning of his *Commentary*, in DQC I:2 and 3, he uses it to define the three categories of monks: those who live in quietude, those who though sick and weak (and thus unable to undertake strenuous asceticism) give thanks and those who willingly act as servants to the other two categories and he comes back to it on several other occasions in his work (DQC I:100; II: 9, 14). It is thus highly probable that it is Dadishoʿ who is using one of his own leitmotifs taken from the very texts he is explaining to complete Theodore's arguments. Indeed the technique of using one apophthegm to explain another is one of Dadishoʿ's standard practices. Thus we shall conclude that the quote from the *Book of Perfection* is limited to block C.

[90] Graffin, 'Une page retrouvée de Théodore de Mopsueste', p. 33.

[91] Bedjan, *Acta martyrum et sanctorum*, p. 786. In the Greek alphabetical collection it appears as Poemen 29 (Regnault, *Les sentences des Pères du Désert*, p. 229).

DQC I:33[92]

The brothers' question concerns ascetics who are so emaciated through fasting that the sun can be seen through their rib-cages. Our commentator replies that he also has seen such cases and that the great Theodore himself witnessed such extraordinary feats.

ܗܘ ܓܝܪ ܐܦ ܛܘܒܢܐ ܡܦܫܩܢܐ ܒܟܬܒܐ ܕܓܡܝܪܘܬܐ ܕܕܒ̈ܪܐ. ܟܕ ܡܫܒܚ ܛܒ ܠܐܘܛܘܟܝܣ ܘܠܩܘܪܝܠܠܘܣ ܝܚܝ̈ܕܝܐ. ܐܚ̈ܐ ܒܒܣܪܐ ܕܥܡܪܝܢ ܗܘܘ ܒܐܢܛܝܘܟܝܐ: ܘܐܡܪ: ܕܡܠܠ ܡܠܠܬܐ ܕܐܝܟ ܡܙܕܟܝܐ ܡܢ ܬܫܥܝܬܐ ܕܓܡܝܪܘܬܗܘܢ. ܒܚܪܬܐ ܕܝܢ [93] ܐܡܪ ܐܦ ܗܕܐ. ܗܟܢܐ ܟܡܐ ܡܢ ܝܨܝܦܘܬܗܘܢ ܝܬܝܪܬܐ ܘܩܫܝܬܐ. ܐܬܡܚܠ ܦܓܪܝܗܘܢ ܘܐܬܢܟܦܘ ܠܓܡܪ. ܐܝܟ ܕܩܠܝܠ ܕܚܙܝܢ ܟܕ ܚܙܘ ܠܗܘܢ ܡܣܬܟܠܝܢ ܡܢ ܙܘܥܐ. ܢܣܒܪܘܢ ܕܛܠ̈ܠܐ ܚܙܝܢ ܗܘܘ ܘܠܐ ܒܢܝ̈ܢܫܐ. ܐܡܪܐ ܕܝܢ ܗܕܐ ܕܥܠ ܐܚܪ̈ܢܐ. ܐܦ [94] ܐܢܐ ܟܕ ܥܡܗܘܢ ܗܘ [95] ܐܣܒܪܬ ܠܟܠܗܘܢ ܕܐܝܟ ܗܕܐ ܟܡܐ ܙܒ̈ܢܝܢ.

> 'The Blessed Interpreter, in his *Book on the Perfection of Disciplines*, greatly praises the monks Eutyches and Cyril—two brothers in the flesh who lived in Antioch—when he says that "words are overcome by the story of their perfection" and ends by saying also, "Because of their long and harsh abstinence, their bodies had become so weak and frail that people who looked at them [only] rapidly thought they saw shadows and not men. Although I mention this about other people, I myself when I was with them often thought the same thing"'.

This provides us with some interesting biographical information about Theodore. We know that he entered a monastery in Antioch which he subsequently left to get married but was later persuaded

---

92 A f° 12v°, G f° 16v°.

93 ܕܝܢ] *om* G

94 ܐܦ] ܕܐܦ G

95 ܗܘ] *om* G

by his friend John Chrysostom to go back again.[96] Our text here seems to reflect his personal monastic experience and the kind of highly ascetic companions he frequented.

DQC II:100[97]

The brothers ask their abba what distinction exists between 'Satan, enticement, sin and passion'. To this Dadishoʿ gives a lengthy reply which is interesting material in itself because of the spiritual analysis he gives and the difference he establishes between the first stirrings of desire and the danger of letting the desire linger on which leads to actual sin. He quotes several passages from Evagrius, Mark the Hermit and finally Theodore who is sandwiched between an Evagrian and a glossed Psalm text at the end of his reply.

ܐܦ ܛܘܒܢܐ ܡܦܫܩܢܐ ܒܟܬܒܐ ܕܓܡܝܪܘܬܐ ܕܡܪ̈ܕܘܬܐ ܗܟܢ ܐܡܪ. ܕܘܠܐ ܗܘ.
ܕܒܟܠܝܘܡ ܢܗܘܐ ܐܓܘܢܐ ܠܐܝܠܝܢ ܕܪܚܡܝܢ ܡܝܬܪܘܬܐ. ܟܕ ܢܦܫܐ ܚܒܝܫܐ[98]
ܒܨܒܘ̈ܬܐ ܕܡܝܬܪܘܬܐ. ܫܐ̈ܕܐ[99] ܕܝܢ[100] ܟܕ ܚܙܝܢ. ܡܥܟܒܝܢ[101] ܠܢ
ܘܡܟܠܝܢ[102] ܠܢ ܡܢ ܦܘܠܚܢܐ ܕܙܕܝܩܘܬܐ. ܡܛܠ ܗܢܐ ܕܡܥܟܒܝܢ ܠܢ ܕܝܘ̈ܐ.
ܘܡܥܝܩܝܢ ܠܢ ܚܫ̈ܐ. ܟܕ ܚܙܝܢ ܕܚܒܝܫܐ ܢܦܫܢ ܠܐܠܗܐ ܡܢ.

'The Blessed Interpreter also says the following in *The Book of Perfection of Disciplines*, "It is necessary that those who desire virtue have warfare every day. When the soul occupies itself with matters of virtue, the demons hinder us by means of the passions and impede us from the practice of justice. When the devils

[96] He addressed two impassioned letters to Theodore on the subject, see Dumortier, *Jean Chrysostome. À Théodore*, pp. 46–79, 220–239; Quasten, *Patrology*, p. 401.

[97] B f° 85v°, C f° 42r°, G f° G92r°.

[98] ܚܒܝܫܐ] ܚܒܝܫܐ CG

[99] ܫܐ̈ܕܐ] *add waw* G

[100] ܕܝܢ] *om* G

[101] ܡܥܟܒܝܢ] ܡܥܟܒܝܢ BG

[102] ܘܡܟܠܝܢ] ܘܡܟܠܝܢ BG ■ *add* ܠܢ G

> make war on us and stir up in us the passions, we must thrust away from us their importunity through labour and prayer'".

The glossed text of Psalm 20:7 which immediately leads on reads as follows. The glossed parts have been highlighted in italics in the translation.

ܘܛܘܒܢܐ ܕܘܝܕ ܐܦ ܐܡܪ. ܕܫܐܕܐ ܒܝܕ ܡܚܫܒܬܐ ܡܩܪܒܝܢ ܥܡܢ ܘܕܝܘ̈ܐ
ܒܚ̈ܫܐ. ܘܚܢܢ ܒܫܡܗ ܕܡܪܝܐ ܐܠܗܢ ܢܚܝܢ. ܕܠܗ ܫܘܒܚܐ ܠܥܠܡܝܢ ܐܡܝܢ

> 'and the blessed David also says, "*The devils make war against us through thoughts and the demons through passions*, but we shall prevail through the name of the Lord our God; *to him be glory for ever amen*"'.

Here we can be quite sure that the Psalm is not part of the *Book of Perfection* but betrays Dadishoʿ's own hand for two reasons. Firstly the fact that we have a series of independent proof texts introduced by 'so-and-so says' following one after another: Evagrius, Theodore, David—so the Psalm is an independent unit which is part of DQC's structure and not a Biblical rider incorporated from Theodore. Secondly, the type of gloss used where a Biblical text is quoted qua Scripture but gets glossed with monastic terminology is quite typical of Dadishoʿ's own style. So we can rest assured that the Theodore quote is only the first block of text.

DQC II:200[103]

The object of the discussion is why it is harder to live in a monastery with other brothers than to tame wild animals or remain unscathed in the middle of a burning fire. Dadishoʿ replies that it is because of the dissolute members of the community whom the devils use as means of harassing the virtuous. The idea is a classic one among our monastic writers and he quotes first from Evagrius and then from Theodore.

---

[103] B f°176r°, C f°129r°, G f°133v°.

ܐܦ [104] ܩܕܝܫ ܕܘܟܪܢܐ [105] ܛܘܒܢܐ ܬܐܕܘܪܘܤ [106] ܡܦܫܩܢܐ. [107]
ܒܟܬܒܐ ܕܥܠ ܓܡܝܪܘܬܐ ܕܝܘܠܦܢ̈ܐ ܐܡܪ [108] ܗܟܢܐ. ܕܐܝܟܢܐ ܕܓܒܪ̈ܐ
ܡܬܟܠܝܢ [109] ܡܢ ܪܗܛܐ ܟܕ ܪܕܝܢ ܥܡ ܛܠܝ̈ܐ ܙܥܘܪ̈ܐ: ܗܟܢܐ ܐܦ ܐܢܫ̈ܐ [110]
ܓܡܝܪ̈ܐ [111] ܡܢ ܗܘܝܐ ܕܥܡ ܐܚ̈ܐ ܣܓܝ̈ܐܐ. ܡܢ ܨܠܘܬܗܘܢ [112] ܘܐܓܘܢܗܘܢ [113]
ܘܢܛܘܪܘܬܗܘܢ.

A 'The blessed Theodore the Interpreter, of holy memory, also says the following in the *Book of Perfection of Disciplines*, "Just as grown men are hindered in a race when they travel with young children, so the perfect are hindered in their prayer, their combat and their observance by being with many brothers."'

The text then continues immediately with:

B 'Those who live alone, even if they are sorely afflicted by the devils through the warfare of thoughts, visions and even blows, yet it is easier for them to endure such things rather than the vexations and trials that befall them in communities because of dissolute and slandering brothers.'

Then:

C 'Hence we see that many famous fathers did not prolong their stays in communities, but abandoned the

---

104 ܐܦ] *add waw* C
105 ܩܕܝܫ ܕܘܟܪܢܐ] *om* C
106 ܬܐܕܘܪܘܤ] ܐܘܓܪܝܤ B ■ ܡܪܩܘܤ C
107 ܡܦܫܩܢܐ] *om* C
108 ܐܡܪ] ܐܡܪ G
109 ܡܬܟܠܝܢ] ܡܬܟܠܝܢ BG
110 ܐܢܫ̈ܐ] *sine seyame* CG
111 ܓܡܝܪ̈ܐ] *add* ܡܬܟܠܝܢ BC
112 ܨܠܘܬܗܘܢ] *cum seyame* G
113 ܘܐܓܘܢܗܘܢ] ܘܐܓܘܢ̈ܝܗܘܢ B

> assemblies of brothers because of them and also the few fathers who shared their discipline and companionship and went away to dwell on their own.'

So the question arises: where does the quote end? It seems safe to assume that C is a separate unit written by Dadishoᶜ's own hand because of the introductory ܡܟܝܠ 'hence' with which it starts, and the change to the 1st person plural. C is in fact an introduction to a series of examples, given by Dadishoᶜ, of Desert Fathers who, tired of community life, returned or went into the desert, we are thus firmly on the grounds of the *Commentary on the Paradise*.

Block B is rather more problematic to decide. I suspect however that we are dealing with Dadishoᶜ's rather than Theodore's writing. Block A is using a metaphor and stands in its own right somewhat after the manner of an aphorism. Block B is somewhat more prosaic and simply restates the argument with which the reply began. The style and vocabulary could also be qualified as being characteristic, or at least not uncharacteristic, of the *Commentary*: devils inflicting blows or wounds (ܡ̈ܚܐ), dissolute (ܪ̈ܦܝܐ) brothers and in particular 'vexations' (ܚ̈ܫܐ) which is used twice again in this very section by Dadishoᶜ—it is not a rare word, to be sure, but it is not such a frequent one as to occur everywhere. I would therefore plead for caution and consider that the quotation from the *Book of Perfection* is limited to block A.

CONCLUSION

This paper has given us the opportunity to make a first perusal of Dadishoᶜ Qatraya's *Commentary on the Paradise of the Fathers* in search of texts written by Theodore of Mopsuestia. For practical reasons this preliminary study has had to be limited to *The Book of Perfection of Disciplines*. As a monastic work, it is not unsurprising that the *Commentary*, itself a monument to monastic scholarship, should prove to be a fruitful source. Though mentioned in other of Dadishoᶜ's works, we never find such a textual wealth of citations as here. This study has thus been able to shed new light on an otherwise almost completely lost work and piece together the fragments in a way never done before. From a methodological point of view, great care has been taken to be able to try and delimit as precisely as possible the textual areas to be attributed to Theodore rather than to Dadishoᶜ.

This however is only the beginning. The other identified texts attributed to Theodore remain to be studied in detail. Interesting and rewarding work thus remains to be undertaken.

THE BOOK OF MONKS: ETHIOPIAN MONASTICISM VIA BETH QATRAYE

ROBERT A. KITCHEN
KNOX-METROPOLITAN UNITED CHURCH

ABSTRACT

The Ethiopian Orthodox Church underwent a remarkable renaissance starting in the 13th century, featuring a major translation movement of earlier Christian patristic texts along with a revival of the monastic calling and institutions. Emerging from this period was the collection of three texts originally composed in Syriac for the education of novice monks in the Ethiopian Church, acquiring the name of The Book of Monks*:* The Commentary on the Paradise of the Fathers *by Dadisho Qatraya;* The Monastic Writings *by Isaac of Nineveh; and the* Writings of the Spiritual Elder *(John Saba or John of Dalyatha). Each of the three texts were likely translated from Christian Arabic into Ge'ez. This paper discusses a version of Dadisho Qatraya's Commentary on the Paradise, Ethiopian Manuscript Microfilm Library no. 1387, examining the character of the translation and editorial decisions of Dadisho's Commentary, as well as how the Ge'ez translators/editors manage the Syriac originals of the other two texts by Isaac of Nineveh and John of Dalyatha.*

IN SEARCH OF BETH QATRAYE

The road to Beth Qatraye began while searching for Ethiopia in the middle of Minnesota. Aware that Philoxenos of Mabbug, the sixth century anti-Chalcedonian bishop and controversialist, was revered in the Ethiopian Church, I traveled to the Hill Museum and Manuscript Library (HMML), St. John's University, Collegeville, Minnesota, and consulted the catalogues of the Ethiopian Manuscript Microfilm Library (EMML) collection of microfilms. I discovered a number of texts attributed to Filekseyus[1] or Philoxenos: a short prayer,[2] a homily of questionable authenticity,[3] and about a dozen long texts with the identifier "Philoxenos of Mabbug, Questions and Answers of the Egyptian Fathers". The Syrian Philoxenos must have known the Desert Fathers, but his writings make little or no reference to these classical stories, so I concluded this was just another pseudonymous text.

A seminar conducted by Sebastian Brock introduced me to Dadisho Qatraya and his *Commentary on the Paradise of the Fathers* (DQC), and referred me to an article by Nicholas Sims-Williams.[4] I was astonished to find one of the representative question/answer units addressed not to an anonymous *sābā* or elder, but to Philoxenos. Sims-Williams noted that there were Ge'ez translations, so connections between the two versions became clear. Going back to HMML, I saw that the Ge'ez manuscripts ('the *Filekseyus*') were indeed translations from the Syriac via Christian Arabic of Dadisho's *Commentary*.

---

[1] Regarding the Ge'ez spelling of Philoxenos, see Witold Witakowski, "Filekseyus, the Ethiopic Version of the Syriac Dadisho Qatraya's Commentary on the Paradise of the Fathers" in *Rocznik Orientalistyczny* 49.1 (2006) 281–296. "The ending *-yus*, instead of the supposed (*Filəksə)-nus* comes from the error, or rather deficiency, of Arabic writing at this time seldom making use of diacritical points. When deprived of their respective diacritical points, Arabic letters *Ya* and *Nun* look the same, and the Ethiopic translator had no clue as to which was the right pronunciation" (285).

[2] "Prayer of Philoxenos"—EMML 1867, 133a–137b; EMML 2213, 169b–175b.

[3] "Homily on how Simeon carried Jesus in his arms" – EMML 1763, 129a–132b.

[4] Nicholas Sims-Williams, "Dādišoᶜ Qatrāyā's Commentary on the *Paradise of the Fathers*", *Analecta Bollandiana* 112 (1994) 33–64.

AFTER-LIFE OF DADISHO'S COMMENTARY: THE BOOK OF THE THREE MONKS

On the surface, Dadisho's work appears to be of a secondary level—a commentary directly building upon previous authors' works, including Ananisho, the early-seventh century East Syrian compiler of the *Paradise of the Fathers*,[5] and of course, the various collections of desert father stories and anecdotes included in that work. Nevertheless, this is more than "just a commentary" which will be evident in how Dadisho's afterlife in Ge'ez is utilized by the Ethiopian Orthodox Church.

The focus here will center upon the *Filekseyus* (F), Dadisho's Ge'ez alter ego, but it was not allowed to remain a solitary text. Following the late 13th century renaissance in Ethiopia, the *Filekseyus* became part of the large *The Book of the Three Monks*, the other two 'monks' being Isaac of Nineveh and John Saba of Dalyatha. This book became the ascetical manual for novice monks for centuries in the Ethiopian Church. Syriac students will immediately notice that all three original authors were from the Church of the East. It has been suggested that Philoxenos' authorship was substituted to provide an orthodox miaphysite or anti-Chalcedonian name to a text otherwise very useful.[6] Yet there is no such veil for Isaac of Nineveh (another Beth Qatraye author) or for John of Dalyatha, and no one seemed to mind or even mention the issue of confessional tradition. All three texts were written from a monastic setting, and the content addresses the practical theology involved in forming an ascetical discipline of prayer and work in the search for the presence of God while living in a community.

---

[5] Budge, Ernest A. Wallis, *The Paradise or Garden of the Holy Fathers, Being Histories of the Anchorites, Recluses, Monks, Coenobites, and Ascetic Fathers of the Deserts of Egypt between A.D. CCL and A.D. CCCC circiter*. London: Chatto & Windus, 1907.

[6] Phillips, David, "The Syriac Commentary of Dadisho' Qatraya on the Paradise of the Fathers: Towards a Critical Edition", *Bulletin de l'Académie Belge pour l'Etude des Langues Anciennes et Orientales* 1 (2012): 1–23.

TEXTS AT HMML

The examination of these three Ge'ez texts is based upon single texts, not a critical edition for the time being, which almost certainly harbour idiosyncratic features. Two come from the same manuscript, Ethiopian Manuscript Microfilm Library No. 1387, Institute of Ethiopian Studies, Addis Ababa, Ethiopia, 18th century. This manuscript begins (1a–81a) with one of the longest versions of the *Filekseyus*, 245 numbered questions by Egyptian monks. The description of the manuscript notes that this text is understood to have been translated initially by Abuna Abba Sälama Matargwem (1348–1388 A.D.). Abuna Sälama was the Coptic patriarch of the Ethiopian Church who unlike some patriarchs took his role seriously, learned Ge'ez and translated a number of important works from Arabic into the Ethiopian language. He was given the title "the Interpreter/Translator" or "*Matargwem*" to whom most of the monks' questions are directed. He is not to be confused with the other "Blessed Interpreter" or Theodore of Mopsuestia, the Biblical exegete of the Church of the East, who is also referred to as *Matargwem*.

Notably, EMML 1387 continues with a short text of Evagrius Ponticus on the author's "Eight Thoughts" (81a–84b), followed by a short homily of Evagrius on aspects of the Christian life (84b–86b). The Monastic Rules of Pachomius (86b–90b) are the next relatively short text. The manuscript concludes with the *Writings of the Spiritual Elder* [Aragāwi Manfasāwi] or John Saba of Dalyatha (91a–201b), a late-eighth century writer. Several units comprise this long text: 37 homilies (*dersān*) (91a–156b); 45 letters (*male'ekt*) (156b–191b); then three treatises on knowledge (191b–200b); and finally a short letter of John Saba to his brother (200b–201a). The *Letters* conform in this manuscript more or less to the Syriac order, although on occasion several *Letters* are given the same number in different locations in the text and seldom match the number of the canonical Syriac order, along with several Ethiopic *Letters* being transcribed out of place.

The *Homilies* begin the text and include 37 *dersān* or discourses. The Syriac version has only 15 homilies, but the Christian Arabic

(29 homilies) and the Ge'ez supply more.[7] Again, the Ethiopic version contains the extant Syriac homilies, but not in their original order. The themes of monastic spirituality and dogmatic issues include essays on the nature of demonic temptations and their avoidance and defeat, the flight from the world, prayer and the necessity and benefit of silence, the attainment of *theoria*, an understanding of the Eucharist within the ascetical and monastic setting, and on his conception of the vision of God. This latter theory would be pivotal in John's condemnation by Timothy I (786/787) on charges of "messalianism".

A second manuscript, Ethiopian Manuscript Microfilm Library No. 1836, Monastery of Ḫayq Esṭifānos, Ambāssal, Wallo, 17th century, contains only two texts: the first being the *Monastic Writings of Isaac of Nineveh [Mār Yeshaq]* (1a–112b), divided into 33 sections or homilies of varying lengths of the so-called First Part of Isaac's corpus, dealing with a familiar range of monastic and contemplative subjects. There is a recent critical edition of this text edited and translated into German by Dawit Berhanu.[8]

It is not all Isaac, however. There are four homilies of John Saba of Dalyatha, followed by an abbreviated version of Philoxenos of Mabbug's *Letter to Patricius*.[9] The authentic Philoxenos had finally found a place in Ge'ez literature, not just in name only. The source of the material for this manuscript almost certainly derives from the textual tradition generated from two Syriac manuscripts: Sinai Syr. 24 and Vatican Syr. 125.[10] The two texts are closely related, both containing

[7] *Jean de Dalyatha. Les Homélies I–XV. Édition critique du texte syriaque inédit, Traduction, introduction et notes by* Nadira Khayatt (Antelias, Lebanon: Centre des Études et de Recherches Orientales – CERO, Université Antonine – UPA, 2007); Brian E. Colless, *The Mystical Discourses of John Saba*, University of Melbourne, 1969 (unpublished dissertation).

[8] *Das Mashafa Mar Yeshaq von Ninive: Einleitung, Edition und Übersetzung mit Kommentar*, ed. Dawit Berhanu (Hamburg: Verlag Dr. Kovač, 1997).

[9] *La lettre à Patricius de Philoxène de Mabboug*, ed. & transl. René Lavenant, *Patrologia Orientalis* 30.5 (Paris: Firmin-Didot, 1963).

[10] Grigory Kessel, "Sinai Syr. 24 as an important witness to the reception history of some Syriac ascetic texts" in *Sur les pas des Araméen chré-*

the principal text of Isaac of Nineveh's First Part, plus four homilies of John of Dalyatha and the abbreviated version of the *Letter to Patricius*. Moreover, this shortened version of *Patricius* would be translated into Greek under Isaac's name and circulate widely.[11]

Another version of the *Filekseyus* (112a–203b) concludes EMML 1836. This latter *Filekseyus* is divided into 13 divisions, numbers 5–13 are thematically organized on the model of the Systematic versions of the *Apophthegmata Patrum*.

ORAL HISTORY AND MEMORY IN THE COMPILATION OF THE TEXT AND MANUSCRIPT

All three texts have multiple copies of varying lengths in the EMML/HMML collections, as well as in the British Library and other libraries.[12] The creation of a critical edition for the *Filekseyus*, for example, will be time-consuming and challenging because of the variations in numbering the question/answer units and among other things, spelling.

Getatchew Haile, the principal cataloguer of the Ethiopian collection at HMML, showed me a large printed volume, published in recent years in Addis Ababa, of *The Book of the Three Monks* with Amharic commentary. I asked from which manuscripts were these texts transcribed. Dr. Haile shook his head and said, "There were no manuscripts; it was transcribed from memory". The scribe was not utilizing a printed copy, but writing down the questions and answers from memory or dictation. This can be readily seen in the

---

tiens. Mélange offerts à Alain Desreumaux, eds F. Briquel-Chatonnet & M. Debié (*Cahiers d'études syriaques 1*; Paris: Geuthner, 2010) 207–218.

[11] See, Sebastian P. Brock, "Syriac into Greek at Mar Saba: The Translation of St. Isaac the Syrian" in J. Patrich, ed., *The Sabaite Heritage in the Orthodox Church from the Fifth Century to the Present* (OLA 98; Leuven, 2001) 201–208.

[12] Manuscripts of the *Filekseyus* in HMML are: EMML 15, 17th or 18th century, 183r–247v; EMML 418, 18th or early 19th century, 3r–80v; EMML 1387, 18th century, 1r–81r; EMML 1836, 17th century, 112r–203v; EMML 1848, 20th century (1951/52), 2r–112r; EMML 2100, 17th century, 163r–223r; EMML 2127, 19th–20th century, 10r–162v; EMML 2837, 17th or 18th century, 4r–81v.

spelling of EMML 1387 that operates from a phonetic, not orthographic basis. The scribe is most likely reciting to himself the text and recording it, but Geʿez has a number of pairs of letters with distinct Semitic roots, but over time these have lost their phonetic distinction. So the scribe writes what he hears himself reciting and on the same page will often spell the same word in several different ways, yet these words all are pronounced homophonically.

Another piece of evidence for this transcription from memory is the frequent occurrence of a lengthy answer by Dadisho or by an elder/*sābā* in which the Syriac text contains a complex of ideas and recollection of stories from the *Paradise*. The Ethiopic edition omits some of these sections and rearranges the order of the elements of the answer, not always in a manner that flows coherently with the original narrative. This needs further analysis and comparison with the Christian Arabic versions and could be the result of scribal variants, but just as likely it is the Ethiopian scribe transcribing what he remembers and then remembers later on a story or apophthegm he had forgotten and writes it down out of the original order. Typically, the first and last sentences or statement function as the theme and conclusion for the Ethiopic version of what is a lengthy, anecdote-filled Syriac question/answer unit—pithy propositions easier to remember.

The *Filekseyus* of EMML 1387 is a lengthy text that follows the Syriac version in order and in structure with two books or parts of uneven length. The first part has 53 question/answer units; the second part has 192 units. Whereas the translator of the *Filekseyus* follows the trajectory of the DQC this is not a full and complete version, although much larger than a translation of the shorter Epitome version of DQC.[13] The DQC in David Philip's critical edition has 399 question/answer units, divided between 108 for the first part and 291 for the second part, so that the editor/translator of *Filekseyus* made a number of choices regarding which units to include or omit, and within a question/answer unit there is a great

[13] This shorter version is found in two manuscripts: British Library Add. 17175 & Vatican Syr. 126. Paul Bedjan transcribes the latter manuscript in *AMS* VII: 895–963. See, Phillips, "The Syriac Commentary of Dadisho", 16–18.

deal of omission of details, events and names from the Syriac, as well as attempts to summarize and abbreviate the original narrative. A single Ge'ez unit's answer sometimes includes the answers of several units of DQC, and a few units in the second part of the *Filekseyus* are taken from the first part of DQC. The translator/editor generally follows the sequence of DQC with a few exceptions, but there is a lengthy section in which *Filekseyus* selects every second question/answer of DQC.

A number of apophthegmata concern a famous abba traveling with another well-known abba in the Syriac version, but in the Ge'ez version the second name is often not remembered and reduced to "a companion" at best. Periodically dispersed throughout the DQC is the formulaic question of the monks, "How many people were called Macarius?" The elder responds with a summary description of the various abbas with the same name. One assumes that these trivia questions are intended as mnemonic devices for the novices, but the *Filekseyus* dispenses with all of these questions. If the medium is the message, the editor does not need to have the monks simply memorizing lists of names.

The critical hermeneutical key to understanding the purpose and use of this translation is that seven and more centuries later, the Ethiopian Orthodox Church is not primarily interested in the scholarship of the Desert Father legacy of stories and personalities. The intent of the *Filekseyus* is to immerse the novice monk in the spiritual lore of the monastic vocation, and to saturate his mind and spirit with advice and warnings about the pitfalls of aiming to be perfect while remaining nevertheless an imperfect human being. The names of the great Egyptian ascetics, to be sure, are recited as spiritual models and heroes, through both their positive and negative adventures.

EVAGRIUS PONTICUS

Despite *Filekseyus* avoiding trivial names, the translator does not refrain from citing two major theologians—Theodore of Mopsuestia and Evagrius Ponticus. Theodore (d. 428) was adopted by the Church of the East as its Biblical exegete and theologian, and was conferred the title "the Blessed Interpreter". Nevertheless, it is to Evagrius that Dadisho and *Filekseyus* turn most frequently for wisdom and counsel.

The most remarkable aspect of Evagrius' life and writings is his posthumous reception in Eastern Christian thought. The Greek intellectual of the early Desert Fathers, Evagrius died in 399 as a consequence of his severe asceticism just as the so-called Origenist controversy erupted. At the Second Council of Constantinople, 553, Origenism was formally condemned, but it was really against Evagrius' ideas that the Council was reacting. Evagrius' writing and concepts did not go away and were adopted by spiritual writers in both Greek and Syriac traditions, Armenian, Arabic and Ethiopian as well. The Church of the East was particularly attracted to Evagrius' concepts, and all three of our writers here utilize Evagrius persistently. In an article on Philoxenos of Mabbug's engagement with Evagrius, Robin Darling Young observed that the stigma of Evagrius' reputed heterodoxy was not evident to Philoxenos and other writers because they appeared to know or use only his writings on the prayer and spiritual life.[14] The passages in DQC and *Filekseyus* where Evagrius is cited are mostly anecdotes of his conversations and advice to other monks from the *Apophthegmata Patrum* and *Lausiac History* of Palladius.

In F 6 (DQC 1.16) the brothers ask about Abba Ammonias who was reported to burn himself and other severe austerities, including cutting off his right ear, whenever the passion of fornication afflicted him. The Interpreter concludes by observing that "Abba Evagrius said regarding him, 'I have not seen anyone who has surpassed passion more than him.'" Students of Evagrius will recognize the variant expression 'surpassing passion' or passionlessness or apatheia in Greek, *lā ḥāšūšūtā* in Syriac.

F 96 (DQC 2.74) consists only of a question by the brothers, which in the Syriac version is the response of Dadisho, one way or another a citation of Evagrius. "Only when one begins in the battle of thoughts does his soul come to be purified and enlightened by the light of grace. Mar Evagrius said, 'Just as Satan petitioned God

[14] Robin Darling Young, "The Influence of Evagrius of Pontus" in *To Train His Soul in Books: Syriac Asceticism in Early Christianity*, edit. Robin Darling Young & Monica J. Blanchard (CUA Studies in Early Christianity 5; Washington, DC: Catholic University of America Press, 2011) 157–175, esp. 170.

regarding Job, in the same way Satan seeks out every soul that is beginning to be enlightened and shine so that grace may be a little too far from it and [the soul] becomes stronger than [grace] in order to show its steadfastness and love which is in God, but then suddenly many evil things will come upon it.'" This is not theological speculation, but Evagrius' practical experience that enables him to alert the brothers to the inevitable struggles and perils of faith. However, in F 119 (DQC 2.112) Evagrius is cited for what appears to be the opposite sentiment. "The wise Evagrius said, 'One will be better when he does not enter into conflict.'"

In terms of ascetical discipline, Evagrius summarizes a premodern conception of the human physiology especially pertinent to monks. F 43 (DQC 1.98) has the brothers ask, "[Why was] Mar Evagrius commanding the brothers not to be satiated with water? *The Interpreter said:* … the fathers said that those who do not reduce eating and drink too much water do not defeat the spirit of fornication nor perfect righteousness. There is nothing that dries up the flesh and prevents one from dreaming and waking and wandering and still the impure thought during the daytime. Although one may be thirsty if one fasts and reduces drinking, he does not benefit by drinking a great amount of water, filling his stomach and increasing the moistness of his flesh. [It is] then the demon will find an occasion to seduce him with thoughts during the day and with dreams at night. Mar Evagrius said, 'If you wish to be pure, then reduce [your] eating and it will restrain you from drinking water, and at once purity of heart will shine and your mind will shine like a star you will see in your prayer.'"[15] Again, Evagrius is received as one who brings practical methodology to the monastic life, even though we are no longer certain it is correct advice.

PERFECTION AGAIN

Dadisho/*Filekseyus*' commentary turns out to have something surprising tucked into a corner out in full view or "in between the

---

[15] See *Evagrius Ponticus. The Greek Ascetic Corpus*, transl. Robert E. Sinkewicz (New York: Oxford University Press, 2003) – *Praktikos* no. 17, p. 101.

lines". In the first logia, F 1 (DQC 1.2)—a rambling introductory discourse punctuated with a few apophthegmata—an elder declares that there are two levels in the Christian life: the Upright (*kēnē/ḫīrān*) and the Perfect (*gmīrē/feṣūmān*) and discusses and compares the qualities of these two groups. "The perfect way of life is thus the way of life of Elijah and Matthew and Hanna and Mary the sister of Martha. The way of life of Matthew and Elijah is better than the way of life of Abraham and Zacchaeus. And the labour of Hanna and Mary is better than the labour of Sarah and Martha. It is not in [his manner of] thinking, but in [his] way of life because Abraham was perfect in his thinking with regard to the friendship of God and humanity and his animals in the world. God loved this person because Christ would come to be from his seed".

Dadisho and *Filekseyus* employ the same vocabulary regarding the institution of the Upright and Perfect described in only two earlier Syriac works: the late fourth-century *Book of Steps/Liber Graduum*[16] and the late fifth/early sixth-century *Discourses* of Philoxenos of Mabbug.[17]

For Isaac of Nineveh and John of Dalyatha, perfection is only accomplished by a person in the eschaton, in the kingdom of heaven. One can mimic perfection in this worldly life, but the authentic theological status is always elusive here and so must await fulfilment in the New World, an eschatological state of divine completeness and fullness. The phenomenon seen in these texts in front of and behind the scenes is the difficult practice of structuring these ideals into a worldly physical way of life in church and society. However, once acquiring the regularities and routines of institutional existence, these levels become prone to human inadequacies and even to sin!

---

[16] *The Book of Steps: The Syriac Liber Graduum*, English translation and Introduction by Robert A. Kitchen & Martien F. G. Parmentier (Cistercian Studies 196; Kalamazoo, MI: Cistercian Publications, 2004), xxxviii–xlix.

[17] *The Discourses of Philoxenos of Mabbug: A New Translation and Introduction* by Robert A. Kitchen (Cisterican Studies 235; Collegeville, Minnesota: Cistercian/Liturgical Press, 2013) xliv–lvi.

Since there were no other known witnesses to its occurrence in later texts or chronicles, the adaptation of the Upright and Perfect to a monastic situation appears to indicate that this ecclesiastical innovation was no longer active in the secular church.

In F 3 (DQC 4–5), the definition of the Perfect is given: "As it is written: 'If you wish to become perfect, take up your cross and come after me' which is his boundary—renunciation from place and family and possession and wife and children, and the departure from the world and the endurance of the austerities of solitude.' Someone in the world, the Upright, who is married and serves the sick and afflicted, is never equal to those three solitaries mentioned earlier. Christ calls the 'virtuous worldly ones' 'the sons of the world' and the holy ones or solitaries 'the sons of light.'"

A brief simile in DQC 6 offers an important fact: "just as the worldly faithful ones *bring the solitaries into their houses and receive and comfort [them]*; in the same way also the solitaries bring the faithful ones to the kingdom of heaven and receive them in their tabernacles of light and comfort and give [them] pleasure". This reference to the Upright providing for and assisting the Perfect mirrors the practice in the *Book of Steps* of the Upright serving the physical needs of the Perfect, though the practice is mentioned only a few times. Notably, *Filekseyus* omits this passage, which might indicate that this institution was no longer in favour in such an organized physical manner in the Ethiopian Church. Nevertheless, in *F* 239 [DQC 2.280] a clear picture of interdependence between the worldly Christians and the solitaries is outlined. "The worldly ones care for the solitaries with their alms through their possessions, and the solitaries care for the worldly ones through their prayers for them and their concern for them. The solitaries share physical [concerns] with the earthly ones, and with the spiritual ones the worldly ones share in heavenly [concerns]". Although this is an irenic statement without specific details, it implies an ideal mode of relationship to be promoted in the Ethiopian church.

In the *Book of Steps* this service of the inferior to the superior becomes an apparent source of jealousy, rivalry and conflict, even violent reprisals. This theme is rehearsed in several subsequent questions: Are the virtuous worldly ones inferior in virtue and reward to beginning solitaries, even the disturbed and dissolute solitaries sometimes noted by Dadisho? Dadisho/*Filekseyus* reply without hesitation that the virtuous worldly are inferior even to those

Perfect of imperfect ascetical fibre. The author of *Book of Steps* is insistent upon a significant gap between Upright and Perfect which can only be bridged by the radical renunciation of possessions and of family life, i.e., celibacy, no matter how good the Upright may have become and how poorly and imperfectly the Perfect have behaved. Philoxenos does not draw such strict boundaries since the Upright are for the most part novice monks who have already renounced the world and family—they are still living mentally in the world and just have not forgotten what they have left behind.

These passages unveil a third chapter of the 'categories/levels/steps' previously only evidenced in the *Book of Steps* and the *Discourses* of Philoxenos, another 150–175 years after Philoxenos, still based in the monastery—Church of the East rather than Miaphysite, but as with *Book of Steps* located in the Persian/Islamic empires—yet apparently in relationship with the worldly Upright. Are there witnesses to its existence in other contemporary texts, perhaps in an unedited or un-translated manuscript?[18] In the interim, a more complete picture needs to be constructed regarding how this institutional paradox of the Virtuous Upright of the world being inferior to the Less Than Perfect of the monastery was al-

---

[18] Nicholas Marinides has directed me to the Syriac Life of Maurice the Emperor: "Histoire de Saint Maurice, Empereur des Romains", edited & translated by L. Leroy & F. Nau in *Patrologia Orientalis* 5 (1910) 773–778. Also, John Wortley, "The Legend of the Emperor Maurice", *Actes du XVe Congrès Internationale d'Études Byzantines, Athènes – Septembre 1976*, vol. 4 (Athens, 1980) 382–391. The latter article deals with the Greek version, but refers to the quite different Syriac. Maurice prays to God constantly for assurance and guidance on how to attain perfection. An angel appears and tells him he has sinned enough that he won't reach perfection, but will still be counted with the righteous (*zadīqē*) at his death. If he desires the higher degree, however, he must submit to martyrdom. Maurice would agree, and was murdered by Phocas (602 C.E.). Regardless of the hagiographical elements, this indicates the continued existence of the upright and perfect dichotomy, a lower level of salvation and a higher existence, in the seventh century, roughly contemporaneous with Dadisho Qatraya.

lowed to exist and for how long, another piece to the puzzle of early Syriac asceticism.

EUCHARISTIC ENCOUNTERS

The emergence of the monastic movement, especially with the phenomenon of the desert fathers in Egypt and beyond, seemed to discourage, even denigrate Eucharistic celebrations. Phil Booth argues that after the Council of Chalcedon in 451, the Eucharist revived as the central identifier for several emerging traditions.[19] Holy men were no longer focusing solely upon their inner spiritual development and athletic ascetical feats, but also in their faithfulness to the liturgical unity of their church. In the late-seventh century Dadisho would have been living during this period in which the validity of Eucharistic celebration for monks and solitaries would no longer be neglected, but would be considered an essential aspect of authentic holiness. Two stories which both Dadisho and *Filekseyus* elect to include in their question/answer units are not the usual depictions of a Eucharistic communion, yet portray an unusual engagement and passion in the sacrament. Celebrating communion in both instances emphasizes, not diminishes, the holy man's sanctity.

F 10 (DQC 1.27) *The brothers said*: "Why is it that Abba Macarius the Alexandrian did not spit for 60 years from the time he was baptized until the time he died?

The Interpreter said: On account of his reception of the holy mysteries. In this way it was fitting that he would drink water or eat consecrated bread after his reception of the holy mysteries. Look, did not the fathers say to us when saliva comes up after the Eucharist, before one drinks water or eats the consecrated bread, then let him swallow it? But if his soul is great, let him wipe it on a piece of his clothing".

This answer is greatly abbreviated from the Syriac, but still retains accurately the essence of the original. Omitted from the Syriac

---

[19] Phil Booth, *Crisis of Empire: Doctrine and Dissent at the End of Late Antiquity* (Transformation of the Classical Heritage 52; Berkeley: University of California Press, 2013).

version is the further option for the monk who finds himself expectorating saliva at the wrong moment is to wipe the saliva on his beard. The visceral nature of this answer indicates a strong belief in the Real Presence of Christ during the Eucharist, and whether sixty years is hagiographical exaggeration or not, the intent of the story is to illustrate that the Eucharist is an integral part of the monastic life and identity which must not be engaged in a casual manner.

F 17 (DQC 1.34) *From the second division. The brothers said*: "Interpret for us the word of Abba Macarius the Elder who said, 'Now, I have never offered [the Eucharist] to Mark the mourner, for an angel of the Lord was presenting it to him with his hand from the altar.'

The Interpreter said: In ancient times in the Egyptian desert there was one governing the monastery who alone was consecrating the Eucharist until the time of his departure. According to what Palladius said, eight priests were governing the monastery of Barnug, but as long as the first one was living there was no functioning as a priest for any of [the others]. There was only one priest and one deacon ministering the entire year to the solitaries who were in the cells of Antioch, and Macarius the Elder was consecrating [the Eucharist] by himself. There appeared the hand of an angel between him and the hand [lit. skin] of Mark, just as one of the seraphim had done when he took the fiery coal from the altar and placed it into the mouth of Isaiah the prophet,[20] and an angel was acting in this way because angels do not have the authority to consecrate the Eucharist and give it to people. But on account of Mark's great purity and humility by which another might imitate him and the fame of his struggles, he possessed four virtues which do not fall upon any other due to his struggles, for his purity in his soul and body and his humility is greater—two gifts are of God which strengthened the Old and New [Testaments] in his heart and his knowledge of their faithful interpretation, and the reception of the Eucharist from the hand of an angel".

The point of this hagiographical tale is to underline the sanctity of Mark since the sacred mysteries of the Eucharist are not shared with him by a mere human being, but by an angel. There

[20] Isaiah 6:6–7

could be other ways in which to exemplify Mark's holiness, but it is significant that his holiness is manifested specifically in the reception of the Eucharist, not in an ascetical accomplishment. Needless to say, Macarius the Elder's monopolization of the celebration of the Eucharist may not witness to his generosity, but it does emphasize what he believed to be of fundamental importance to his ascetical pilgrimage.

QUESTIONS AND ANSWERS

The obvious distinctiveness about these texts of Dadisho and *Filekseyus* is that they are examples of the question/answer genre which Classical and Byzantine scholars call *erotapokriseis*". Recent years have seen a revival in the study of this genre of literature in Late Antiquity, which occurs in Syriac literature as well, Bas ter Haar Romeny being the principal scholar of this phenomenon.[21] Romeny describes a number of the occurrences of this genre, largely in Church of the East circles, and notes that the questions of most of these examples are based upon a text, the Biblical text the most frequent. The DQC and *Filekseyus* are in fact based upon a text, the *Paradise of the Fathers*, itself a compilation of other texts of a similar genre.

Form does lead to function. The *Sitz Im Leben* of these questions and answers appears to be located in a monastic setting in which mostly novice monks are seated around an abba and playing with the text that is already very familiar to them. Their questions are at times simple trivia, yet often inquiring about the deeper and sometimes plain meaning of challenging stories and conversations from the *Paradise*. Certainly, the structure of this commentary provides an excellent tool for the monks to memorize and master the various apophthegmata, absorbing eventually the spiritual direction written in the answers, as well as in between the lines.

---

[21] Bas ter Haar Romeny, "Question-and-Answer Collections in Syriac Literature", in *Erotapokriseis: Early Christian question-and-answer literature in context*, edited by Annelie Volgers & Claudio Zamagni (Leuven: Peeters, 2004) 145–163.

I wish to pose what are likely unanswerable questions. Was Dadisho's *Commentary* an artificial construction of the author or did it derive out of actual questions and answers put forth by the novice monks in his monastery? That might help explain the selection of passages, deriving from the needs of the monks rather than the didactic instincts of the old man. Certainly, *Filekseyus* was making even more of these decisions and selection. Most likely the truth lies somewhere in between, although ultimately indiscernible.

What I have touched upon is the nature of the questions in these different examples of *erotapokriseis* and their social provenance. Dadisho focuses more emphatically on monastic culture and conundrums than the famous questions and answers of Barsanuphius and John,[22] and those of Anastasios of Sinai,[23] both of whom provided practical and spiritual counsel primarily to lay people who came to the monastery seeking advice. On one level, this is a commentary on a set text and the text sets the substance of the questions. But there is a persistent tone throughout this lengthy work that the questions arise out of the needs, concerns and anxieties of the brothers. Dadisho has much to say regarding many of their questions and sometimes even answers the point of their question. In the long run, however, in the original Syriac setting in the monasteries of the Persian Church of the East living amidst the new political and religious reality of Islam, and then among the Arabic-speaking Syrian churches, and finally in the Ethiopian Church, those who read and profited most from Dadisho's answers were the less-experienced monks who found in reading this *Commentary* the kind of questions they needed to ask in order to progress in the monastic and spiritual life, and sometimes the very questions they were burning to ask.

---

[22] Barsanuphius and John, *Letters.* Volumes 1–2, transl. John Chryssavgis, (The Fathers of the Church 113/114; Washington, DC: The Catholic University of America Press, 2006/2007).

[23] M. Richard & J. Munitiz (eds), *Anastasii Sinaïtae: Quaestiones et responsiones (*CCSG 59; Turnhout, Belgium: Brepols 2006); English translation: J. Munitiz (transl.), *Anastasios of Sinai: Questions and Answers* (CCT 7; Turnhout, Belgium: Brepols, 2011).

Manuscripts of the *Filekseyus* in the Hill Museum & Manuscript Library collection:

EMML 15, 17th or 18th century, 183r–247v.
EMML 418, 18th or early 19th century, 3r–80v.
EMML 1387, 18th century, 1r–81r.
EMML 1836, 17th century, 112r–203v.
EMML 1848, 20th century (1951/52), 2r–112r.
EMML 2100, 17th century, 163r–223r.
EMML 2127, 19th-20th century, 10r–162v.
EMML 2837, 17th or 18th century, 4r–81v.

THE INFLUENCE OF CHRISTIANITY AMONG THE ARAB TRIBES IN THE GULF AREA DURING THE SIXTH AND SEVENTH CENTURIES A.D.

SAIF SHAHEEN AL-MURIKHI
QATAR UNIVERSITY

ABSTRACT

This study surveys the role and activity of Nestorian Christian scholars and clerics in spreading Nestorian Christianity in the Gulf region throughout the sixth and seventh centuries. It also examines the role, influence and contribution of the Arab tribes that witnessed the spread of Christianity in east Arabia before and after they embraced Islam; namely, on the political, economic and social life of the Gulf region.

Before the advent of Islam, Christianity spread in the Gulf region mainly through the Syriac Church of the East, known in sources as "Nestorianism". Christianity was then embraced by many Arab tribes living in the Bahrain region which, at that time, stretched in east Arabia from Kazma in Kuwait to Ras-al-Khayma in the United Arab Emirates. In the Syriac sources the Bahrain region was known as *Beth Qatraye*, and was politically a part of the Sasanian Empire. Churches, monasteries and missionary centers were found in the larger, prosperous cities and villages, and the Christians of the Church of the East also maintained good political, religious and economical relations with the Christians of Iraq and Persia.

When Islam appeared in the seventh century and the Arab Muslim state was established, Muslims in the Gulf region faced two different faith communities: one was pagan and the other had embraced Christianity. Followers of paganism quickly and decisively converted to Islam and became integrated into the newly established Muslim society, finding in Islam reason and ethical content, as well as a strong organizational structure that was lacking among the scattered pagan tribes. However Islam spread slowly among followers of monotheistic religions, especially Christianity, because of its strong, coherent ecclesiastical organization, its network of shelters and monasteries, and the education and health care provided by Christian institutions. A sizeable portion of the Christian population in the region therefore held on to their religion until the ninth and tenth centuries.

This paper surveys Nestorian Christianity's spread of influence, and examines the role and activity of Nestorian Christian scholars and clerics in spreading Nestorian Christianity in the Gulf region throughout the sixth and seventh centuries. It sheds light on the role, influence and contribution of the Arab tribes that witnessed the spread of Christianity in east Arabia before and after their embrace of Islam; namely, on their political, economic and social life in the Arab Muslim state.

This study covers the end of the fifth century to the seventh century—one of the most prolific periods of prosperity and expansion for the Syriac Church of the East. In this period, monks, clerics and merchants succeeded in spreading Christianity, especially the Nestorian doctrine, throughout the so-called Bahrain region: from Kazma (Kuwait) to the northern part of the Omani coast (Ras Al-Khayma – United Arab Emirates).

THE HISTORICAL SOURCES

There are a number of historical sources which deal with Qatar and Bahrain during the seventh century: *Tarikh al-Tabari*, al-Tabari's History, the book on the Apostles and Kings, by Muhammad ibn Jarir al-Tabari (d. 825), and the book *Futuh al-Buldan* by al-Baladhuri (d. 909). These are important sources that provide information concerning the activity of religious, political, economic and cultural development of the population of Qatar and its neighboring regions since the advent of Islam in the seventh century and until the nineteenth century

Muruj al Dhahab wa ma'aden al Jawhar by Abu al-Hasan Ali bin Al Hussein al-Masudi (d. 958) is another important historical source. Al-Masudi discusses the incidence and prevalence of Christianity in the Arabian Peninsula before Islam and the names of a number of men of Arab tribes who professed the Christian religion at the advent of

Mujam al-Buldan and *al-Khazal wa al-Dal bain al-Dur wa al-Darat wa al-Diarah*, by Yāqūt al-Hamawī (d. 1228) are also of great importance in providing us with valuable information about sites and geographic regions, cities and villages, in the Arab Gulf region before Islam and during the Islamic conquests, as well as the names of certain sites and areas, and some churches and monasteries and religious centers in the Gulf region.

THE GULF IN THE SASANIAN PERIOD

The Sasanian state was established on the ruins of the Parthian Empire at the beginning of the second century and assumed control of large parts of its borders and its properties. It was considered a continuation and extension of the Persian Empire. Its capital city was al-Mada'in and its influence extended across large areas of the Arabian Peninsula and in particular the areas and regions which overlooked the Arabian Gulf, the Arabian Sea, and the Red Sea. Sasanians took control of Yemen, Oman and Bahrain, and these regions were subjected politically, militarily, and economically to Sasanian sovereignty from the second century until the beginning of the seventh century.

As a result of its geo-strategic location, the province of Bahrain captured the attention of the Sasanian State and trade relations and economic and religious ties between the inhabitants of this province and the inhabitants of the Sasanian state were strengthened.

The province of Bahrain in that period extended along the east of the Arabian Peninsula of Kazma (Kuwait) to the northern coast of Oman (today's United Arab Emirates). Ibn Manẓūr's dictionary (*Lisān al-ʿArab*) describes Bahrain as: "a territory between Basra and Oman".[1] al-Bakri's description of the territory of Bahrain is as follows:

---

[1] Ibn Manzur, *Lisān al-Arab*, (article by Bahr).

> It is a vast country to the east, has a sea coast and to the west it is connected to Al-Yamamah and to the north Basra and Oman, and to the south it is connected to the province of Oman. It has plains and many rivers as well as wells gushing forth fresh water one man or even two men in height, henna and cotton plants on its river banks are like lilies, a land with myriad palm trees and fruits".[2]

The most important cities and villages of the province of Bahrain were:

> al-Khat, al-Qatif, al-Arra, and Hajer and its capital (al-Safa), al-Baynuna, al-Zara, Jowana, al-Sabour, Darin, al-Ghaba, al-Moshaqar, al-Haws, al-Kathif al Akbar and al-Kathib al-Asghar. Ard Nouh, dhou-al-Naar, al-Maleha, al-Zaraeb Kazma and Qatar.[3]

Yaqout al-Hamawi simplifies his description of the geographic borders of the Gulf (which he called the 'Persian Sea'), saying:

> It is a division of the great Indian Sea … borders with al-Tiz from the side of Makran on the shores of the Persian Sea along to Abadan, this is the bed of the river, which the Tigris flows into. It is also the first arm of the Persian Sea on the coast from the side of Basra and Abadan.

On the eastern coast of the Persian Gulf were the Persian Sea, the Bahraini Sea and Oman, and on the western side as well as to the north and the south was the Land of the Arabs.[4]

The city of Hajer was the provincial capital of Bahrain and the place where the political ruler, who was appointed by the Persians, resided. Before Islam the land of Bahrain had been a part of the Persian Empire. During this period Bahrain enjoyed a degree of political autonomy and this was evident in the rapid embrace of

---

[2] Al-Bakri (ʿAbd Allāh b. ʿAbd al-ʿAziz) *al –Masālik wa-ʿl-mamālik*, vol 1, pp. 370–371.

[3] Ibn Al-Faqih, *Mukhtasar kitāb al-buldān*, p. 89; Al-Hamadani, sifat Jazirat al-ʿArab, p. 84.

[4] Yaqut, *Muʿjam al-buldān*, vol.1, pp. 346–348.

Islam by the people of Bahrain and its leaders and the absence of any political or military resistance to this from the Sasanian state and its rulers in the region.

THE RISE OF ISLAM

During the time of the Prophet Muhammad, the Persian ruler Sibukhit governed the province of Bahrain, and ruled from the city of Hajer. There were a number of Arab tribes living in the area surrounding Hajer, the most famous of which were the tribes of ʿAbdul Qays, Bakr Bin Wael and Tamim. They had two appointed rulers from the Persians, namely al-Munzer Bin Sawa al-ʿAbdi and Abdullah Bin Zayd al-Asbadhi.[5]

When Islam gained popularity in the Peninsula, and spread among the Arab tribes, a delegation from the tribes of Abdul-Qays in Bahrain led by al-Jaroud Bin al-Maʾli (who was a Christian)[6] met with the Prophet Muhammad and accepted Islam. Islamic resources narrate that al-Jaroud remained as a pious Muslim who strictly followed Islam until the end of his life.[7]

The Prophet Muhammad sent al-ʿAlaa al-Hadrami to Bahrain to invite its people to embrace Islam. He also sent a personal letter to al-Munzer Bin Sawa and another to Sibukhit, the ruler of Hajer, as well as to the whole population of Bahrain. They all accepted Islam—both the Arab and non-Arab tribes.[8] Louis Cheikho mentions that al-Munzer Bin Sawa al-ʿAbdi was a Christian before he embraced Islam.[9]

Prior to the advent of Islam, Christianity had spread among the Arab tribes such as ʿAbdul Qays, Bakr Bin Wael and Tamim, who lived in the province of Bahrain. Among the prominent dignitaries from ʿAbdul-Qays, was Bohira al-Raheb (The Monk). Bohira, who embraced Christianity before the rise of Islam in the region,

---

[5] Al-Baladhuri, *Futuh al-Buldan*, pp. 106–107; Yaqut, *Muʿjam al-buldān*, vol.1, p. 348.

[6] Al-Tabari, *Tārikh*, vol. 3, p. 136.

[7] Al-Tabari, *Tārikh*, vol. 3, p. 136.

[8] Yaqut, *Muʿjam al-buldān*, vol.1, p. 348.

[9] Cheikho, *Al-Nasraniah wa Adabaha*, p. 71.

was known among the Christians as Gergis Bin Abdul-Qays. He had a monastery where he worshiped called al-Baqe'i (also known as Deir al-Raheb)[10] in the city of Bosra in the Levant on the trade route of the tribes coming from al-Hijaz and Yemen.[11]

Islamic resources narrate that when Muhammad was twelve years old he met Bahira in the town of Bosra in Syria, during his travels with a Meccan caravan, accompanying his Uncle Abu Talib ibn ʿAbd al-Muttalib. A miraculous occurrence indicated to the monk that Muhammad was to become a prophet and that he would have great fame. The monk revealed his visions to the boy's uncle (Abu Talib) and urged him to hurry back to Mecca with the child.[12]

CHRISTIANITY IN THE GULF

The Nestorian church emerged in Antioch at the beginning of the fifth century, around 428, and then spread gradually to the Levant, Persia, and subsequently to the province of Bahrain. Nestorian church traditions were spread widely through Bahrain by Nestorian missionaries.

The Nestorian church tradition emphasizes the disunion between the human and divine natures of Jesus. According to the Nestorians, the nature of Christ is divided equally between His divine nature and His human nature, but the two are distinct and separate. This idea goes against the beliefs of other Christian dominations who believe in the hypostatic union, which states that Christ's one nature was fully God and fully man.

Although Zoroastrianism and Monism—the official religions of the Persian Empire—were pagan religions, Persian authorities demonstrated a great deal of religious tolerance. The establishment of churches was sporadically permitted in different parts of the Empire, and followers of the Nestorian church tradition were permitted to preach Christianity among the people of Persia, Iraq and different parts of today's Gulf region.

---

10 Yaqut, *Kitab al-Khazal wa al-Dal*, vol. 1, p. 282; vol. 2, p. 40.

11 Al-Masudi, *Muruj al-Dhahab*, vol. 1, pp. 89–90.

12 Ibn Ishaq, *Sirat Ibn Ishaq*, pp. 53–55.

Furthermore, the province of Bahrain and its inhabitants were known for their intellectual openness due to the close ties and rapport between the Bahraini tribes and the people of Hira, and in particular the Christians among them. The Christians of Hira, referred to as *ʿIbad* ('servants' of Christ or worshippers of God), belonged to different tribes and were known for their knowledge, religion and culture. At this time, more than fifty Christian schools were active in Iraq.[13] These Christian schools taught—alongside religious studies—Greek philosophy, medicine, chemistry and mathematics. Furthermore, the al-Moshaqar market in Bahrain would attract a large number of traders from Hira and other cities and states in the Arab Peninsula and beyond:

> in the city of al-Moshaqar, the Arabs have a market that starts on Jumada al-Akhira and lasts until the end of the month. Then market visitors would leave to Jmai at Qabel, Arabs from all around come to attend…whenever there are passersby they stay behind for the market, they would go to Hajer, they come from everywhere in Arabia and elsewhere.[14]

Syriac was the official religious language for the followers of the Nestorian church tradition.[15] Ibn Habib tells us:

> Syriac[16] was the spoken tongue of five of the prophets: Idris (traditionally identified with the Biblical Enoch), Noah, Ibrāhīm (Abraham), Lūṭ, (known as Lot) and Yūnus (also spelled Younis).

Ibn al-Nadeem mentions that the Syrians had three typefaces:

> al-Maftouh which is called the *Asternagala* being the most elaborate and beautiful, it is also called the Heavy script which resembles the *mushaf* script. Then the *al-Tahrir al-Mukhafaf*, known as *Iskolthia* which is called the Rounded typeface which is equivalent to *al-Waraqeen*. Thirdly, al-*Sarta* and it is used for

---

13 Rafael Babu Ishaq, *Tarikh Nasara al-Iraq*, pp. 20–22.
14 Al-Afghani, *Aswaq al- ʿArab fi al-Jāhiliyyah wa-ʾl-Islām*, p. 241
15 Jawād Ali, *al-Mufassal fi tārikh al-ʿArab qabla al-Islām*, vol.6, p. 628.
16 Ibn Habib al-Salami, *Kitab al-Tarikh*, p. 20.

formal correspondences and is equivalent to *al-Raqaa* script in Arabic.[17]

Prayers and worship were written and recited in Syriac in the Gulf region. Syriac was also used as the language of teaching and learning in churches and monasteries, and it began to be used in cultural and intellectual writings. Most of the manuscripts, writings and intellectual heritage of the religious and intellectual Christians who lived at the time, e.g. Isaac the Syriac, Gabriel, and others from among the clergy, scientists and intellectuals, were written in Syriac.

A large number of churches and monasteries were scattered amongst the towns and villages of Iraq and Persia, indicating the spread of Christianity in these areas and its spread among the local population. In his book *al-Khazal and al Dal: Bayna al Dour wal Daraat wal Diyarah*, Yāqūt al-Hamawī cites and describes in excess of 275 monasteries, including seventeen monasteries located in the area between Ahwaz, Khuzestan and al-Hira.

Among the most famous of these monasteries are the monastery at Ablaq in Ahvaz and the monastery of Khindev in the realms of the province of Khuzestan, which is attributed to Leila, daughter of the king Helwan Ibn Imran Ibn Ilhaaf Ibn Quda'ah, the monastery of Ibn Waddaah on the outskirts of Hira, attributed to Ibn Waddaah al-Alehyana who was one of the kings of Hira, as well as the monastery of Aloscon, also in Hira. In Qalali, lived many monks known for their hospitality.[18]

As Louis Cheikho has noted, Arab communities competed in the reconstruction of churches and parishes, boasting among themselves who would build more in their neighborhoods. They not only celebrated their festive occasions in those places of worship,[19] but monasteries were also famous among the Arabs for their vineyards and would be visited for wine tasting.[20]

---

[17] Ibn al-Nadeem, *al-Fahrast*, p. 38.

[18] For more, see, Yaqut, *al-Khazal wa al-Dal*, vol. 1, pp. 252–313, vol. 2, pp. 5–254.

[19] Cheikho, *Al-Nasraniah wa Adabaha*, p. 85.

[20] Gergis Dawood, *Adian al-Arab Qabl al-Islam*, p. 263

Bishops and monks enjoyed the love of the people in these areas as a result of the variety of services they provided, including religious care through schools, and health care due to their knowledge of medicine and its application in the treatment of people. They also provided humanitarian aid, such as providing shelter and providing merchants and owners of caravans with water and food. The Islamic sources point out that Bohira the monk held a feast and invited the convoy of Quraish (including Abu Talib and his nephew Muhammad) which had stopped near his hermitage in Bosra in the Levant.

Whenever a new Episcopal See was established, a variety of other local services were also established—for example, a new school and a library, as well as a hospital to provide health services.[21] The building of churches and monasteries relied heavily on the charitable donations offered by Christians, as well as from the funds of the Byzantine state. The churches—in addition to being houses of piety and worship—were also houses of policy and action, benefiting the Romans directly and strengthening their influence and increasing the number of their subjects.[22] The building of churches and monasteries was an important source of income for local people who were involved in the construction work and received salaries to help them meet the cost of living.

The spread of Christianity in the Gulf region goes back to the beginning of the fourth century, during the reign of Persian king Shapur II (309–79) in Persia and Iraq and subsequently to the rest of the Gulf region.[23]

One of the most important factors that led to the spread of Christianity, and in particular the Church of the East, in the Gulf region, is the fact that there was a developed and well-pointed economic and political relationship with the Sassanid Empire. This situation had been in place for several centuries. The trade between Persia and Hira from one side and the Bahrain region from the other played a significant role in the spread of Christianity and the Church of the East.

---

[21] Atiya, *A History of Eastern Christianity*, p. 257.

[22] Jawād Ali, *al-Mufassal fi tārikh al-'Arab qabla al-Islām*, vol. 6, p. 650.

[23] Healey, "The Christians of Qatar in the 7th A.D", pp. 225

Both Christian missionaries and traders benefited from that level of trade. They used the land and sea trade routes in order to reach cities and commercial centers all over Bahrain. Wherever missionaries arrived, they established centers for spreading the Christian religion. Christian clergy and traders found in Bahrain a suitable climate to spread Christianity among peoples who followed pagan religions that lacked logical and ethical content.

Pagan religions lacked both the discipline and cohesion that Christianity offered. There were public health services as well as shelters and centers of education, which connected the followers of Christianity with the clergymen through churches and monasteries.

Christian clergymen in the province of Bahrain succeeded in attracting a large portion of the population there and persuaded them to embrace Christianity. Sources mention that Bishop Barbasem: (343–347) built a monastery on one of the islands located between Beth Qatraya and Oman. Monk Mar Awdisho (Abdisho of Nisibis) was also able to spread Christianity on one of the province's islands and persuade some of the inhabitants of that island to accept Christianity.[24] The large number of churches and monasteries in the province of Bahrain in the period from the fifth century until the seventh century is proof of this.

A number of recent excavations have revealed the ruins of large churches and a complex of church monasteries in strategic locations to the entrances of some of the Gulf islands, as well as sources of potable water that date to before the sixth and seventh centuries. Two such sites were found on the island of Sair Bin Yaas and in Meraweh (an island in Abu Dhabi, in the United Arab Emirates).[25] Excavations have also revealed monasteries, churches and Christian living quarters on Filaka Island (in modern day Kuwait) and in Jubayel and Thaj (in the eastern region of the Kingdom of Saudi Arabia).[26]

---

[24] For more see Bin Seray, "Christianity in the East", *ARAM*, Vol. 8, 1996, pp. 315–332.

[25] For more, see Joseph Elders, "The lost Churches of the Arabian Gulf", *Proceedings of the Seminar For Arabian Studies*, Vol.31, 2000, pp. 47–57.

[26] For more see Bin Seray, "Christianity in the East", *ARAM*, Vol. 8, 1996, pp. 315–332.

Historical sources also speak of churches and religious centers in Hajar[27] and in Darin[28] (part of the eastern region of the Kingdom of Saudi Arabia) and on the island of Samahij[29] (currently in the Kingdom of Bahrain). There were also churches and bishops in al-Khat[30] (a small town in Al-Ahsa).

Although there is currently no clear evidence about the scope and nature of life in those quarters and areas, it can be concluded from these surveys and excavations that the churches had properties and agricultural lands under their supervision. Monks, priests and clergymen in those locations did not spend their lives in isolation from the rest of society; they were active in commerce, educational roles, health services and religious duties that they performed in the nearby Christian societies. They also were active in their missions in pagan areas, and churches were an important bridge for the transference of medicine, astronomy and philosophy to the province of Bahrain at that time.

RELIGIOUS TOLRERANCE IN THE GULF

A translation has recently been published by Dr Mario Kozah of a Syriac manuscript containing religious letters addressed to the people of Qatar by the Christian patriarch Ishoʿyahb III (patriarchate 649–59) to Christians who lived in Qatar in the seventh century.[31] This manuscript is of great importance. Messages in it are addressed to all the people of Qatar of various religions and affiliations, with sermons exhorting the followers of Christianity to adhere to their religion and to reflect on the principle of man and

---

[27] The city of Hajer during the 7th century A.D. was the capital of Bahrain province. For more see Yaqut, *Muʿajm al-Buldan*, vol. 5, p. 393.

[28] Darin was described by Yaqut as a major port famous for the import of Musk from India. See *Muʿjam al-Buldan*, vol. 2, p. 432.

[29] Samahij is an island lying in the middle of the Gulf between Oman and Bahrain. For more sea Yaqut, *Mu`jam al-Buldan*, vol. 3, p. 246.

[30] Al-Khat was a seaside in the province of Bahrain. For more see Yaqut, *Muʿjam al-Buldan*, vol. 2, p. 378.

[31] For more see Kozah, "A Translation of the Syriac Text of Ishoyahb III's Letters to Qataris", pp. 1–22.

fate. These letters clearly show tolerance and religious coexistence in this region during the sixth–seventh century.

They also show particular tolerance towards the Arab tribes that had entered Islam, which was ruling during in that period in the province of Bahrain. Muslim tribes did not interfere with the church clergymen, and allowed them to compose religious books, and to publish and circulate their contents across the region.

As already mentioned, in spite of the prevalence of the use of Arabic, Persian and Syriac among the population in the province of Bahrain, the Syriac language was the most commonly used among Christians. In addition to it being the language of Christianity in the region, it was also the language of science and culture. This is shown by the large number of manuscripts and books written in Syriac, which emerged during the sixth and seventh centuries, and talk about the social conditions of people and their religious life.

Were the Christian clergymen who were born in the province of Bahrain Arab? Did they write and speak Arabic? In spite of the prevalence of these three languages among the population, the Christians in the Gulf region only used the Arabic language in their writings on rare occasions. No Arabic Christian writings that deal with the social and religious aspects of the Gulf region have reached us, nor do we find mention of missionary activity in the writings of early Muslim Arab historians from the likes of Ibn Khayyat (d.854), ʾAḥmad Ibn Yaḥyā al-Balādhurī (d. 892) and Ibn Habib (d.859).

There is no doubt that before and during the sixth and seventh centuries the Nestorians in the province of Bahrain had influence on the province's religious and political authorities. The Church of the East's general council meetings, held in different regions of the Byzantine empire, took important decisions affecting the status and religious and political matters of the people of the province. For example, during the general council of 585 it was discussed that the Sunday should be a day of rest for Christians in the province of Bahrain, if possible refraining from work on that day, and being pardoned from work when necessary.[32]

---

[32] Cheikho, *Al-Nasraniah wa Adabaha*, p.71.

The Syriac Church of the East bishopric in Beth Qatraye appears to have been active since 225.[33] It also had authority over a number of other bishoprics in the region, for example the bishopric Samahij and Darin. There were also bishoprics in al-Khat and another on the island of Tarot.[34] All of these bishoprics were subject to the religious control of the Archbishop of Persia. After a period of disagreement, Ishoʿyahb III encouraged the liberation of Beth Qatraye from the religious influence of the bishops of Persia and it became a sovereign independent religious authority.[35]

'Beth Qatraye' means 'the country of Qataris' in Syriac, although in this period the term was given to specific parts of the province of Bahrain, as well as Qatar, Abu Dhabi, the islands of Bahrain and parts of the Eastern Province of Saudi Arabia.

This region was famous due to the presence of a large number of bishops and monks with prominent, influential, and active roles in the Church of the East's large religious synods that were held in major Christian cities such as Constantinople, Nicaea and Ephesus and others. The bishops and monks of Beth Qatraye attended these church synods and discussed the fads and heresies of the day, disputing such matters with those who were skeptical about the Christian religion, in the churches and monasteries scattered in the area. Louis Cheikho provides a list of many of the bishops of the province of Bahrain who were present at these church meetings or had their names in church lists, including Archbishop Thomas of Qatar and Isaac of Hajer, Jacob, Paul and Ishoʿyahb of Darin, Elias, Sarkis of Samahij and Shaheen of al-Khat.[36]

Many of these bishops were leading scientists and were very cultured, having studied in the schools of Edessa and Nusaybin. They were able to converse in multiple languages and invited people to worship God, sharing with them stories about the creation of the earth and man as appeared in the Bible and encouraging

---

33 Atiya, *A History of Eastern Christianity*, pp. 258; J.F. Healey, "The Christians of Qatar in the 7th A.D.", pp. 227.

34 al-Ani, A., *al-Bahrain fi Sadir al-Islam*, p. 67.

35 Cheikho, *Al-Nasraniah wa Adabaha*, p. 71

36 Cheikho, *Al-Nasraniah wa Adabaha*, p. 71. Bin Seray, "Christianity in the East", *ARAM*, Vol. 8, 1996, pp. 315–332.

them to lead an ascetic life, not to cling to this worldly life. They were also informed astronomers and had knowledge of the stars and plants, and were knowledgable about medicine and philosophy. Accordingly, the impact of these bishops on the Arab tribes in the province of Bahrain before Islam was significant.

Historical sources indicate that some monks and priests were involved in trade, working for the sale, purchase, and transfer of local goods to areas as far away as India and China.

Pearls[37] were the most important of the commercial goods to attract the attention of monks and priests, because of their high value and popularity in the overseas markets, in addition to their properties and health benefits in the treatment of diseases. Pearls also had some religious connotations especially with the monks of the Church of the East, who saw in the pearls symbolism relating to the soul. Al-Ahmed mentions the involvement of certain individuals in trade: a Church of the East monk from Beth Qatraye named Bar-Sadi would join the merchants on their sea journey to India,[38] and a sixth-century monk called Ibrahim from the Gulf region made several trips to India before joining the Church and did not stop until the pirates seized his ship.[39]

Churches and monasteries were effective educational and cultural institutions. In the pre-Islamic era, they were instrumental in the development and prosperity of the scientific movement in the province of Bahrain. The works of writers from Beth Qatraye flourished and spread. Their compositions brought them fame in distant horizons. Isaac the Syriac (also known as Isaac of Nineveh, where he later became a bishop) was also the most famous of its writers, and the most scholarly and productive of them all.

---

[37] Brock, "Syriac Writers from Beth Qatraye", pp. 86-87; Kozah, "The Syriac Writers of Beth Qatraye in the 7th Century C.E."

[38] Al-Ahmed, *Tārikh al-Khalij al-Arabi min aqdam al-azinah hattāal-tahrir al-'Arabi*, 392-393.

[39] Al-Ahmed, *Tārikh al-Khalij al-Arabi min aqdam al-azinah hattāal-tahrir al-'Arabi*, 392-393.

Isaac the Syriac

We have little information about the emergence of Isaac and his studies, beside the fact that he was born and raised in Qatar at the beginning of the seventh century and joined a monastery there. When he was young, he dedicated his life to the practice of asceticism, learned the religious traditions of the Church of the East, and took advantage of the library attached to the monastery. He continued to do so until he became an authority in theology. He then turned to monasticism and engaged in religious education in the region. As time passed, Isaac become more famous for his spiritual writings, especially those dealing with monasticism and a life of contemplation and stillness.

When the Bishop Georges (680–659) visited Beth Qatraye in the middle of the seventh century to attend the local synod in the region,[40] Isaac attracted his attention. Isaac later took up the bishopric of the city of Nineveh in Iraq, possibly influenced by the fact that one of his relatives (a monk called Gabriel) was a resident Bible commentator in the church in Iraq.

Isaac took up the bishopric of Nineveh for five months, after which he resigned and chose to live a life of isolation in Khuzestan and the surrounding mountains with the monks and hermits that lived there.[41] He lived a life of hardship and dedication to the study of the Bible.

After being affected by blindness in the last days of his life, he dedicated his books to his disciples, and then died whilst at a retreat in the monastery of Rabban Shapur where he was buried.[42]

Isaac the Syriac wrote a number of books relating to the religious aspects of Christian spirituality, the majority of which are in manuscripts written in Syriac. One of his works consists of three books that have been translated from the Syriac into English, French and Italian. Dr. Kozah presented a solid scientific study under the title of "The Syriac Writers of Beth Qatraye in the 7th

---

[40] Brock, "Syriac Writers from Beth Qatraye", pp 86-87.

[41] Wensinck,A.J. *Mystic Treatises by Isaac of Nineveh*, pp xvii-xix

[42] Bin Seray, "Christianity in the East", *ARAM*, Vol.8,1996,pp. 323-324

Century". Kozah relied mainly on the Syriac sources and writings and was unique in the tracking of published and non-published works of Bishop Isaac the Syriac.

Although most of the works of Isaac the Syriac were religious and theological in content, it is clear from reading his vocabulary that he was familiar with philosophy, medicine, literature and astrology. He also had a collection of poems printed in his name.[43]

Ahob (Job) of Beth Qatraye

Ahob (Job) of Beth Qatraye is mentioned on the list compiled by Abdisho.[44] Ahob grew up in Qatar and studied in its churches and monasteries during the seventh century when Qatar possessed the main scientific centers in the region. It competed with the schools in Edessa and Nisibis as another location to study the traditions of the Church of the East.

Ahob is known for his commentaries, exegesis and scholarly marginal notes that he added to the New Testament. His exegesis included the divine laws and all the prophets and messengers mentioned in the Bible.[45] This exegesis had a tangible influence on the religious life, and, in particular, among the priests and monks who began to exchange them among themselves, benefiting from them through study and research.

Ahob's writings reflected the religious and scientific status that Qatar enjoyed during that period. One of Ahob's most famous writings is *The Cause of Psalms*, translated into English and edited by Professor Bas ter Haar Romeny from Leiden University in the Netherlands.

---

[43] Rafael Babu Ishaq, *Tarikh Nasara al-Iraq*, p.64.

[44] Brock, "Syriac Writers from Beth Qatraye", pp 92-93; Kozah, "The Syriac Writers of Beth Qatraye in the 7th Century CE", p. 16

[45] Kozah, "The Syriac Writers of Beth Qatraye in the 7th Century CE", p. 16.

Dadisho the Qatari

Dadisho, or Dadisho the Qatari, lived towards the end of the seventh century, and was a contemporary of Bishop Isaac the Syriac.[46] Dadisho was known for his many works and religious writings in the Church of the East tradition.

Unfortunately the majority of his works are missing and only a few have survived. Some of his most important works are the *Commentary on the Asceticon of Abba Isaiah* translated into English by R. Draguet, and his book the *Commentary on the Paradise of the Fathers*. This book is currently being translated from its Syriac original.[47] Dr Robert Kitchen is currently working on translating the first section of the book from the ancient Abyssinian language into English.

Other examples of his writings include his *Discourse on Stillness* and his *Letter to Abqosh*. Dadisho spent most of his life as a monk in a monastery in the north of Iraq where he died and was buried. Unfortunately little is known about his dates of birth and death.

Gabriel of Beth Qatraye

Gabriel of Beth Qatraye lived in the seventh century, and was a relative and a contemporary of Isaac the Syriac. Gabriel worked as a priest in one of the large churches in Iraq, and his responsibility was to provide exegesis commentaries on religious books. The first mention of Gabriel is from the visit to Beth Qatraye of Bishop Georges (659–680) in order to attend a local Synod in the region.[48] Gabriel, an exegete in the Church of the East in Beth Aramia, is mentioned as a relative of Isaac the Syriac.

---

[46] Bin Seray, "Christianity in the East", *ARAM*, Vol.8,1996,pp. 323-324.

[47] Kozah, "The Syriac Writers of Beth Qatraye in the 7th Century CE", p. 16.

[48] Brock, "Syriac Writers from Beth Qatraye", pp 88-89.

Gabriel bar Lipah

Gabriel bar Lipah lived during the first half of the seventh century, before Ishoʿyahb III started his liturgical reforms.[49] The most famous of Gabriel's religious works is his *Commentary on the Liturgy*.[50]

Abraham Qatraya bar Lipah

The Qatari monk Abraham Qatraya bar Lipah was born and lived in Qatar during the second half of the seventh century. His most famous work is the exegesis and commentaries that he wrote on the monk Gabriel bar Lipah's religious work, the *Commentary on the Liturgy*. For further explanation and in order to make things clearer, Abraham Qatraya bar Lipah put these commentaries and exegesis in the form of questions and answers. These were written in Syriac and are currently being translated into English by a group of researchers led by Abdulrahim Abuhusayn and Mario Kozah. They aim to publish and distribute it, so that it is available for researchers with an interest in Qatari history before Islam.

SUMMARY

The findings of this study can be summarized as follows:

Since the fourth century, Christianity and in particular the Church of the East tradition had spread widely in the Gulf region, and Christianity continued to be practiced even after the advent of Islam in the sixth century and before its spread in the Gulf region and the surrounding areas. Christian religious centers such as parishes, churches, bishoprics and monasteries in the towns and villages can be found in a number of places in the province of Bahrain. Those centers contributed to the flourishing of the economic and cultural life as well as the development of health services in the region. Many writers among the Christian priests and monks had a

[49] Brock, "Syriac Writers from Beth Qatraye", pp89.

[50] Brock, "Gabriel of Qatar`s Commentary on the Liturgy, Journal of Syriac Studies", Vol.6.2, 2009, pp. 197-248.

great impact on the development and prosperity of the scientific and cultural movement in the region.

The territory of Bahrain during the sixth and seventh centuries was characterized by tolerance and religious coexistence and intellectual openness, through the multiplicity of religions in the region and the freedom to practice religious rites.

Finally, Syriac was the prevalent religious language among the Arab tribes in the region. Prayers and worship were conducted and written in Syriac, and it was the language of culture and thought for many Christian priests and monks.

BIBLIOGRAPHY

Anon. (1912) *The Periplus of the Erythraean Sea*, tr. W. H. Schoff, Longmans, New York.

Abramowski, L. and A. Goodman, (1972) *A Nestorian Collection of Christological Texts*, Vol. II. Cambridge University Press.

Al-Afghani, S. (1993) *Aswaq al-ʿArab fi al-Jāhiliyyah wa-ʾl-Islām*

Al-Ahmed, Sāmi Sa'id. (1985) *Tārikh al-Khalij al-Arabi min aqdam al-azinah hattāal-tahrir al-ʿArabi.* Basrah.

al-Ani, Abdul-Rahman Abdul-Karim. (2000) *Bahrain fi Sadir al-Islam.* Beirut.

Al-Azraqi. (1969) *Akhbar Makka.* Ed. Rushdi S. Malhas. Beirut: Dar al-Andalus.

Al-Bakrī, ʿAbd Allāh b. ʿAbd al-ʿAziz. (1992) *al-Masālik wa-ʾl-mamālik*, ed. A.P. Van Leeuwen and A. Ferre, 2 vols. Ministry of Culture, Tunisia.

Al-Baladhuri. (1987) *Ansab al-Ashraf, Vol. 1.* Ed. Muhammad Hamidullah. Cairo: Dar al-Maʿarif.

———. *Ansab al-Ashraf, Vol. 4.1.* Ed. Ihsan ʿAbbas. Wiesbaden: Franz Steiner, 1979.

———. *Ansab al-Ashraf, Vol. 5.* Ed. Ihsan ʿAbbas. Wiesbaden: Franz Steiner, 1996.

———. *Futuh al-Buldan.* Beirut: Maktabat al-Hilal, 1988.

Al-Balhuri, Ahmed b. Yahyā (1987) *Futūh al-Buldān*, ed. Abdullah and Omar Anis al-Sabagh. Beirut.

Al-Hamawi, Yaqut. (1998) *Kitab al-Khazal wa al-Dal bain al-Dur wa al-Darat wa al-Diarah*, ed. Yahya Zakria Abarah and Muhammed Adib Jamran, 2 vols. Ministry of Culture, Damascus.

———. (1979) *Muʾjam al-buldān*, 5 vols. Beirut.

Al-Jahiz. (1991) *Hujaj al-Nubuwwa.* In *Rasaʾil al-Jahiz.* Ed. ʿAbd al-Salam Harun. Beirut: Dar al-Jil. Vol. 3: 221–281.

———. (1991) *Al-Radd ʿala al-Nasara.* In *Rasaʾil al-Jahiz.* Ed. ʿAbd al-Salam Harun. Beirut: Dar al-Jil. Vol. 3: 301–351.

Al-Masʿudi. (1966) *Muruj al-Dahab wa-Maʿadin al-Jawhar.* Ed. Charles Pellat. Beirut: The Lebanese University.

Al-Tabari M. (1979) *Tārikh al-rusūl wa-ʾl-mulūk*, ed. M.A.F. Ibrāhim, fourth ed., 10 vols. Cairo.

Al-Tabari. (1991) *Taʾrikh al-Umam wa-l-Muluk.* Beirut: Dar al-Kutub al-ʿIlmiyya.

———. (1992) *Jamiʿ al-Bayan fi Tafsir al-Qurʾan.* Beirut: Dar al-Kutub al-ʿIlmiyya.

Al-Waqidi. (1984) *Kitab al-Maghazi.* Ed. Marsden Jones. Beirut: ʿAlam al-Kutub.

Al-Yaʿqubi. (1992) *Taʾrikh al-Yaʿqubi.* Beirut: Dar Sadir.

Assemani, J. (1725) *Bibliotheca Orientalis Clementino-vaticana*, vol. 3.1, Rome: Typis Sacrae Congregationis de Propagande Fide.

Atiya, A. S. (1991) *A History of Eastern Christianity.* Kraus Reprint, N.Y.

Baum, W. and D. Winkler (2003) *The Church of the East a Concise History.* Routledge Curzon, London.

Bernard, V and J-F Salles. (1991) "Discovery of a Christian church at al-Qusur, Failaka (Kuwait)" *PSAS* 21: 7–21.

Beaucamp, J. (2000) "Les deux prières de la Passion d'Aréthas de Najrân". In *Prières méditerranéennes hier et aujourd'hui: Actes du colloque par le Center Paul-Albert Février.* Eds. G. Dorival and D. Pralon. Aix-en-Provence: Publications de l'Université de Provence. Pp. 223–236.

Beaucamp, J., F. Briquel-Chatonnet and C. J. Robin. (1999–2000) "La persécution des chrétiens de Nagrân et la chronologie himyarite". *Aram* 11–12: 15–83.

——— (eds.) (2010). *Juifs et chrétiens en Arabie aux Ve et VIe siècles: Regards croisés sur les sources.* Paris: Association des amis du Centre d'histoire et civilisation de Byzance.

Bell, R. (1926) *The Origin of Islam in its Christian Environment.* London: Macmillan & Co.

Bedjan, P. (1968) *Acta martyrum et sanctorum: Tomus septimus vel Paradisus Patrum*, reprint, Hildesheim: Olms

Bedjan, P. (1897) ed., *Acta Martyrum et Sanctorum Syriace*, Vol. VII (Paris & Leipzig: Otto Harrasowitz).

Berhanu, D. (ed.) (1997) *Das Mashafa Mar Yeshaq von Ninive: Einleitung, Edition und Übersetzung mit Kommentar*, (Hamburg: Verlag Dr. Kovač).

Beulay, R. (1987) *La lumière sans forme: Introduction à l'étude de la mystique chrétienne syro-orientale.* L'Esprit et le Feu, Chevetogne: Éditions de Chevetogne.
Bin Seray, H. M. (1996) "Christianity in East Arabia". *Aram* 8: 315–332.
———. (1997) "The Arabian Gulf in Syriac Sources", *New Arabian Studies* vol. 4.
Booth, P. (2013) *Crisis of Empire: Doctrine and Dissent at the End of Late Antiquity.* Transformation of the Classical Heritage 52; Berkeley: University of California Press.
Bosworth, C. E. (trans.) (1999) *The History of al-Tabari, Vol. 5.* Albany: SUNY Press.
Bowman, J. (1964–1965) "The Debt of Islam to Monophysite Syrian Christianity". *Nederlands Theologisch Tijdschrift* 19: 177–201.
Bri, W. C. (1981) *An Historical atlas of Islam.* Leiden.
Brock, S. P. (1999–2000) "Syriac Writers from Beth Qatraye". *Aram* 11–12: 85–96.
———. "Syriac into Greek at Mar Saba: The Translation of St. Isaac the Syrian" in J. Patrich, ed., *The Sabaite Heritage in the Orthodox Church from the Fifth Century to the Present* (OLA 98; Leuven, 2001) 201–208.
———. (2006) *The Wisdom of St. Isaac of Nineveh.* Gorgias Press.
Budge, E. A. W. (1907) *The Paradise or Garden of the Holy Fathers, Being Histories of the Anchorites, Recluses, Monks, Coenobites, and Ascetic Fathers of the Deserts of Egypt between A.D. CCL and A.D. CCCC circiter.* London: Chatto & Windus.
Carter, R. A. (2008) "Christianity in the Gulf during the first centuries of Islam". *Arabian Archaeology and Epigraphy* 19: 71–108.
Carlson, T. A. (2011) "A Light From 'the Dark Centuries': Isḥaq Shbadnaya's Life and Works". *Hugoye*, vol. 14, pp. 191–214.
Chabot, J-.B. (ed. and trans.) (1902) *Synodicon orientale ou Receuil de synodes nestoriens.* Paris: Imprimerie Nationale.
Cheikho, L. P. L. (1989) *Al-Nasraniah wa Adabaha Bain Arab al-Jahelia.* Beirut.
Chronicon anonymum in *Chronica minora, part 1* (CSCO Vol. 4). Paris: Typographeo Reipublicae, 1903. Pp. 15–39.
Chryssavgis, J. (transl.) (2006–2007), *Barsanuphius and John. Letters.* Volumes 1–2, (The Fathers of the Church 113/114; Washington, DC: The Catholic University of America Press).

Colless, B. E. (1969) *The Mystical Discourses of John Saba*, University of Melbourne (unpublished dissertation).

Conrad, L. I. (1987) "Abraha and Muhammad: Some Observations Apropos of Chronology and Literary *Topoi* in the Early Arabic Historical Tradition". *Bulletin of the School of Oriental and African Studies* 50.2: 225–240.

Cowley, R. W. (1980) "Scholia of Ahob of Qatar on St. John's Gospel and the Pauline Epistles". *Le Muséon*, vol. 93, pp. 329–43.

De Blois, F. (2002) "Nasrani and Hanif: Studies on the Religious Vocabulary of Christianity and Islam". *Bulletin of the School of Oriental and African Studies* 65: 1–30.

Draguet, R. (1972) *Commentaire du Livre d'abba Isaïe (logoi I-XV) par Dadišo Qatraya (VIIe s.)*. Corpus scriptorum christianorum orientalium 327, Louvain: Secrétariat du CorpusSCO.

Dumortier, J. (ed.) (1966) *Jean Chrysostome. À Théodore*. Sources chrétiennes 117, Paris: Cerf.

Duval, R. (ed. and trans.) (1904–1905) *Išoʿyahb Patriarchae III, Liber Epistularum (CSCO Volumes 11–12)*. Paris: Typographeo Reipublicae.

Elders, J. (2001) "The Lost Churches of the Arabian Gulf: Recent Discoveries on the Islands of Sir Bani Yas and Marawah, Abu Dhabi Emirate, United Arab Emirates". *Proceedings of the Seminar for Arabian Studies* 31: 47–57.

Elders, J. (2003) "The Nestorians in the Gulf. Just Passing Through? Recent Discoveries on the island of Sir Bani Yas, Abu Dhabi Emirates, U. A. E." Pages 230–236 in D. Potts, H. Al-Naboodah, P. Hellyer (eds), *Archeology of the United Arabs of Emirates. Proceedings of the First International Conference of the Archeology of the U.A.E.* London, Trident Press.

Fahd, T. (1976) "Qatar wa-nawāhihā fi al-jughrāfiyyah al-qadimah" in *Mu'tamar dirāsāt tārikh sharqi al-Jazi rah al-ʿArabiyyah*, vol. I. Doha.

Fiey, J. M. (1983) "Rabban Bûya de Shaqlâwâ, et de Jéricho". *Proche-Orient Chrétien* 33: 34–38.

Finkel, J. (1933) "Jewish, Christian and Samaritan Influences on Arabia". In *The Macdonald Presentation Volume*. Princeton: Princeton University Press. Pp. 145–166.

Fishbein, M. (trans.) (1997) *The History of al-Tabari, Vol. 7*. Albany: SUNY Press.

Gachet, J. (1998) "Akkaz (Kuwait), a site of the Partho-Sasanian period. A preliminary report on three seasons of excavation (1993–1996)" *PSAS* 28: 69–79.

Geerard, M. (1974) *Clavis patrum Graecorum*, vol. 2: *Ab Athanasio ad Chrysostomum*, Turhout: Brepols.

Geerard, M. and J. Noret (1988) *Clavis patrum Graecorum: Supplementum*, Turnhout: Brepols.

Graffin, F. (1977) 'Une page retrouvée de Théodore de Mopsueste', in R. Fischer (ed.) *A Tribute to Arthur Vööbus: Studies in Early Christian Literature and Its Environment, Primarily in the Syrian East*, Chicago: The Lutheran School at Chicago, pp. 29–34.

Geagea, N. (1984) *Mary of the Koran*. Trans. and ed. Lawrence T. Fares. New York: Philosophical Library, 1984. [Originally published as *Maria nel messagio coranico*. Rome: Edizioni del Teresianum, 1973.]

Gergis, D. (1988) *Adian al-Arab Qabla al-Islam*. Beirut.

Griffith, S. H. (2008) "Christian Lore and The Arabic Qur'an" The "Companions of the Cave" in *Surat al-Kahf* and in Syriac Christian Tradition". In *The Qur'an in Its Historical Context*. Ed. G. S. Reynolds. New York: Routledge. Pp. 109–137.

———. (2013) "When Did the Bible Become an Arabic Scripture?" *Intellectual History of the Islamicate World* 1: 7–23

Havenith, A. (1988) *Les arabes chrétiens nomads au temps de Mohammed*. Louvain-la-Neuve: Cerfaux Lefort.

Hawting, G. (2011) "Pre-Islamic Arabia / The Jahiliyya". In *Oxford Bibliography Online* (www.oxfordbibliographiesonline.com). Pp. 1–22.

Healey, J. and H. Bin Seray (1999–2000) "Aramaic in the Gulf: Towards a Corpus". *Aram* 11–12: 1–14.

Healey, J. (2000) "The Christians of Qatar in the 7th Century A.D.". In *Studies in Honour of Clifford Edmund Bosworth, Vol. 1*. Ed. I. R. Netton. Leiden: Brill. Pp. 222–237.

———. (2009) "The Patriarch Išoʿyahb III and the Christians of Qatar in the first Islamic Century". In *The Christian Heritage of Iraq: Collected Papers from the Cristianity of Iraq I–V Seminar Days*. Ed. E. C. D. Hunter. Piscataway: Gorgias Press. Pp. 1–9.

Herodotus, *The Histories*, tr. Aubrey De Selincourt. Penguin Books (1996).

Hoyland, R. G. (2001) *Arabia and the Arabs: From the Bronze Age to the Coming of Islam*. London: Routledge.

Heil, G. and A. Ritter (ed.) (1991) *Pseudo-Dionysius Areopagita: De coelesti hierarchia* [...]. Patristische Texte und Studien 36, Berlin: De Gruyter.

Ibn al-Athir (2010) *Al-Kamil fi al-Tarikh*. Ed. ʿAbd Allah al-Qadi. Beirut: Dar al-Kutub al-ʿIlmiyya.

Ibn Al-Faqī Al-Hamhānī, Abi Bakr Ahmad b. Muhammed. (1988) *Mukhtasar kitāb al-buldān*. Beirut.

Ibn Habib. *Kitab al-Muhabbar*. Beirut: Dar al-Afaq al-Jadida, n.d.

———. (1964) *Kitab al-Munammaq fi Akhbar Quraysh*. Ed. Khurshid A. Fariq. Haydarabad: Daʾirat al-Maʿarif al-ʿUthmaniyya.

Ibn Habib, Abdul Malik Ibn Habib. (1999) *al-Salami al-Andalusi*, Kitab al-Tarikh. Beirut.

Ibn Hisham (1990) *Al-Sira al-Nabawiyya*. Ed. Ibrahim al-Saqqa et al. Beirut: Dar al-Khayr.

Ibn Ishaq (1967) *The Life of Muhammad: A Translation of Ishaq's* Sirat Rasul Allah. Trans. Alfred Guillaume. Lahore: Oxford University Press.

Ibn Ishaq. (1976) *Sirat Ibn Ishaq*, ed. M. Hamid allah. Fez .

Ibn Manzur. (1988) *Lisān al-Arab*, 7 vols. Beirut.

Ibn al-Mujawir (1936–1950) *Tarikh al-Mustabsir*, in *Arabische texte zur kenntnis der stadt Aden im mittelalter*. Ed. Oscar Löfgren. Uppsala: Almqvist and Wiksells.

———. (2008) *A Traveller in Thirteenth-Century Arabia: Ibn al-Mujawir's* Tarikh al-Mustabsir. Trans. G. Rex Smith. London: the Hakluyt Society.

Ibn al-Neem, (1985) *al-Fahrast*, ed. Nahid Abass Uthman. Doha.

Ibn Saʿd (1958) *Al-Tabaqat al-Kubra*. Beirut: Dar Sadir.

Ishaq, R. B. I. (1948) *Tarikh Nasara al-Iraq*. Baghdad.

Kaplan, A. (2013) 'Expertise paléographique du ms. Syr Bagdad 210 en vue de sa datation : Dadisho Qatraya. Commentaire sur le Paradis des Pères', *BABELAO*, [Online], vol. 2, pp. 105–121, available http://www.uclouvain.be/441380.html.

Kessel, G. (2010) "Sinai Syr. 24 as an important witness to the reception history of some Syriac ascetic texts" in *Sur les pas des Araméen chrétiens. Mélange offerts à Alain Desreumaux*, F. Briquel-Chatonnet & M. Debié, eds (*Cahiers d'études syriaques 1*; Paris: Geuthner) 207–218.

Khayatt, N. (ed. and transl.) (2007) *Jean de Dalyatha. Les Homélies I–XV. Édition critique du texte syriaque inédit, Traduction, introduction et notes* (Antelias, Lebanon: Centre des Études et de Recherches Orientales – CERO, Université Antonine – UPA).

King, G. R. D. (1997) "A Nestorian Monastic Settlement of the Island of Sir Bani Yas, Abu Dhabi: a preliminary report" *BSOAS*, 60: 221–235.

Kitchen, R. A. & M. F. G. Parmentier (transl.) (2004), *The Book of Steps: The Syriac Liber Graduum*, English translation and Introduction (Cistercian Studies 196; Kalamazoo, MI: Cistercian Publications).

Kitchen, R. A. (transl.) (2013), *The Discourses of Philoxenos of Mabbug: A New Translation and Introduction* (Cisterican Studies 235; Collegeville, Minnesota: Cistercian/Liturgical Press).

Kozah, M. (forthcoming) "The Syriac Writers of Qatar in the 7th Century CE: An Overview of the Current State of Studies". In *Syriac in its Multi-Cultural Context*. Eds. H. Teule, E. Keser-Kayaalp, K. Akalın, N. Doru, and M. S. Toprak. Louvain: Peeters.

———. (forthcoming) "An Edition and Translation of the Syriac Text of Ishoyahb III's 'Letters to the Qataris'". In *The Syriac Writers of Qatar in the 7th Century CE: An Anthology*. Piscataway: Gorgias Press.

Lammens, H. (1917) "Les Chrétiens à la Mecque à la veille de l'Hégire". *Bulletin de l'Institut Français d'Archéologie Oriental* 14: 191–230.

Langfeldt, J. A. (1994) "Recently discovered early Christian monuments in North-eastern Arabia", *AAE* 5:32–60.

Luxenberg, C. (2009) *The Syro-Aramaic Reading of the Koran: A Contribution to the Decoding of the Language of the Koran*. Amherst: Prometheus Books. [Originally published as: *Die Syro-Aramäische Lesart des Koran: Ein Beitrag zur Entschlüsselung der Koransprache*. Berlin: Das Arabische Buch, 2000.]

Lavenant, R. (ed. and transl.) (1963) *La lettre à Patricius de Philoxène de Mabboug*, *Patrologia Orientalis* 30.5 (Paris: Firmin-Didot).

Leroy L. & F. Nau, (ed. and transl.) (1910) "Histoire de Saint Maurice, Empereur des Romains", *Patrologia Orientalis* 5: 773–778.

Luibheid, C., P. Rorem and R. Roques (eds.) (1987) *Pesudo-Dionysius.The Complete Works*. The Classics of Western Spirituality, New York: Paulist Press.

Al-Mulayki, R. "*Al-Masihiyya fi al-islam: tafsir jamiʿ al-ayat al-qurʾaniyya al-lati yastashid biha al-masihiyyun*". *Muntadayat Hurras al-ʿAqida* http://www.hurras.org/vb/showthread.php?t=9384 (accessed on 3 February 2014).

Mourad, S. A. (1999) "On the Qurʾanic Stories about Mary and Jesus". *Bulletin of the Royal Institute for Inter-Faith Studies* 1:2: 13–24.

———. (2002) "From Hellenism to Christianity and Islam: The Origin of the Palm tree Story concerning Mary and Jesus in the Gospel of Pseudo-Matthew and the Qurʾan". *Oriens Christianus* 86: 206–216.

———. (2009) "Christians and Christianity in the *Sira* of Muḥammad". In *Christian-Muslim Relations: A Bibliographical History, Volume 1 (600–900)*. Eds. David Thomas and Barbara Roggema. Leiden: Brill. Pp. 57–71.

Marsh, F. (1979) *The Book of the Holy Hierotheos* […], reprint, Amsterdam: Philo Press.

Migne, J.-P. (1863) *Patrologiae cursus completus: Series graeca*, vol. 40: *Patres Aegyptii saeculi IV*, Paris: Migne.

Munitiz, J. (trans.) (2011) *Anastasios of Sinai: Questions and Answers* (CCT 7; Turnhout, Belgium: Brepols).

Nöldeke, T. (1879) *Geschichte der Perser und Araber zur Zeit der Sasaniden*. Leiden: Brill.

O'Leary, D. L. (1973) *Arabia Before Muhammad*. New York.

Payne, R. (2011) "Monks, Dinars and Date Palms: Hagiographical Production and the Expansion of Monastic Institutions in the Early Islamic Persian Gulf". *Arabian Archaeology and Epigraphy* 22: 97–111.

Potts, D. T. (1990) *The Arabian Gulf in Antiquity, Volume 2: From Alexander to the Coming of Islam*. Oxford: the Clarendon Press.

———. (1984) "Northeastern Arabia: From the Seleucids to the Earliest Caliphs" *Expedition*, Vol. 26, No.3.

———. (1994) "Nestorian Crosses from Jabal Berri" *AAE* 5: 61–65.

———. (2008) "The Deacon and the Dove: On Some Early Christian (?) Grave Stelae from al-Maqsha and Shakhura (Bahrain)". *Arabian Archaeology and Epigraphy* 19: 109–119.

Pregill, M. E. (2007) "The Hebrew Bible and the Quran: The Problem of the Jewish 'Influence' on Islam". *Religion Compass* 1.6: 643–659.

Phillips, D. (2012) 'The Syriac Commentary of Dadisho' Qatraya on the *Paradise of the Fathers*: Towards a Critical Edition', *BABELAO*, [Online], vol. 1, pp. 1–23, available http://www.uclouvain.be/408559.html.

Quasten, J. (1963) *Patrology*, vol. 3: *The Golden Age of Greek Patristic Literature*, Utrecht: Spectrum.

The Qur'an. Trans. Tarif Khalidi. New York: Penguin Books, 2009.

Rabbath, E. (1980) *L'Orient chrétien à la veille de l'Islam*. Beirut: Librairie Orientale.

Raven, W. (1988) "Some early Islamic texts on the Negus of Abyssinia". *Journal of Semitic Studies* 33.2: 197–218.

Regnault, L. (1981) *Les sentences des Pères du Désert*, Solesmes: Abbaye Saint-Pierre de Solesmes.

Reinink, G. J. (1979) *Studien zur Quellen- und Traditionsgeschichte des Evangelienkommentars der Gannat Bussame*. Corpus Scriptorum Christianorum Orientalium, vol. 414; Subsidia, t. 57. Secrétariat du CorpusSCO, Louvain.

Richard M. & J. Munitiz (eds.) (2006) *Anastasii Sinaïtae: Quaestiones et responsiones* (CCSG 59; Turnhout, Belgium: Brepols).

Rizzardi, G. (1982) *Il problema della cristologia coranica*. Milano: Istituto Propaganda Libraria.

Robin, C. (2000) "Arabia, Christians and Jews in". In *Encyclopedia of the Middle Ages, Vol. 1 (A–J)*. Eds. A. Vauchez, B. Dobson and M. Lapidge. Trans. A. Walford. Chicago: Fitzroy Dearborn. Pp. 89–90.

Romeny, B. ter Haar (2004) "Question-and-Answer Collections in Syriac Literature", in *Erotapokriseis: Early Christian question-and-answer literature in context*, ed. A. Volgers & C. Zamagni (Leuven: Peeters) 145–163.

Roolvin, R. et al. (1957) *Historical Atlas of the Muslim People*. Amsterdam.

Roques, R., G. Heil and M. de Gaudillac (ed.) (1970) *Denys l'Aréopagite: La Hiérarchie céleste*. Sources chrétiennes 58bis, 2nd ed., Paris: Cerf.

Rubin, U. (1990) "Hanafiyya and Ka'ba: An Inquiry into the Arabian Pre-Islamic Background of Din Ibrahim". *Jerusalem Studies in Arabic and Islam* 13: 85–112.

———. (1995) *The Eye of the Beholder: The Life of Muḥammad as Viewed by the Early Muslims, A Textual Analysis*. Princeton: The Darwin Press.

Ryckmans, J. (1964) "Le Christianisme en Arabie du Sud préislamique". In *Atti del convegno internazionale sul thema l'Oriente christiano nella storia della civilità*. Rome: Accademia Nazionale dei Lincei. Pp. 413–454.

Scher, A. (ed. and trans.) (1908–1950) *Histoire nestorienne inédite: Chronique de Séert*. Paris: Firmin-Didot.

Sims-Williams, N. "Dādišoʿ Qatrāyā's Commentary on the *Paradise of the Fathers*", *Analecta Bollandiana* 112 (1994) 33–64.

Sinkewicz, R. E. (transl.) (2003), *Evagrius Ponticus. The Greek Ascetic Corpus*, (New York: Oxford University Press).

Solomon of Akhlat. 1886. *The Book of the Bee*. Ed. E. A. Wallis Budge. Anecdota Oxoniensia, Semitic Series, vol. 1, pt. 2. Clarendon Press, Oxford.

Shahid, I. (1971) *The Martyrs of Najrân: New Documents*. Brussels: Société des Bollandistes.

Shoemaker, S. J. (2003) "Christmas in the Qur'an: the Qur'anic Account of Jesus's Nativity and Palestinian Local Tradition". *Jerusalem Studies in Arabic and Islam* 28: 11–39.

Thomas, D., (2007) *Arab Christianity*, The Blackwell Companion to Eastern Christianity, Blackwell Publishing Ltd.

Trimingham, J. S. (1979) *Christianity among the Arabs in Pre-Islamic Times*. London: Longman.

Tsafrir, Y. (2009) "70–638: The Temple-less Mountain". In *Where Heaven and Earth Meet: Jerusalem's Sacred Esplanade*. Eds. O. Grabar and B. Z. Kedar. Jerusalem: Yad Ben-Zvi, and Austin: Texas University Press. Pp. 73–99.

ten Napel, E. (1989) "Some Remarks on the Quotations from Emmanuel Bar Shahhare's Hexaemeron in Isḥaq Šbadnaya's Prose-Commentary on the Divine Providence". *Studia Patristica*, vol. 20, pp. 203–10.

Van der Velden, F. (2011) "Early Eastern-Syriac Perception of Islam in Ishoyahb III Letter Epistularum (640–660): No Earlier Christian Sources for a Christian-Muslim Relationship?" In *Byzantium in Early Islamic Syria*. Eds. N. M. El Cheikh and S. O'Sullivan. Beirut: American University of Beirut Press). Pp. 43–57.

Vööbus, A. (1958) *History of Asceticism in the Syrian Orient, Vol. 1: The Origin of Asceticism. Early Monasticism in Persia (CSCO Vol. 184, part 14)*. Louvain: Secrétariat du Corpus Scriptorum Christianorum Orientalium.

Watt, W. M. (1967) "The Christianity Criticized in the Qur'an". *Muslim World* 57:3: 197–201.
Whittow, M. (1996) *The Making of Orthodox Byzantium, 600-1025*. London.
Wigram, W.A. (1910), *An Introduction History of the Assyrian Church*. London.
Witakowski, W. (2006) "Filekseyus, the Ethiopic Version of the Syriac Dadisho Qatraya's Commentary on the Paradise of the Fathers" in *Rocznik Orientalistyczny* 49.1: 281–296.
Witztum, J. (2011) "Joseph among the Ishmaelites: Q 12 in Light of Syriac Sources". In *New Perspectives on the Qur'an: The Qur'an in Its Historical Context 2*. Ed. G. S. Reynolds. New York: Routledge. Pp. 425–448.
Wortley, J. (1980) "The Legend of the Emperor Maurice", *Actes du XVe Congrès Internationale d'Études Byzantines, Athènes – Septembre 1976*, vol. 4 (Athens) 382–391.
Young, R. D. (2011) "The Influence of Evagrius of Pontus" in *To Train His Soul in Books: Syriac Asceticism in Early Christianity*, edit. R. D. Young & M. J. Blanchard (CUA Studies in Early Christianity 5; Washington, DC: Catholic University of America Press) 157–175.
http://deaconswithoutboarders.blogspot.co.uk/2012/01/blog-post_13.html
http://forums.catholic.com/showthread.php?t=625600
Unpublished report from Qatar National Historic Environment Record, Birmingham University (QNHER 1268). Excavations at Qasr Al-Melaihat, south of Al-Wakra: a 7th Century building, 2013.

INDEX

BIBLICAL REFERENCES

Gen 1:1–28:6	138
Gen 15:9–10	141–143
Gen 50:10	141–143, 151
Exod 9:32	140
Ps 5:4	148
Ps 20:7	227
Rom 8:28	219
Eph 1:21	219
Col 1:16	219
3 Enoch	119–120

ANCIENT SOURCES

Acts of the Synod of Seleucia-Ctesiphon, 5

al-Khazal wa al-Dal bain al-Dur wa al-Darat wa al-Diarah, 251

Anonymous Commentary, 18–20, 134, 137–138, 140–144, 151

Apodeiktikos (Posterior Analytics), 164

Apophthegmata, 163, 208, 224, 236, 238–239, 241, 246

Asceticon, 136, 160, 164, 265

Baghdad, Dawra sir. 694, 126

Baghdad, Dawra sir. 938, 126

Basil's Letter to Gregory, 160

Book of Chastity, 7, 9–10

Book of Governors, 110

Book of Grace, 78

Book of Perfection (Sahdona), 96, 200, 207, 209–210, 215, 219, 223–229

Book of Steps/Liber Graduum, 101, 241–243

Book of the Aims of the Psalms, 146, 148–150

Book of the Bee, 191

Book of the Main Points of the History of the Temporary World, 146

Book of the Three Monks, 233, 236

Catalogue of ʿAbdishoʿ bar Brikā, 18, 125, 135, 196, 198, 200, 210

Catalogue of ecclesiastical writers, 18, 125, 128, 131,

Categories, 161, 163–164, 224

Cause of the Psalms (by Aḥūb Qaṭraya), 19, 134, 264

Celestial Hierarchy, 219

Codex Syriacus Primus, 84

Codex Syriacus Secundus, 83, 90–92

Collectio Coisliniana, 142

Commentary on the Asceticon of Abba Isaiah, 135–136, 164, 200, 265

Commentary on the Four Gospels, 136

Commentary on the Liturgical Offices, 155, 157, 159, 266

Commentary on the Paradise of the Egyptian Fathers, 60, 163, 195, 197–198, 200, 203, 207–210, 220, 224, 229, 231–233, 237, 246, 265
Commentary on the Psalms attributed to Denha or Gregory, 134, 144–149, 151
De. Musica, 162
Discourses (John of Dalyatha), 79
Discourses (Philoxenus), 95, 116, 241, 243
Discourse on the Spiritual Life, 161
Diyarbakir Commentary, 137, 140–143, 151
Eisagoge, 163
Epitome, 203–205, 212, 237
Expositio Officiorum, 149
Filekseyus (Ethiopic version of *Commentary on the Paradise of the Fathers*), 232–234, 236–242, 244, 246–248
Futuh al-Buldan, 250
Garshuni corpus, 11–12, 22, 195, 197, 199–206
Hekhalot Rabbati, 115–116, 119–120
Hekhalot Zutarti, 119
History of the founders of monasteries in the realms of the Persians and the Arabs, 7
Jami'al-bayan fi ta'wil al-Qur'an, 68, 53
Kephalaia Gnostica, 160–161
Lausiac History, 239
Law Book of Mar Shemʿūn, 21
Letter 50 (by John of Dalyatha), 97
Letter XVIII (to the Qatari people), 4
Letter XXI (To the Monks of the Beth Qaṭraye), 3–4
Letter to Abqosh, 265
Letter to Patricius, 79, 235–236
Lexicon (of Bar Bahlul), 150
Life of Īšōʿsabran, 112
Mardin 46, 8, 75, 89
Maʿaseh Merkavah, 119–120
Merkavah Rabbah, 119–120
MS (olim) Diyarbakır 22, 18, 137–138, 140, 142–143
MS 181 (Holy Mar Isaac Qaṭraya), 1, 89
MS Mingana 553, 18
MS Sʿert 27, 136
Mujam al-Buldan, 251
Muruj al Dhahab wa ma'aden al Jawhar, 250
On the peoples of India and on the Brahmins, 165
On Stillness, 78, 164, 198, 265
Peri Hermeneias, 164
Poem on the [divine] economy from the beginning to the end, 125
Poem on the Divine Government of the World from the Creation to the Consummation, 150, 169
Quaestiones, 142
Qur'an, 38, 40, 42–43, 47, 49, 51–53, 61–62, 64–68, 98, 104, 106
Seert 76, 8
Selected Questions, 144
Sharfet, Rahmani 80, 126
Sira literature, 38, 40
Synod of Dayrīn 676, 6
Synodicon Orientale, 6
Syro-Hexapla, 142
Tetrachtys, 162
The Chapters of Knowledge, 80
The Chronicle of Seert, 39
The Fifth Part (of the works of Isaac of Niniveh), *possible*, 10–11, 123–128, 131
The First Part (of the works of Isaac of Niniveh), 9, 72–74, 76–83, 85–87, 123–124, 128–130

The Fourth Part (of the works of Isaac of Niniveh), *possible*, 11
The History of Peoples and Kings, 40
The Khuzistan Chronicle, 59
The Life of Jonah, 39
The Life of the Messenger of God, 40
The Monastic Writings, 231, 235,
The Pedigrees of Aristocrats, 40
The Second Part (of the works of Isaac of Niniveh), 9, 72, 80–83, 87, 123–124, 127, 129
The Third Part (of the works of Isaac of Niniveh), 9, 72, 83–84, 87, 123–124, 126
Vat. Sir. 24 f. 153, 20
Vaticano, sir. 592, 126
Writings of the Spiritual Elder, 231, 234

SUBJECTS

Abbasid era, 33, 205
Abd al-Qais (tribe), 23
Abu Dhabi, 24, 31, 56, 258, 261
Addis Ababa, 234, 236
Akkaz, 25, 55
al-Dayer, 29
al-Ḥasā (al-Aḥsāʾoasis), 24, 53, 250
al-Hufūf, 6
al-Khaṭṭ (al-Qaīf), 24
al-Qaṭīf, 6, 27, 57, 252
al-Qusur, 25–26, 31, 55
al-Wakra, 30
anchorites, 9, 218, 233
Antiochene School, 152–153
apokatastasis, 123, 130
Arabian Peninsula, 2–3, 21, 37–39, 51, 56, 251
Ardai, 27
Arkkiyat, 31–34
Baghdad, 82, 84, 90–92, 123, 126, 138, 203–204, 212
Bahrain, 2, 5–6, 24–25, 27–29, 31, 38, 44, 53, 57, 249–255, 257–262, 267
Baker b. Wail (tribe), 23
Beth ʿAbe, 9, 110
Beth Aramaye (See Seleuca-Ctesiphon)
Beth Hūzaye, 8–9, 135, 195
Beth Mawtbe, 18
Beth Mazunaye, 7, 24, 55, 57
Beth Parsaye, 158
Beth Qaṭraye, 1–8, 14–15, 17, 19–23, 35, 39, 53–60, 78, 133–136, 141, 151, 153, 155–156, 158, 163, 165–166, 169–171, 176–177, 191–192, 206, 231, 233, 249, 261–265
Bodleian Library, 11, 80–81, 90, 174
Bushire, 24, 27, 252, 259, 261
Byzantine Empire, 159, 166, 257, 260
Byzantines, 41, 158–159
Byzantium, 2, 22, 41
Cambridge University Library, 11, 81, 146, 198
Church of the East (Nestorian Church), 1, 3, 6, 20, 23–24, 29, 33, 35, 71, 74, 77, 82, 110, 133–134, 155, 158, 162–163, 165–166, 171, 195–196, 198, 201, 203, 212, 233–234, 238–239, 243, 246–247, 249, 250, 257, 260–266
Council of Chalcedon, 244
Council of Constantinople, 162
Council of Nicaea, 159

Dair Mar Elia (St. Elijah's Monestary), 34
Dayr Ḥamīm, 12
Dayrīn, 4, 6–8, 15, 24, 27, 252, 259, 261
Dionysius, 117, 159, 161
Dūlāb, 12
Eastern Province (of Saudi Arabia), 31
Edessa, 2, 151, 159, 162, 201, 261, 264
Egypt, 11, 38, 75, 77, 80, 84, 244
Ethiopian Orthodox Church, 231, 233, 236, 238
Ethiopic (Geʿez), 192, 205–206, 231–235, 237–238
Eucharist, 235, 244–246
Failaka, 6, 25, 55
Fars, 2–3, 7, 15, 24
Gehenna, 162, 186, 192
Hagar, 4, 6–7, 57
ḥanif/ḥunafa', 47, 61–69
ḥanīfiyya, 61–62, 64
Ḥaṭṭa, 3–4, 6–7, 57
Hijaz, 38, 44–46, 48, 59, 254
Hinnah, 27, 55
India, 8, 25, 31, 252, 262
Iran, 25–26, 31, 55–57, 158
Iraq, 31, 33–34, 38, 55–56, 76, 96–97, 123, 150, 169, 170–193, 249, 254–257, 263–265
Jabal Berri, 27, 55
Jericho, 179
Jerusalem, 1, 77, 86, 165, 179, 183, 190, 199
Jordan, 38
Jubayl, 25–27, 31, 55
Karka d-Beth Slokh, 14, 16
Kaslik collection, 11
Kharg, 25–26, 55
Khusistan (See Beth Hūzaye)
Kirkuk, 95–96, 139, 156
Kush, 31
Kuwait, 25, 38–39, 55, 57, 249–251
Levant, 62, 254, 257
Mashmahīg (Mešmahik, Mešmahig), 4–5, 28
massacre of the Christians of Najran, 49–50
Matout, 9
Mecca, 40, 44–49, 254
Medina, 40, 44, 47–48, 50–51, 65, 104
Mesopotamia, 2, 25, 75, 79–80, 81–82, 112–113, 141
Monastery of Izla (Monastery of Abraham Kashkar), 158
Monastery of Our Lady of the Sowings, 126
Monastery of Rabban Shabūr, 10, 12, 109, 158, 195–197
Monastery of Mar Saba, 79
Monastery of Rabban Hormizd, 82
Monastery of St. Catherine, 165
Mosul, 34, 73, 76, 89, 126, 138, 140, 145–146, 174
Mount of Olives, 179
Mount Qardu, 157
Muḥarraq, 5, 28–29, 31, 57
Najran, 38, 41, 48–53, 60, 65
Nestorian Church(es), 23–26, 55, 58, 254–255
Nestorian cross, 26, 29–30
Nestorian Office, 20
Nestorians, 23, 60, 254, 260
Nineveh, 1, 7–9, 20, 198
Oman, 24, 38, 55, 57, 251–252, 258–259
Origenist controversy, 239
Palestine, 38, 79–80, 83
Passion of Christ, 149, 171, 181, 226–227, 239, 244
Pentateuch, 18, 134, 136, 138–140, 143, 151

Persia, 22, 59, 249, 254, 256, 257, 261
Peshitta, 139, 144, 152, 217
Pseudo-Dionysius, 188–189, 219
Qasr al-Malehat, 27, 30–31
Qatar, 2–3, 19, 21–24, 27–30, 33–35, 37, 39–40, 54, 56–58, 60–61, 109, 124, 133–137, 139–143, 145–147, 149–153, 196, 249–250, 257, 259, 261, 263–264, 266
Monestary Rab Kennare, 135, 196
Resurrection, 103–104, 149, 171, 187, 191
Rev Ardashir, 7, 21, 57, 24
revolt against the Catholicosate, 7
Roman Empire, 166
Roman Empire (Eastern), 159
Romans, 23, 181, 257
Rum Orthodox Church, 71
Sabiʾa, 62, 69
Samahiğ, 28
Sar Torah (Prince of the Torah), 113, 119–120
Sasanian(s), 113, 120, 158–159, 249, 251, 253, 195
Sassanids (period, empire), 29, 59, 195, 257
Saudi Arabia, 26, 31, 38, 53, 55, 57, 258, 259, 261
School of Edessa, 2, 151, 159, 261, 264
School of Nisibis, 2, 58, 150, 159, 264, 110
School of Seleucia, 140
Second Council of Constantinople, 239
Seleuca-Ctesiphon, 3, 5, 8–9, 15, 24, 39, 57–59
Septuagint, 152
seraphim, 188–189, 219, 245
Shahrzur, 149
Sir Bani Yas, 24–26, 31, 56
Šouštar (Tustar), 12
St. Mark's Monestary, 1
St. Mary al Sourian Monastery, 11
Ṣuḥhār , 24
Syria, 2, 41, 46–47, 254
Syrian Orthodox Church, 71, 74–78, 80, 82–84, 86
Talmud, 112–113
Tārūt, 6, 27
Thāj, 6, 27, 55, 258
Tilūn, 4, 6
Torah, 114, 184
Ṭrīhan, 7
Umm al-Maradim, 29–30
United Arab Emirates (UAE), 24, 38–39, 56, 249–251, 258
Upright and Perfect, 241–243
Vatican Library, 2, 11, 123, 201–202
Yemen, 38, 46, 49–50, 251, 254
Zaydūn (See Rev Ardashir)
Zoroastrians/Zoroastrianism, 54, 112–113, 254

NAMES

Abba Arsenius, 202
Abba Isaiah, 136, 164, 197, 199, 208–209
Abba Moses, 202
ʿAbd al-Masih, 51
ʿAbd Allah ibn al-Thamir, 49
ʿAbdisho bar Brika, 18, 39, 57, 125, 134–136, 147, 150, 196, 198, 200, 210
Abdisho of Nisibis (Monk Mar Awdisho), 257
Abqosh, 198, 265

Abraham, 61, 62, 64–68
Abraham bar Lipah, 1, 13–17, 39, 58
Abu al-Hasan Ali bin Al Hussein al-Masudi, 250–251
Abu Haritha, Bishop of Najran, 51
Abuna Abba Sälama Matargwem, 234
Aḥūb Qaṭraya, 1, 18–20, 39, 58, 60, 133–137, 141–153, 169, 177, 179–181, 183, 190–192, 264
al-Mundhir ibn Sawa (al-ʿAbdi), 53–54
al-Ayham, 51
al-Baladhuri, 40, 45, 47, 54, 250, 260
al-Hadi ila al-Haqq, 50
al-Shahristani, 69
al-Yaʿkoubi, 69
Alexander the Great, 165
Ammonias, 239
Archelaus, 181
Aristotle, 160, 162–164, 166–167
Ascetikon, 209
Assemani, 134–136, 153
Babai the Great, 158, 160–161, 165–166
Bar Bahlul, 150
Bar Timaeus, 179
Barabbas, 181
Barbasem (Bishop), 258
Barsanuphius, 201, 247
Basil of Caesarea, 159–160
Bishop Moses, 9
Boethius, 166
Bohira al-Raheb, 253–254
Būshīr, 10, 197–198
Caesar, 181
Caliph ʿUmar, 50
Constantine, 159
Dadisho' Qaṭraya, 1, 8, 12–13, 39, 55, 58, 60, 78, 109–110, 135, 155–156, 158, 160, 163–164, 165, 195–233, 237–247, 265
Daniel Bar Tubanita, 123, 125, 128, 131
Dhu Nu'as (Jewish king of Yemen), 49
Dindamis, 165,
Emmanuel bar Shahhare, 191
Emperor Heraclius, 41
Emperor Julian, 161
ʿEnanishoʿ, 164
Ephrem, 93, 110, 141, 151, 164, 171, 179, 196
Estaphanūs (Bishop of Mazunaye), 7
Euphemius, 48
Eusebius of Emesa, 152–153
Evagrius Ponticus, 94–96, 98–99, 107–108, 118, 159–161, 163–164, 201, 207–208, 226–227, 234, 238–240
Gabriel Arya, 1, 20, 39, 58, 156
Gabriel bar Lipah Qaṭraya, 1, 8–9, 13–17, 20, 39, 58, 133, 135, 151, 155–157, 159, 169, 176–177, 179–181, 187–190, 192, 266
Gabriel Qaṭraya (see Gabriel bar Lipah Qaṭraya)
George I (Nestorian Patriarch), 57–58
Gīwargīs I (Patriarch of the Church of the East), 6–8, 15, 146, 164
Gregory, 20
Gregory of Nazianzus, 159, 161
Gregory of Nyssa, 130
Herod, 181
Hieronimus, 201–202
Hnana of Adiabene, 145

Hnanishoʿ II, 166
I. E. Rahmani, 8, 10
Ibn al-Athir, 54
Ibn al-Mujawir, 50
Ibn al-Salt, 131
Ibn at-Tayyib, 136–137, 150
Ibn Habib, 44–45, 255, 260
Ibn Hisham, 40
Ibn Ishaq, 40, 45–46, 48, 51–52, 61, 69
Ibn Jarir al-Tabari, 40, 54, 68, 250
Isaac III, 93–121
Isaac Eshbadnaya (see Shbadnaya)
Isaac of Nineveh, 1, 7–12, 20, 39, 55, 58, 60, 71–92, 93–121, 123–131, 135, 155–156, 158, 162–165, 169, 176, 185–186, 192, 196–198, 231, 233, 235, 241, 256, 262–265
Isaac Qaṭraya (see Isaac of Nineveh)
Isaac Shebadnaya (see Shbadnaya)
Isaac the Syriac/Syrian (see Isaac of Nineveh)
Ishoʿ bar Nun, 20, 144–145
Ishoʿdad, 135, 137, 140–145, 147–148, 150, 152, 177–178, 192
Īshōʿdnaḥ, 7, 9–10
Īshōʿyahb (Bishop of Dayrīn), 7, 59, 135
Īshōʿyahb III (Patriarch of the Church of the East), 3–4, 6, 13–15, 58, 110, 112, 157, 259, 261, 266
Īšōʿsabran, 112
Jacob of Serug, 93, 196
Jaʿfar al-Sadiq, 104, 106
Jesus, 43, 46, 51–53, 117, 177, 179, 181, 183–184, 217, 254
John bar Penkaye, 146
John Chrysostom, 171, 226
John of Dalyatha, 79, 97–98, 106, 231, 233–236, 241
John of Zoʿbi, 171
John the Baptist, 43, 177–178
John the Evangelist, 179
John the Solitary (of Apameia), 95, 102, 164
Josephus, 171
Khosrau, 150
Kumai, 189
Lazarus, 179, 216
Mar Abba Gabriel Qaṭraya (See Gabriel bar Lipah Qaṭraya)
Mar Dāzedeq, 10, 197–198
Mar Gūrgīs, 8
Mar Shabūr, 10
Mar Zadoe, 57
Macarius the Elder, 163, 238, 245–246
Mark the Hermit, 207–208, 226
Mary, mother of Jesus, 43, 46, 52–53, 146, 216
Maximus the Confessor, 130
Muhammad ibn Jarir al-Tabari, 40, 54, 68, 250, 253
ʿNānishoʿ, 198, 201–202
Narsai, 159, 164, 172
Negus of Abyssinia, 41
Nimparūk bar Dūstar (from Hatta), 3
Origen, 130, 189, 239
Palladius, 165, 201–202, 239
Philoxenus of Mabbug, 79, 95, 97, 116, 199, 201–202, 205, 231–233, 235, 239, 241, 243
Pilate, 181
Porphyry, 163

Prophet Muhammad, 33, 38, 40–42, 44–47, 49–51, 53–54, 64, 66, 155, 250, 253–254, 257
Pūsai (Bishop of Hagar), 7
Pythagoras, 160, 162
Rabban Denḥa, 19
Rabban Gabriel Qaṭraya (See Gabriel bar Lipah Qaṭraya)
Sahdona, 96–97
Šapur II, 56, 257, 263
Sargīs (Bishop of Ṭrīhan), 7
Sergius of Reshʿaina, 161, 163, 166, 219
Shahīn (Bishop of Ḥaṭṭa), 7
Shahrastani, 131
Shbadnaya, 169–193, 150, 125
Shemʾūn, 7, 21
Shemʿon d-Ṭaybuteh, 78
Shubḥalmaran, 14, 16, 156
Sibukhit, 253
Simon of Beth Arsham, 50
Solomon of Basra, 191–192
Theodore bar Koni, 146, 150, 171
Theodore of Karkh Juddan, 162
Theodore of Mopsuestia, 20, 95, 102, 110, 116, 119, 130, 133–134, 140, 142, 144, 146–148, 150–153, 159, 162, 189, 200–201, 207–209, 229, 234, 238
Theodoret of Cyrrhus, 142
Timothy I, 15, 143, 235
Tūmā (Metropolitan of Beth Qaṭraye), 7
ʿUbayd Allah ibn Jahsh, 45, 61
ʿUthman ibn al-Huwayrith, 44–45, 61
Waraqa ibn Nawfal, 44–45, 61
Yāqūt al-Hamawī, 251–252, 256, 259
Yazdigrid, 24
Zayd Ibn ʿAmro Ibn Nufayl, 61

www.ingramcontent.com/pod-product-compliance
Lightning Source LLC
Chambersburg PA
CBHW022052160426
43198CB00008B/208
* 9 7 8 1 4 6 3 2 0 3 5 5 9 *